Women in Modern America
A Brief History

Women in Modern America

A Brief History

Lois W. Banner
Douglass College, Rutgers University

Under the General Editorship of
John Morton Blum, Yale University

HARCOURT BRACE JOVANOVICH, INC.
New York   Chicago   San Francisco   Atlanta

Preface

Until the mid-1960s the history of women was neglected by historians. A few general works were written from time to time, but most authors assumed that the women's suffrage movement was all there was to it. Increasing concern with social history on the part of historians and the advent of a new feminist movement coincided to stimulate studies about women. The result has been to create a field of historical investigation that seeks to rescue both major figures and the ordinary woman from obscurity and provide a corrective to the traditional histories from which women are absent.

This book examines the history of women in America from 1890 to the present. Three periods, each characterized by distinctive qualities, seem to stand out. The first, from 1890 to 1920, was one of energy and innovation. Many of the traditional discriminations against women came to an end, and an impressive number of women's feminist and reform groups were organized. The second period, from 1920 to 1960, was one of greater complacency about women's problems; the nation struggled with depression and war, and feminist groups declined in size and vitality. The third period, from 1960 to the present, witnessed the emergence of a feminism more radical than any of its predecessors.

In my study of this era, I have three aims: to explore the reasons why feminism rose and fell and rose again; to examine the history of various groups of women, including the working class, blacks, immigrants, farm women, and the middle class, each of which responded to the pressures and opportunities of the times in a different way; and, finally, to focus on the dramatic and continuing struggle waged by determined, innovative women to achieve their rights.

I have attempted to examine and correlate the complex factors that have affected women's lives. Common strains run through every period.

One has been the influence of a society undergoing rapid changes: the progress of industrialization and the move to the cities; changing attitudes toward sex and marriage; the growing power of the mass media as cultural conditioners; the expansion of the economy and of certain occupations within it, such as secretarial work; two world wars that opened up new jobs for women; a depression and a war that made the family seem a haven of stability and security; technological advances that offered women more leisure time. A second factor that influenced women in America throughout these years has been the deep and abiding image of woman as the "good" wife, mother, homemaker, and the repository of human virtue on the one hand, and as the "evil" temptress, the Pandora of classical mythology and the Eve of Judeo-Christian belief, on the other—two stereotypes that have dominated thinking about women throughout the history of Western culture and that continue to prevail today. A third factor is the overriding discrimination against women in every area of their lives, whether they have been seeking education, jobs, justice under the law, or simply the freedom to lead their lives as they see fit.

This history of women is also a history of feminism, a term that is difficult to define precisely. Generally it has meant the advocacy of the rights of women. But the view of what constitutes those rights has often changed since the mid-nineteenth century. To solve that problem, I have used different terms for the various kinds of feminist. I use the term *feminist* broadly to apply to all those men and women who have consciously worked on women's behalf. *Radical feminist* refers to those whose perspective approximates the contemporary feminist viewpoint: they support abortion, day-care centers, complete equality for men and women; they believe that the differences between the sexes are primarily cultural, not innate. For those feminists whose position is uncompromisingly hostile to patterns or institutions of discrimination, I use the term *militant. Social feminist* (a term first coined by historian William O'Neill) applies to women for whom social reforms take priority over strictly women's causes. Finally, *domestic feminists* are those who argue that the solution to women's problems lies in the professionalization of homemaking.

To help the reader who wishes to pursue any particular aspect of this history more fully, I have provided a critical bibliography at the end of each chapter.

I am grateful for the assistance I received when preparing this volume. I am particularly thankful for the careful critical reading given all or portions of the manuscript by Carl N. Degler, John M. Blum, Daniel J. Walkowitz, Judith Walkowitz, Nancy J. Weiss, and James M. Banner, Jr. Finally, I would like to acknowledge the superb editorial assistance of Elizabeth Holland and Irene Pavitt and of art editor Yvonne Steiner.

LOIS W. BANNER

For O. P. B.

Contents

The Emergence of 1
the Modern American
Woman: The 1890s

"At the opening of the twentieth century," wrote suffragist Ida Husted Harper, women's status "had been completely transformed in most respects."[1] Her judgment was only partially correct. For most women by the 1890s, much had been gained, but much remained to be achieved. The 1890s were years of transition, during which the advances women had made in the preceding decades began to add up to significant progress, and women's organizations entered a period of rapid growth. But in every area of women's experience discrimination still existed.

1 Suffragist executive committee, including foreign delegates, that arranged the first International Council in 1888. In the front row are Susan B. Anthony (second from left) and Elizabeth Cady Stanton (fourth from left).

WOMEN'S STATUS IN 1890

Legal Codes

The legal codes pertaining to women had not undergone a transformation, but states had gone a long way in amending discriminatory laws. For example, by 1890 many states had substantially modified the common law doctrine of *femme couverte*, under which wives had been chattels of their husbands, with no direct legal control over their own earnings, children, or property, unless a premarital agreement had been negotiated and their property placed in trust.* New laws in many states gave wives control over their inherited property and their earn-

---

* Under the normal trust, the husband had control over his wife's income but not over her property, which was under the guardianship of trustees, usually male relatives or associates of her father. Such prohibitions on property ownership and income did not apply to single women, who were classified as *femme sole* under the common law.

ings. In the case of divorce, women in most states had a reasonable chance of being awarded at least joint custody over their children.

But there were laws in every state that still discriminated against women. Among the most important were the voting laws. In some states women could vote in local school board elections and in municipal elections, but in only four states—Wyoming, Utah, Colorado, and Idaho—could women vote in general state and federal elections. In 1875 in *Minor v. Happensett* the Supreme Court had ruled unanimously that voting was not coextensive with citizenship (as feminists argued) and that the states could withhold the right to vote from women as they did from criminals and mental defectives. Because they could not vote, women could not sit on juries or hold public office. There were state laws that decreed that women could not enter into business partnerships without the consent of their husbands; that husbands had the right to decide where the family would live; and that adultery on the part of the husband was not sufficient grounds for divorce, although it was when committed by the wife. The abolition of such discriminatory laws, which vary from state to state, has taken a full century of determined feminist agitation, and many of them are still on the books. As legal beings, then, women had made substantial progress by the 1890s, but full equality under the law was still not theirs.

Educational Opportunities

In education, women had made more promising gains. At the beginning of the nineteenth century, it was difficult for women to secure any education. No colleges accepted them. In many areas of the country, public grammar schools as well as private academies restricted their pupils to boys or allowed girls to attend only in the summer when sons were needed to work on their families' farms, and classrooms were vacant. It was considered sufficient that girls learn to read and write—skills they could acquire from their mothers or at local "dame" schools established for that purpose. The educated woman was generally looked on with derision and suspicion for stepping outside of the domestic role.

By the end of the century, however, elementary and secondary education was generally available to women. In fact, because boys more often

3

than girls dropped out of high school to seek gainful employment, by 1890 more girls than boys regularly graduated from high school. Higher education, too, was by then open to women. Before the Civil War enterprising men and women had founded private academies for women, while a number of states had established teacher-training institutes, known as normal schools, which attracted mostly women students. A few colleges, too, had opened their doors to women in the antebellum period, notably Oberlin in 1837 and Antioch in 1853. In the years after the Civil War numerous colleges for women were established, including Vassar in 1861, Wellesley in 1870, Smith in 1871, and Bryn Mawr in 1885. In 1888, Mount Holyoke Seminary, founded in 1837 as a high school, gained collegiate status. In these same years many state institutions, particularly in the Midwest and West, ended their restrictions against women, and new private colleges dedicated to the principle of

2   A domestic science class in a public school during the early 1900s.

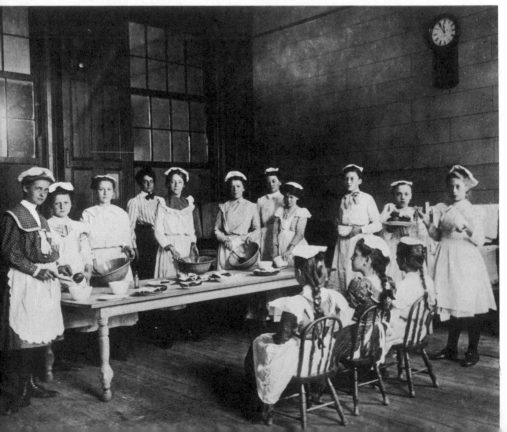

3   Vassar College advertises for students in *The American Agriculturist,* April 1877.

coeducation appeared. Notable among these was Cornell University, founded in 1865. According to historian Arthur Meier Schlesinger, by 1900, 80 percent of the colleges, universities, and professional schools in the nation admitted women.[2]

This significant gain was crucial to the expansion of women's roles in the 1890s and 1900s. For not only were women now able to enter relatively esteemed professions like law and medicine, but their new-found education gave them the self-confidence and critical perception that would lead them to question their position in American society. The fact that women were going to school, that they were gaining knowledge and confidence in themselves, was fundamental to the growth of the woman's movement in the late nineteenth and early twentieth centuries. Most college-trained women became elementary-school teachers, and most professional schools admitted only a small number of women. Still women had not had these opportunities before.

Occupations

The employment situation for women was more ambiguous. True, more women had jobs: in 1870 about 15 percent of women over sixteen years of age were regularly employed away from home for wages; by 1900 the figure had risen to 20 percent. Women were being taught new employment skills like typing and stenography, and they were coming to dominate professions like nursing and teaching. Women had even forced their way into the professions of ministry, law, and medicine over the course of the century. In 1840 Harriet Martineau, prominent English feminist and author, had contended that there were only seven occupations in the United States open to women: teaching, needlework, keeping boarders, setting type, working as servants, or laboring in book binding and cotton factories. But by 1890, according to the census of that year, of the 369 occupations listed, there were only 9 in which women were not represented.

In exceptional fields like the theater, well-known prima donnas like Lillian Russell and Lily Langtry commanded huge salaries for their appearances, while newspapers avidly gave them publicity. There was still an aura of disrespectability about the actress, but the profession offered some mobility for women, and the actress was beginning to as-

4 and 5   *(above)* A silk hat factory, which employed only women who did all the work by hand. *(right)* Lillian Russell, idol of theater audiences around the turn of the century.

6 Women harvesting hops on an upstate New York farm in the 1880s.

sume the role of cultural model that by the 1930s she would so powerfully play.

Yet there was still significant discrimination against working
women. In almost every profession and occupation, skills were divided
into men's and women's jobs. This phenomenon was partly a product
of women's propensity to seek employment related to their traditional
work in the home. Thus in the field of manufacturing, which employed
a sizable minority of working women by 1900, the majority were employed in clothesmaking, textile, and millinery factories; in commercial
food production; and in the cigar, tobacco, and shoemaking industries,
for which women had often done piecework in their homes.

In all these industries, women performed the less prestigious and
lower-paid tasks. For example, in the ladies' garment industry, which

7 Woman employed in a shoe factory, circa 1905.

became one of the largest employers of factory women by the early twentieth century, men were the cutters and pressers, positions of higher authority and pay, while women did the sewing and finishing. This situation resulted partly from the fact that most factory women were young and unmarried and thus transient members of the work force. Yet in general, women had little chance for advancement. They were the assemblers, not the skilled operatives. At best, a long-term female employee might be promoted to the position of foreman over a group of female workers. But in that position she could expect to be paid less than male foremen, just as women workers across the board were paid less than male workers, even when their jobs were similar.

This division between men's work and women's work was also characteristic of the professions. The few women who became doctors

9

and lawyers typically undertook tasks related to conventional feminine roles. Most women lawyers found their place in quasi-office work: collecting claims, redressing minor grievances, preparing probate papers. Most women doctors were gynecologists or pediatricians. One woman doctor in general practice, who found it almost impossible to attract patients, recounted a tale that she thought characteristic of women doctors in her situation. Gratified to be sought out finally by a mother with a sick child, the doctor in fact discovered that the mother's choice was not motivated because of her own reputation. Rather the woman presumed, incorrectly as it turned out, that the rates of a "lady" doctor would be less than those of a "real doctor."[3]

The overwhelming majority of women who entered the professions,

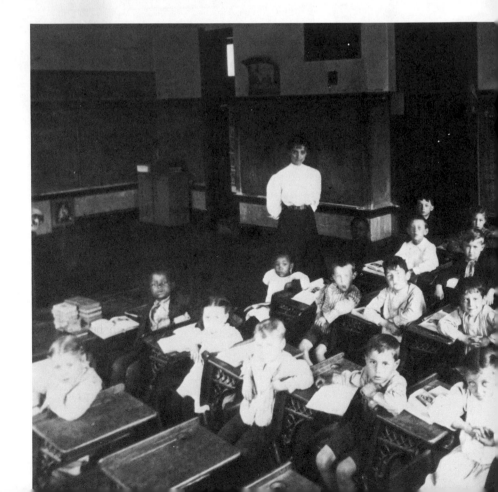

10

however, became teachers and nurses. Thus, they still followed women's traditional family role of teacher of the young and nurse to the ailing. And as women moved into these occupations in large numbers, men either left the field for other pursuits or moved up to the elite positions in the profession. For example, by 1910, 77 percent of teachers were women. Like women factory workers, they were mostly young and single, and many school systems prohibited them for continuing to teach once they married. They clustered in elementary-school positions, while men dominated university teaching and administrative positions in elementary and secondary schools. A similar pattern was apparent in nursing and in librarianship, professions that women have also dominated throughout the twentieth century. So common has this development become that, to denote it, sociologists have coined the term *femi-*

8 An elementary-school classroom in Valley Falls, Kansas, in the early 1900s.

9 A typical office scene, when men still dominated the clerical labor force.

nization. It refers to the process whereby, as women become a majority within a profession, a small number of men take the leadership roles, while most men desert it. This desertion inevitably lowers the status of the profession.

This pattern is evident even in clerical labor—the occupation that more than any other has come to characterize women's work in the twentieth century. This field first opened to women because typewriter manufacturers discovered that attractive women demonstrators sold more machines than male demonstrators had. Moreover, clerical work underwent a rapid expansion in this period of general business growth, and it was clear to employers that women could be paid less than men. Once women became typists and stenographers, men left the clerical field, which they had previously dominated. Some moved up to sales and managerial positions, which gave them higher salaries and more

10 and 11   As the field of clerical work expanded, increasing numbers of women where hired. *(above)* A lunchroom in the Metropolitan Life Insurance Company, New York. *(right)* Lady "typewriters" spend their fifteen-to-thirty minute lunch break on the steps of Trinity Church, New York.

prestige, while others simply sought work in nonfeminine occupations. But office work, despite its obvious advantages over factory labor of higher pay and a shorter work day, held out its embarrassments: for several decades typists were known as "typewriters," and the confusion between this appellation and the name of the machine they used occasioned considerable merriment at their expense in offices and in popular journalism alike.

Medicine and Sexuality

The 1890s were also a time of advancement in the medical treatment of women and in the medical and popular views of female sexuality. The fact that from 1850 to 1900, life expectancy at birth for women rose from forty to fifty-one years was partly due to considerable improvements in medical care for them. The introduction in the latter decades of the century of antiseptic techniques in delivering babies had greatly lessened the danger of puerperal fever, a common infection of childbirth that for centuries had killed thousands of women and their newborn babies. Developments in gynecological surgery had also made curable such a chronic and debilitating female disorder as prolapsed uterus, or displaced uterus, a condition common among women who have borne a number of children, but for which there was no effective cure before the mid-nineteenth century. Moreover, by late century, doctors became less prone to diagnose all female illnesses, including neurosis, as uterine disorders and to treat them by douching, blistering, and bleeding the vagina. The ancient belief that a woman was controlled by her reproductive organs was on the way out. True, the "hysterical" or neurotic woman who was unmarried might still be advised to marry to cure her difficulty, but generally a woman who suffered from a nervous disorder could expect to receive the same rest and counseling therapy prescribed for men.

In some circles, menstruation and childbirth were beginning to be looked on as natural functions and not as illnesses during which a woman simply went to bed. And some progressive doctors, like Edward Bliss Foote, author of numerous popular editions from the 1880s to the 1900s of *Plain Home Talk on Love, Marriage, and Parentage,* openly challenged the Victorian notions that sexual intercourse was unhealthy

14

and often forced on the woman by the man because he could not control his sex drive, that sex was harmful even to him because of the loss of vital body fluid in the semen, and that the only purpose of sex was to produce children. Indeed, Foote even counseled, in the 1904 edition, that it was physiologically damaging for the woman to engage in sexual intercourse if she did not enjoy it.

Yet most members of the middle class, among whom the repressive ideas about sexuality were particularly prevalent, were no more open about sexual matters than they had been before. Few middle-class Americans could regard masturbation as anything other than immoral and unnatural and eventually bound to result in bodily decay and insanity. Few parents, as much as they punished their children for showing even the slightest sign of masturbation, were willing to discuss sex with them. Journalist Rheta Childe Dorr remembered that when a girl turned fourteen, scores of new rules were introduced, "and when you asked for an explanation you met only embarrassed silence."[4] For many girls the onset of menstruation was a severe shock because, given Victorian prudery, they had not been told about it. Children then as later often learned about sex from their classmates, if they learned about it at all. The bride who married knowing nothing about sex was not uncommon. Such was the experience of novelist Frances Parkinson Keyes, who was married in 1904. In her middle-class circle, the mother of the bride was supposed to have "a little talk" with her daughter shortly before the wedding ceremony. But, explained Keyes, mothers were generally so embarrassed at this encounter that they said nothing enlightening. Besides, continued Keyes, "many mothers felt very strongly that prenuptual revelations about the marriage relationship would sully a young girl's innocence and make her less desirable to the 'right man.'"[5]

Nor had attitudes in general about childbirth changed. In the 1890s, Elizabeth Peabody, daughter of the wealthy Peabody family of Boston, was shocked when a schoolmate directly referred to one of her mother's yearly pregnancies.[6] And even suffragist Elizabeth Cady Stanton, who had periodically retreated from the suffrage campaign to bear seven children in all, advanced the age-old argument that pregnant women must remain inactive because their actions and emotions directly influenced the fetus. Do mothers-to-be not know, wrote Stanton in 1900, castigating some young women she had observed drinking and smoking during pregnancy, that "they are making gamblers and drunkards of the next generation? During the nine months of prenatal life, they are stamping every thought and feeling of their minds on the plastic beings."[7] Frances Parkinson Keyes remained in bed for weeks before and after the birth of her first child, and she was stunned to discover that one of the household maids, for whom there had been no hiatus in household labor, had given birth secretly and on her own to an illegitimate child shortly after Keyes' own carefully attended pregnancy and childbirth. The middle class could afford to support the idea of the fragile female; for the working class it was often a different matter.

In the latter years of the nineteenth century restrictions regarding sex became even more severe as most states moved to outlaw the sale of contraceptives and the dissemination of birth-control information. "Social purity" was a major objective of many late nineteenth-century Victorians and even many reform-minded individuals. At their best, social purity advocates—a heterogeneous group that included organiza-

12 "A Clarion Call for World Prohibition": the WCTU presents the Great Temperance Petition to the state legislature in Albany, New York.

13 The temperance campaigns of the WCTU alienated powerful liquor interests from the suffrage movement.

tions like the Women's Christian Temperance Union (WCTU) and the Young Women's Christian Association (YWCA)—worked to eliminate prostitution and to simplify women's dress. Ultimately, they were an important force in bringing the American public to openly discuss social problems like prostitution and venereal disease. On the question of birth control, however, the attitude of even many reformers was puritanical: they saw it as a means, not of liberating women, but of freeing men to pursue their supposedly greater sexual urges outside the marital bond.

In 1873 the anti–birth-control mood gained particular emphasis when Congress passed the so-called Comstock Law, named after its chief proponent, the single-minded, antivice crusader, Anthony Comstock. This law banned the dissemination of pornography, abortion devices, and "any drug, medicine, article, or thing designed, adapted, or intended for preventing conception." Most states thereafter passed

17

their own laws modeled after the Comstock statute. Birth control was, by implication, catalogued along with pornography as lewd and immoral, and there were overtones within the laws of the old belief that birth control, like masturbation, sapped bodily energy and produced physical decay.

Many states also prohibited abortion in the post-Civil War years. Under the common law, abortion had been permitted until the sixth month of pregnancy—the normal time of "quickening," or the first felt movements of the fetus in the womb. The prohibition against abortion made sense: medical techniques were crude; poorly trained men and women set up abortion mills; and many women died at the hands of quacks. But the laws against abortion, in combination with those that forbade the sale of condoms or diaphragms, flew in the face of what historians are beginning to think was the fairly widespread practice of birth control among nineteenth-century Americans, given the decrease in family size over the course of that century. If couples wanted to control the size of their families, they had available to them only fairly primitive techniques—continence, coitus interruptus, the rhythm method, and douching.

Still, women were beginning to be viewed more as human beings and less as fragile creatures, prone to periodic illness and nervous disorders. Some historians view the increasing use of birth-control measures as important evidence of women's growing power within the family. And, after years of debate, reformist doctors and feminists who advocated simplicity of dress for women and attention to diet and exercise were gaining authority. For two decades, educators, doctors, and the general public had hotly debated whether women constitutionally could withstand the rigors of a college education. The argument had intensified after Dr. Edward H. Clarke, in his influential *Sex in Education* (1873), proposed that the strain of learning would make a woman sterile. But by 1900 this debate had become somewhat academic, as statistics began to prove that college women not only maintained a level of scholarly ability and physical health equal to male students but often surpassed them. Moreover, ministers no longer preached sermons, as they had earlier in the century, in which they identified the supposed weaknesses of women and justified the discriminations against them as part of the "curse" of Eve, whom God had more severely punished than Adam because she had first taken the apple from the serpent in the Garden. It was not uncommon among women, however, for menstruation to be called "the curse."[8]

Women's Organizations

Women were beginning to view themselves differently, too, and it led them increasingly to organize, not only to achieve the vote, but for a variety of professional, cultural, and reform goals. The emergence of women doctors, lawyers, and college graduates resulted in the formation of the first professional women's associations, while other women flocked into local women's clubs seeking education, cultural uplift, a better understanding of women's nature, and a chance to involve themselves in civic concerns that went beyond the home.

In 1873 the Women's Christian Temperance Union was formed, and in 1890 the national General Federation of Women's Clubs was organized. In that same year, the two branches of the women's suffrage movement, which had split in great acrimony in 1869, were reunited in the

14 A meeting of the DAR, 1898.

National American Woman's Suffrage Association (NAWSA). During the 1880s and 1890s appeared, among other groups, the Young Women's Christian Association, the Daughters of the American Revolution (DAR), the Association of Collegiate Alumnae (later to become the American Association of University Women), the Congress of Mothers (later to become the National Parent-Teachers Association), and the National Council of Women. In 1893 women captured the public attention with their participation in the Chicago Columbian Exhibition, the world's fair of the century. At the special women's building at the fair, there was a year-long display of arts and handicrafts by women, and there were continual speeches by prominent women and conferences of women's organizations. The participation of women in the fair was a brilliant publicity stroke. Early in the nineteenth century it had been considered a disgrace for a woman's name to appear in public print. Now, as one observer noted, women were constantly "in the glare of publicity."[9]

Public Image: The "Gibson Girl"

The "New Woman" she was termed—by feminists, who lauded her and the press, which both praised and derided her. For the most part she worked only until she married, although she might be one of those who, even in the 1890s, chose a career instead of marriage. She was easily identifiable by her new style of dress. Instead of yards of trailing petticoats and beribboned gowns, which women had laboriously to embroider by hand, she wore a tailored suit or a dark skirt and a simple blouse, or "shirtwaist," modeled after men's attire. Her skirts may not have risen above her ankles, but if she were particularly daring, she might loosen her corset, that torture instrument of Victorian dress, which gave women eighteen-inch waistlines, fainting spells, and sometimes even permanent damage to internal organs.

The "New Woman" of the 1890s was in many ways typified by the popular "Gibson girl" of the period. The creation of the artist Charles Dana Gibson in a series of drawings in *Life* magazine in the 1890s, this healthy and athletic maiden, simply dressed, became a national favorite. Prints of Gibson drawings appeared on the walls of countless American homes. The Gibson girl was not designed to be a sex object, as were the "vamp" of the 1920s and the "siren" of the 1950s. Although she

20

15   The Gibson girl: a hint of rebellion.

16 A Gibson drawing entitled "Picturesque America."

might be permitted some décolletage for evening, her regular attire was chaste and maidenly. Often she wore a shirtwaist blouse and a simple skirt. She was not, however, pictured in employment outside the home. Gibson's pictures centered on love, courtship, and marriage—the traditional themes—but the Gibson girl was also depicted playing tennis and golf, bicycling, and even driving an automobile. The Gibson girl was the American virgin-woman, but around her there was a refreshing hint of health, sensuality, and rebellion.

ROOTS OF CHANGE

Why were women, who in the 1820s had neither legal, professional, nor educational standing, by the 1890s seemingly on the road to achieving equality with men? Most often, change was brought about by the interaction of two factors: new social, economic, and cultural forces on the one hand, and the efforts of individuals on the other. In case after case, feminists and other reformers agitated for change, and their arguments gained force as altered conditions in an industrializing nation made new life styles and relationships for women imperative.

Dress Reform

In the 1840s, health reformers and liberal educators had begun to rail against the middle-class woman's dress, particularly the corset. Few Americans had listened to them. In those years, feminists Susan B. Anthony and Elizabeth Cady Stanton, among others, had adopted a modified version of Victorian dress—the so-called bloomer costume, which consisted of a long-sleeved, high-necked, and loose-fitting tunic over a pair of baggy trousers. They soon found they had to give it up because of public ridicule and the unwillingness of women to follow their example. By the 1890s, however, public attitudes were changing. One reporter at the Columbian Exhibition was amazed to find that the audience responded enthusiastically to fashion shows presented at the

17 A typical 1900 corset made of steel and bone that pushed the bust up, the stomach in, and the rear out.

women's building that featured simple styles and shortened skirts. Standing in the audience, she heard many women express "their great desire to be free from the bondage of skirts—women, too, who would, one would suppose, rather die in long skirts than let the world know they had legs."[10]

By the 1890s, women, with new freedoms, were bolder than they had been before. And after fifty years of crinolines and corsets, these new styles looked fresh and exciting. Besides, women no longer had such a vested interest in adhering to Victorian fashions. Once, to the upwardly mobile middle-class woman who could afford them, they had bespoken status and security: with her wasp waist and her well-defined bosom and hips she bore little resemblance to farmers' or laborers' wives, whose often shapeless figures and simple clothes mirrored a life of hard work and penury. By late century, however, simplicity in dress had come to be associated, not with the poor or with radicals like Stanton and Anthony, but with more exciting and acceptable models: the actress, the working woman, the college woman, the sportswoman.

Women had come to learn the ease and comfort of simple, light clothing as they began to participate in sports. In the early years of the nineteenth century, genteel women exercised as little as possible because of the supposed delicacy of their physical constitutions. But as ice skating became popular in the 1850s and croquet in the 1860s, it seemed foolish to bar women from these simple activities, especially since many doctors were contending that American women did not get enough exercise. In the 1880s bicycling first appeared and soon became a national craze. Everyone who could afford a bicycle rode one, for pleasure and as a means of transportation. To pedal their machines over any distance, women had to wear simpler and shorter garments. In the 1890s, tennis and golf became popular among the wealthy, and the middle class took up these sports after the turn of the century. They soon became acceptable sports for women.

New styles did not appear overnight. Skirts remained generally long until the First World War. Novelist Edna Ferber has recalled that in the 1890s neighbors in her home town of Appleton, Wisconsin, were shocked when her mother, who ran the family store, began to wear shirtwaist blouses and skirts that did not reach the ground.[11] Crino-

24

18   WCTU leader Frances Willard receiving her first cycling lesson.

lines, bustles, and the tight lacing of corsets were slowly abandoned, but most women continued to wear some form of corset until the 1920s. There was not a "revolution" in clothing styles in the 1890s on the order of what some historians discern in the 1920s. But there was a willingness to consider more rational styles of dress. True, Parisian dress designers, fearful that simple clothing would eliminate the elaborate fashions on which their reputations were based, fought the trend. But

19 Photographs taken by Alice Austen in 1896 for Maria Ward's book *Bicycling for Ladies*, showing (from left to right) dismounting, wheeling, the wrong way to take a curve, and the right way.

who could resist the tide of change when even the *Ladies' Home Journal*, the venerable organ of middle-class female opinion, in 1893 endorsed the right of women to choose their own clothes on the basis of comfort? Thus dress reform came into being because of the preachings of doctors and health reformers, because of the rise of sports, because women at work and at school had to have simpler clothes, and because women and men slowly found the notion of the emancipated woman appealing.

Expansion of the Women's Labor Force

In employment, changing demographic and industrial patterns were probably more important than feminist arguments or individual actions in opening up new jobs for women. Even before the Civil War, migration patterns had created sex imbalances in many areas of the country; particularly in areas of older settlement, women outnumbered men. Work had to be found for these women; there were simply not enough husbands, fathers, or brothers available to support them. A

group of cotton manufacturers argued with effect before Congress in 1815 that their mills provided employment to thousands of poor women for whom there was no work in the rural economy and who otherwise would become public charges.[12]

Moreover, recent scholarship suggests that the average age of marriage for women in the nineteenth century was about twenty-two. Thus many women were able for a number of years between maturity and marriage to contribute to the family support with work outside the home or to save money for their own marriages. This situation contributed to the argument for allowing women to seek remunerative employment in a variety of fields, especially as families increasingly moved to cities, where they were more dependent on outside services and less dependent on the labor of family members than they had been in the rural areas.

Within the burgeoning American economy there was a demand for this supply of workers. Owners of the earliest factories in the nation,

20 A cotton factory in the early nineteenth century.

the cotton mills of Lowell and Waltham, Massachusetts, turned to young women as a logical labor source in the 1810s. Later in the century, even after immigration had created a larger labor pool, industrialists continued to employ women, particularly as domestic piecework moved into factory production and because women could be paid less than men. Similarly, the rapid growth of public-school systems created the need for more teachers, while local communities found persuasive the common judgments that women were particularly suited to elementary-school teaching and that, as in manufacturing, they would accept lower salaries than those paid men. Moreover, the Civil War—as have most modern wars—also acted as a social force to extend women's employment. With men at the battlefield, more women were needed in teaching and in manufacturing, while some new job areas, like the federal civil service, began to open up to them.

For the most part, the expansion of women's employment outside the elite professions occurred without significant feminist pressure. In manufacturing, organized women concentrated on attacking its exploitative conditions. Some historians view the movement from home to factory as a step toward self-realization on the part of individual women and thus a feminist act. But to what extent the attitudes of a young woman who worked for a few years as an unskilled laborer and then married were changed is debatable. With regard to teaching, feminists were partly responsible for the extension of this field. Indeed, a number of prominent women leaders in the nineteenth century—like suffragist Susan B. Anthony, temperance advocate Frances Willard, and educator Catharine Beecher—began their careers as schoolteachers.

21   A cotton mill, 1895.

A "Strange New Note"

The reasons for the phenomenal growth of women's organizations in the late nineteenth century are similarly complex. Some recent historians of women have argued that this phenomenon was the result of the advent of labor-saving appliances that gave housewives the leisure time for volunteer activity. This thesis, however, is only partially correct. The advent of canned goods, the sewing machine, and new kitchen appliances did lessen the burdens of housekeeping by the 1890s. But as Robert and Helen Lynd reported in *Middletown*, their study of Muncie, Indiana, many women in the 1890s were still baking their own bread and canning their own fruits and preserves—partly to economize, partly out of habit, and partly because society expected that an able wife should demonstrate extensive housekeeping ability.[13] Even wealthy Maude Nathan of New York City felt so guilty about leaving her home to do volunteer philanthropic work that, to assuage her conscience and the objections of her family, she did all the marketing for the family, closely supervised the servants, and planned and directed the making of sheets and towels as well as her own clothes. Once a year, she herself canned a year's supply of pickles, preserves, and corned beef for the household.[14]

By late century most women were using sewing machines, but they still made their own clothes and those of their children. Indeed, according to economist Robert Smuts, the only mechanical aids in most homes in 1890 were the sewing machine and the egg beater. But the crucial time-savers for the housewife were not sewing machines or canned goods but rather electrical equipment like the vacuum cleaner, the refrigerator, and the washing machine. Although a fully electric kitchen was displayed at the Columbian Exhibition of 1893, it was not until the 1920s that electrical equipment was readily available.

Besides the advent of labor-saving devices, there were other more compelling reasons for women's new leisure in the late nineteenth century. For one thing, a sizable increase in immigration had increased the supply of servants. Equally significant was the decision of women themselves to have fewer children than their mothers. Novelist Mary Austin, of Illinois frontier origin, dated a change in women's attitudes

22 Housekeeping is still hard work and the woman's responsibility.   31

about their roles from about 1868. "The pioneer stress was over," she wrote, and with it had ended "the day of large families, families of from a dozen to fifteen."[15] According to Austin, "a strange new note had come into the thinking of the granddaughters of the women who had borne their dozen or so cheerfully and with the conviction of the will of God strong in them."[16] And this "strange new note," as Austin described it, had little to do with the easier housekeeping, but rather grew out of the yearning of these women for leisure, for culture, and for some world outside the home.

New Inroads

Women in College   Women's entry into higher education was also to a large extent the result of the actions of individual women and men. Eastern women's colleges like Vassar and Smith were founded partly because the major private male institutions—Yale, Harvard, and Princeton, among others—for a long time refused to admit women. In 1889 Barnard College was opened as a coordinate branch of Columbia University, after fifteen years of pressure by women seeking admission and by prominent civic and women's groups made it clear that the male trustees would never tolerate coeducation. Radcliffe College began under similar circumstances as an annex to Harvard.

23   Sophomores at Vassar College commencement carry the traditional "Daisy Chain," which marks the seniors' seats.

The state colleges of the Midwest and West became coeducational in many instances also because women pressured authorities to admit them and then proved their competence. The example of the University of Indiana and Sarah Parke Morrison is characteristic. An 1857 graduate of Mount Holyoke Seminary, Morrison became determined to integrate the public college of her home state. In her favor was the fact that her father, a trustee of the university, was sympathetic to her cause. The administration and the faculty, however, were against her. Even the undergraduates, who did not want women competing in their classes or fraternizing in their clubs, opposed her admission. It took her nine years to achieve her goal.

According to Thomas D. Clark, historian of the University of Indiana, Morrison was equal to the task. She "remembered Lucy Stone and Susan B. Anthony and asserted her rights."[17] Indeed, her victory seemed doubly assured when, two years after her admission in 1866, twelve other women were admitted to the university. But Victorian prejudices did not easily die. As were many women pioneers in education, Morrison was subject to petty annoyances throughout her college career. Commencement, for example, was a difficult experience, for she feared, with good reason, that the graduation audience would subject her to "curious" and "hostile" stares as she walked across the stage to receive her diploma and that her ankles might be exposed to "immodest views."

Sarah Morrison is a minor figure in American history. Yet her feminist determination to advance the cause of women was an important ingredient in the mixture of forces that brought coeducation to the state colleges of the Midwest and West. States that had more recently passed through a frontier stage, it is true, seemed more willing to integrate their colleges after the Civil War than did state legislatures and college administrations in the older states of the Union. But it is incorrect to conclude from this evidence, as many historians do, that it was a democratic "frontier" spirit alone that brought about coeducation in the West. No doubt Western statesmen were proud of their "pioneer" women, but outspoken women—and male allies—were present, too, to put pressure on faculties, administrations, and state legislatures.

Women in Medicine and Law Similarly, individual women were responsible for making the elite professions admit them, often against tremendous odds. The medical profession is a typical example. Harriott Hunt, who was self-trained and who had a private practice in Boston for some years early in the century, was repeatedly refused admission to Harvard Medical School because of her sex. She never received a medical degree. Elizabeth Blackwell, the first licensed woman doctor in the United States, was turned down by medical schools throughout the nation and was admitted in 1848 to Geneva Medical College in Geneva, New York (now part of Hobart College) only because the male students thought it would be "amusing" to have a woman there. Despite the difficulties she encountered, she graduated at the head of her class, although, like Sarah Morrison, she feared the graduation ceremony. Blackwell refused to appear on the stage to receive her diploma. Although Blackwell boarded with a family in Geneva, the townspeople avoided her because they thought that only a woman of loose morality would attend the medical college. This was a charge not infrequently leveled against women in professional training as well as working women in general.

Once women were admitted to professional schools, not only were higher standards demanded of them, but they were regularly subjected in and out of class to hostile jokes and embarrassing off-color stories. Mary Putnam-Jacobi, one of the first graduates of a medical school after Blackwell, even reported that women students in several major Eastern hospitals were able to observe operations only after physically forcing their way through a cordon of male students determined to keep them out of the operating rooms.[18] County and state medical associations, too, were loathe to certify women doctors: only after a twenty-four-year battle did the Massachusetts Medical Society in 1879 admit women to its membership.

The opposition to women lawyers seems to have been less vigorous than the opposition to women doctors, perhaps because the first applicants to the bar did not appear until the late 1860s. The first woman lawyer in the United States, Arabella Mansfield, gained her training by studying with an established lawyer, and in 1869 she was licensed by the Iowa bar with no difficulty. Other women, however, had more

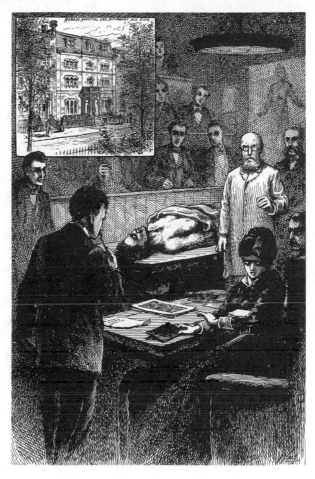

24 Elizabeth Blackwell as a student in the medical school operating room. *(inset)* The Women's Hospital and Infirmary, New York.

difficult experiences. Like many law schools, particularly in the Northeast, the Columbian College of Law (now George Washington University) in 1869 and in 1887 refused to admit women on the grounds that coeducational classes would be an "injurious diversion of the attention of the students" and that "women had not the mentality to study law."[19] In California, the law schools and the state bar admitted women only after a long and expensive legal contest brought a judicial ruling in their favor. In Illinois and Wisconsin, aspiring women lawyers had to secure special legislation to overturn adverse rulings of state bar associations and courts.

Women in Journalism   Among all the professions, that of journalism offers perhaps the most impressive example of women's intrepid persistence in the face of professional hostility. Since mid-century, women had been employed on newspapers as gossip columnists, as editors of women's pages, and sometimes as roving correspondents. But only rarely had a woman been hired as a regular reporter on general news stories. It took a succession of determined women to overcome this barrier. Elizabeth Seaman, who worked for the New York *World*, was the most famous of them. Like most women journalists of her time, Seaman assumed a pseudonym, and hers, Nellie Bly, came from the title of a popular Stephen Foster song. Her persistence in hounding editors brought her initial assignments, and the stories she wrote and submitted were so extraordinary that editors could not reject them. Flamboyant exposés of corruption and exploitation were her speciality: she feigned insanity and spent some time in the state asylum to study conditions there; she made paper boxes in a factory to see how the workers were treated; she had herself arrested to investigate conditions in the city jail; and she feigned being a high-class prostitute to expose the city's roués. In 1889 Bly accomplished her most famous exploit: she traveled around the world in seventy-two days to prove that a woman could complete the trip in less than the eighty days it had taken the fictional Phileas Fogg.

Conservative Arguments Produce Progressive Results   It is incorrect to assume that the vigorous action that Nellie Bly and other women professionals took on their own behalf necessarily implied that they were militant feminists. Women pioneers in the professions and in education were often conservative in their orientation, and their moderate rhetoric served to create a sympathetic climate for them. The most common argument for professional medical and legal training for women, for example, was not that women had the right to it, but that women patients and clients had the right to consult professionals of the same sex in order to protect their womanly modesty. How could any woman, the argument went, submit to a gynecological examination by a male doctor and preserve her sense of honor? When conservatives contended that only a woman of dubious virtue would desire to know about cases of rape, adultery, and prostitution that were matters of daily adjudica-

25 New York *World* reporter
Nellie Bly.

tion in the courts, and that to allow women into the courtroom as lawyers would be "revolting to all female sense of the innocence and sanc-
tity of their sex, [and] shocking to man's reverence for womanhood and
his faith in women," supporters of women lawyers argued that many
of the defendants in these cases were women.[20] They had the right to
female counsel; no woman, whether in a divorce suit or a rape case,
could be expected to discuss the details of her situation openly with a
male lawyer.

Many of the arguments advanced in favor of women's education were similarly moderate in tone. Among other educators, Henry Durant, who founded Wellesley College, felt that women ought to be educated to take a role in shaping society. But L. Clark Seelye, the first president of Smith College, reported that "it is to preserve her [the young woman's] womanliness that this College has been founded; it is to give her the best opportunities for mental culture, and at the same time, the most favorable conditions for developing those innate capacities which have ever been the glory and charm of true womanhood."[21]

The most compelling conservative argument for the education of women, however, was one advanced early in the century by, among others, Catharine Beecher, sister of author Harriet Beecher Stowe and founder of one of the first secondary schools for women in the nation. Beecher wanted to educate women, in the first instance, for their own intellectual profit. But she was more concerned that education render them the intellectual equals of their husbands, better mothers for their children, and experts in proper nutrition and hygiene. Aside from the profession of teaching, she did not envision a future in which remunerative employment would be standard for women. As were many women's leaders in the nineteenth and twentieth centuries, Beecher was concerned primarily with improving the position of women in the home both by upgrading the status of housekeeping and by teaching women more effective domestic techniques. In this quest Beecher and others of her generation were the forerunners of the domestic science movement of the 1910s and the home economics movement of the 1920s. In terms of the debate over women's roles, they might be classified as "domestic feminists"; in terms of women's education, their arguments spoke powerfully to a nation for whom the institution of the family was viewed as crucial to social stability.

Even though the higher education of women was often viewed as a way of extending women's traditional roles, in practice such education often had different results. Particularly among the women's colleges of the Northeast, the belief that women students had to equal and excel male students elsewhere and that college-educated women had a special mission to society and to women was quickly generated. M. Carey Thomas, president of Bryn Mawr, in many ways the most feminist of the Eastern women's colleges, captured its spirit when she wrote in 1901 that the college was "the nursing mother of women yet unborn," that its graduates would chart new paths in the professions, that they would emerge as social innovators, that they would establish marriages based on equality and sharing of roles and not on the traditional division of duties.[22]

Men: A Help and a Hindrance

Men were not always antagonistic to the potential competition of women: one male doctor, the head of the Bucks County Medical Association, led the fight in Pennsylvania for the certification of women doctors; another donated the funds to build the still functioning Women's Medical College in Philadelphia because he wanted his sister, who had supported him through school, to have the medical education she had deferred on his behalf. The original endowments for several private women's colleges in the Northeast, such as Vassar and Bryn Mawr, were provided by wealthy men. In both medicine and law, many of the early women careerists, like Mary Putnam-Jacobi, were married to men in the same field who wholeheartedly supported their wives' endeavors. Indeed, a study of thirty-one of the approximately two hundred women lawyers in the nation in 1896 revealed that a number of them originally became interested in the law after they had married lawyers and worked as clerks in their husbands' offices.[23]

Many men also agitated for the opening of elementary and secondary education to women. Fathers as well as mothers wanted their daughters to be educated. Men, too, took an active part in modifying the common law statutes regarding married women. Given the volatile nature of the American economy in the nineteenth century, fathers of means and influence could not help but be concerned over the legal and economic security of their daughters. After all, the financial ruin of a son-in-law might also include the money his wife had brought to the marriage.

But it was not easy for nineteenth-century men to allow wives and daughters total independence. Anna Howard Shaw—minister, physician, and president of the NAWSA from 1904 to 1914—was afraid to tell her family, who had homesteaded in Michigan, of her invitation to preach her first sermon because "to them it would mean nothing short

26 Anna Howard Shaw: minister, physician, and NAWSA president.

of personal disgrace."[24] M. Carey Thomas fought the opposition of her Quaker father at every step of her educational career, despite the strong Quaker tradition of allowing women to take on public roles. Rheta Childe Dorr's husband wanted her to become a novelist in the tradition of George Eliot, who reflected on public events from a distance, but he could not tolerate her ambition to be a journalist in the center of public controversy. Novelist Mary Austin thought it was the tyrannical attitudes of Victorian men that produced most feminists. As one observer noted, "Women cultivated submission to their husbands as a matter of conscience, and those who defied such authority brought scandal on themselves and dishonor on their 'lords and masters.'"[25] According to Mary Austin, when women meeting at suffrage conferences discussed what made them suffragists they invariably credited the way they and their mothers had been treated in their families. "'Well, it was seeing what my mother had to go through that started me'; or, 'It was being

40

sacrificed to the boys in the family that set me going'; or, 'My father was one of the old-fashioned kind.'"[26] Austin remembered how "women of high intelligence and education went white and black telling how, in their own families, the mere whim of the dominant male member had been allowed to assume the whole weight of moral significance."[27]

Such attitudes were common among men of Victorian times—and later. Frederick Howe, husband of suffragist and feminist Jenny Howe and a reformer in his own right, set down in his autobiography, *Confessions of a Reformer,* a telling statement of the difficulty even a liberal encountered in rising above the traditional attitudes concerning the relationships between men and women. Never, he wrote, was he able to get over his instinctive feeling that his wife ought to stay at home. When they first were married, he persuaded her to give up her career as a minister and a suffragist. However, a move to New York City where the feminist movement was more active prompted a change of heart in both Howe and his wife, and she plunged into suffrage work. Yet, he wrote: "I have sometimes doubted whether many of the men who spoke and worked for the equality of women really desired it. Intellectually yes, but instinctively no; they clung as did I to the property instinct, to economic supremacy, to the old idea of marriage, in which all that a woman got she got through petitioning for it."[28]

Despite the difficulties that Shaw, Thomas, Dorr, and Jenny Howe encountered in pursuing career goals, it is equally important that in the end they were able to do so. Thirty years before, it would have been considerably more difficult. In short, the nineteenth century did witness important changes in the status of women; in a relative sense there was progress. The 1848 Seneca Falls Declaration, the first and most important document of the nineteenth-century women's movement, had contained five major demands. Three of these had more or less been achieved by the 1890s: education was open to women; the professions tolerated them; property rights were theirs to some degree. However, women had failed to achieve the remaining two goals: the vote and the end to the double standard of morality, whereby male sexual indiscretions were tolerated and female indiscretions were prohibited. Both would become major planks in the feminist program; both would prove difficult to win.

41

Notes

[1] Elizabeth Cady Stanton *et al.*, *History of Woman Suffrage*, 6 vols. (New York, 1881, 1922), vol. 5: ed. Ida Husted Harper, p. xvii.

[2] Arthur Meier Schlesinger, *The Rise of the City, 1878–1898* (New York: Macmillan, 1933), p. 205.

[3] Mabel S. Ulrich, "A Doctor's Diary, 1904–1932," *Scribner's* (June 1933). Reprinted in *Ms.*, I (July 1972), 11–14.

[4] Rheta Childe Dorr, *A Woman of Fifty* (New York: Funk and Wagnalls, 1924), p. 50.

[5] Frances Parkinson Keyes, *All Flags Flying: Reminiscences of Frances Parkinson Keyes* (New York: McGraw-Hill, 1972), p. 5.

[6] Marian Lawrence Peabody, *To Be Young Was Very Heaven* (Boston: Houghton Mifflin, 1967), p. 169.

[7] Theodore Stanton and Harriot Stanton Blatch, eds., *Elizabeth Cady Stanton, As Revealed in Her Letters, Diary, and Reminiscences* (New York: Harper and Brothers, 1922), vol. 2, p. 350.

[8] Margaret Mead, *Blackberry Winter: My Earlier Years* (New York: William Morrow, 1972), p. 76.

[9] Lydia Commander, *The American Idea* (1907; reprint ed., New York: Arno Press, 1972), p. 144.

[10] *Arena*, IX (1893), 305.

[11] Edna Ferber, *A Peculiar Treasure* (New York: Doubleday and Company, 1938), p. 33.

[12] Edith Abbott, *Women in Industry: A Study in American Economic History* (New York: D. Appleton, 1915), p. 52.

[13] Helen Merrell Lynd and Robert S. Lynd, *Middletown: A Study in Contemporary American Culture* (New York: Harcourt Brace Jovanovich, 1929), pp. 156–58.

[14] Robert Smuts, *Women and Work in America*, 2nd ed. (New York: Schocken, 1971), pp. 13–14.

[15] Mary Austin, *Earth Horizon: Autobiography* (New York: Literary Guild, 1932), p. 31.

[16] *Ibid.*, p. 101.

[17] Thomas D. Clark, *Indiana University, Midwestern Pioneer* (Bloomington, Ind.: University of Indiana Press, 1970), vol. 1, p. 125.

[18] Mary Putnam-Jacobi, "Women in Medicine," in Annie Nathan Meyer, ed., *Woman's Work in America* (New York: Henry Holt, 1891), pp. 139–205.

[19] Karen Meyer Willcox, "Women Lawyers in the United States, 1870–1900," Unpublished senior honors essay, Douglass College, 1973, p. 28.

[20] Ada M. Bittenbender, "Women in Law," in Meyer, *Woman's Work in America*, pp. 218–44.

[21] L. Clark Seelye, *The Early History of Smith College, 1871–1910* (Boston: Houghton Mifflin, 1923), p. 29.

[22] M. Carey Thomas, Notes for the opening address at Bryn Mawr College, 1901, quoted in Barbara M. Cross, ed., *The Educated Woman in America: Selected Writings of Catharine Beecher, Margaret Fuller, and M. Carey Thomas* (New York: Columbia Teachers College Press, 1965), p. 41.

[23] Willcox, "Women Lawyers in the United States, 1870–1900."

[24] Anna Howard Shaw, *Story of a Pioneer* (New York and London: Harper and Brothers, 1915), p. 60.

[25] Commander, *The American Idea*, p. 144.

[26] Austin, *Earth Horizon: Autobiography*, p. 128.

[27] *Ibid.*

[28] Frederick C. Howe, *The Confessions of a Reformer* (New York: Scribner, 1925), p. 235.

Bibliography

The details of women's changing status in the late nineteenth century, especially in the area of legal rights, have not yet been systematically explored. For education, Thomas Woody, *A History of Women's Education in the United States*, 2 vols. (New York: Science Press, 1929), although outmoded, will suffice. More studies are available covering women in the labor force. The most recent work is Robert Smuts, *Women and Work in America*, 2nd ed. (New York: Schocken, 1971). National Manpower Council, *Womanpower* (New York: Columbia University Press, 1957); Elizabeth Faulkner Baker, *Technology and Woman's Work* (New York: Columbia University Press, 1964); Edith Abbott, *Women in Industry: A Study in American Economic History* (New York: D. Appleton, 1915); and Annie Nathan Meyer, *Woman's Work in America* (New York: Henry Holt, 1891) are also useful. An interesting summary of women as clerical workers is found in Bruce Bliven, Jr., *The Wonderful Writing Machine* (New York: Random House, 1954). On changes in domestic technology, see Robert Smuts and Sigfried Gideon, *Mechanization Takes Command: A Contribution to Anonymous History* (New York: Oxford University Press, 1948).

For demographic analysis, Robert V. Wells, "Demographic Change and the Life Cycle of American Families," *Journal of Interdisciplinary History*, II (Autumn 1971), 273–82 is useful, and Helen Merrell Lynd and Robert S. Lynd, *Middletown: A Study in Contemporary American Culture* (New York: Harcourt Brace Jovanovich, 1929) provides some useful information on the 1890s.

Female sexuality and female medical treatment in the nineteenth century have recently aroused great scholarly interest. See Ben Barker-Benfield, "The Spermatic Economy: A Nineteenth-Century View of Sexuality," *Feminist Studies*, I (Summer 1972), 45–74; Carroll Smith-Rosenberg and Charles Rosenberg, "The Female Animal: Medical and Biological Views of Women in Nineteenth-Century America," *Journal of American History*, LX (September 1973), 332–56; Ann Douglas Wood, "'The Fashionable Diseases': Women's Complaints and Their Treatment in Nineteenth-Century America," *Journal of Interdisciplinary History*, IV (Summer 1973), 25–52; and Regina Morantz's rejoinder to Wood in the Spring 1974 issue of the same journal. The standard history of gynecology is Harvey Graham, *Eternal Eve: The History of Gynecology and Obstetrics* (New York: Doubleday and Company, 1951). The only study of abortion is Lawrence Lader, *Abortion* (New York: Bobbs-Merrill, 1966). On birth control, see Norman Himes, *Medical History of Contraception* (New York: Gamut Press, 1935). The most recent study of the antivice reformers of Victorian America is David J. Pivar, *Purity Crusade: Sexual Morality and Social Control, 1868–1900* (Westport, Conn.: Greenwood, 1973).

There is no adequate study of the dress reform movement or of the relationship between female fashions and social change. Foster Rhea Dulles, *Americans Learn to Play: A History of Popular Recreation, 1607–1940* (New York: Appleton-Century-Crofts, 1940) gives information on women and sports.

Aside from journalism, there are no studies on the entry of women into the professions, although Meyer, *Women's Work in America* gives useful information. For journalism, see Ishbel Ross, *Ladies of the Press: The Story of Women in Journalism by an Insider* (New York: Harper and Brothers, 1936). On women in the South, see Anne Firor Scott, *The Southern Lady: From Pedestal to Politics* (Chicago: University of Chicago Press, 1970).

For every period of the history of women in America, innumerable biographies and autobiographies are available. Particularly useful for the late nineteenth century are Elizabeth Cady Stanton, *Eighty Years and More (1815–1897): Reminiscences of Elizabeth Cady Stanton* (New York: European Publishing, 1898); Helen Thomas Flexner, *A Quaker Girlhood* (New Haven: Yale University Press, 1940); Elizabeth Blackwell, *Pioneer Work in Opening Up the Medical Profession to Women* (London and New York: Longmans, Green, 1895); Maude Nathan, *Once Upon a Time and Today* (New York: Putnam, 1933); Edna Ferber, *A Peculiar Treasure* (New York: Doubleday and Company, 1938); Mary Austin, *Earth Horizon: Autobiography* (New York: Literary Guild, 1932); and the extraordinarily revealing autobiographies of Rheta Childe Dorr, *A Woman of Fifty* (New York: Funk and Wagnalls, 1924), and Frances Parkinson Keyes, *All Flags Flying: Reminiscences of Frances Parkinson Keyes* (New York: McGraw-Hill, 1972).

One might also consult Mary S. Hartman and Lois W. Banner, *Clio's Consciousness Raised: Historical Perspectives on Women* (New York: Harper & Row, 1974), a compilation of articles, some of which pertain to the topics covered in Chapter 1. Especially pertinent are Daniel Scott Smith, "Family Limitation, Sexual Control, and Domestic Feminism in Victorian America: Toward a History of the Average American Woman," and Ruth Schwartz Cowan, "Domestic Technology and Social Change: The Washing Machine and the Working Wife."

The American Woman 2
from 1900 to the
First World War:
A Profile

THE MAIN PROSPECT: MARRIAGE AND
MOTHERHOOD

What was the life of the average woman like in the years before the First
World War (1914–1918)? For women of every class, ethnic group, and
region, it was governed by the simple statistic that the overwhelming
majority would marry and become housewives and mothers. Throughout the twentieth century, approximately 90 percent of American
women have married at some time during their lives. Among those who
worked, most would leave their jobs to look after their homes and families. Of all married women in the nation in 1900, only 5 percent were
gainfully employed outside the home. By 1910, 11 percent were so
employed.

27, 28, and 29 Three wedding pictures: *(above)* an immigrant bride wears a dark-colored gown in contrast with the white gown of a native American; *(below)* young rural newlyweds have their photograph taken in a Nebraska cornfield, 1882.

Thus for almost all women, marriage was a natural goal of life, and adolescence was a time of preparation for it. Many women were undoubtedly content with the expectation and fulfillment of this role. The image of the happy housewife that has dominated the popular media from early women's magazines to the television serials of the 1970s has always been based on a real type. And for the unmarried working woman who spent endless hours as a seamstress or laundress, becoming a housewife and mother offered a release from a life of drudgery for her employer.

The role was not always happily occupied. Some sociologists of the family argue that the appearance of the modern state resulted in a decline in the functions that the family performed. Education became the responsibility of the school; health care the responsibility of the doctor; the production of the family income shifted from the family-centered farm to the office or the factory. The availability of clothing, food, and services outside the home introduced a certain ambiguity into the definition of what the function of the family and its members actually was. New information about sexuality, the new legal and educational status of women, and the influence of the women's movement and its implied critique of the Victorian patriarchal family were operating to increase women's—and men's—expectations of personal satisfaction in marriage. Also, the rise in life expectancy of both men and women meant that marriage partners could anticipate spending a much longer lifetime together. In earlier times, death had provided a release from marital discontent. Now divorce, with its attendant anxieties, was on the rise: according to Arthur Calhoun in *Social History of the American Family,* by 1905 one out of twelve marriages was ending in divorce. Finally, historians estimate that about 20 percent of the American population each year has changed residence throughout the nineteenth and twentieth centuries. This mobility was another unsettling factor.

The Middle-Class Wife

These forces particularly affected middle-class women. Victorian strictures had been difficult for them, but at least nineteenth-century America had clearly defined their role. They were to marry, to have children, to obey their husbands. If they sought power, they did so

30 Women in Black River Falls, Wisconsin, get together for tea, gossip, and sewing.

privately and within the family. But by the 1900s, women's attitudes were changing. Many middle-class women had been to school, and some had worked before marrying. They now had before them the example of many women who devoted their lives to their careers. By the second decade of the twentieth century, studies were showing that close to one-half of the alumnae of the major Eastern women's colleges were unmarried and that many of these women were supporting themselves in professional occupations. By then the spinster was no longer looked on with derision: unmarried women in reform movements, in the professions, and feminists in their writings were proving by their own example that a woman's alternatives to marriage were not only possible, but exciting. In the nineteenth century, the suffragists and career women had been effectively caricatured as ugly, shrewish, and, worst of all, "strong-minded." But the many women, like Jane Addams and Florence Kelley, who in the early twentieth century minis-

tered to the poor and were leaders in social welfare, were lauded by the press and applauded by a humanitarian society that could hardly condemn their activities.

Women's organizations were also affecting the lives of middle-class women. As these groups increasingly turned to feminist and social welfare activities, they drew women out of their homes and introduced them to a broader world of public activity and of shared experience. Some women's organizations—particularly church sodalities and women's auxiliaries to men's clubs like the Elks and the Masons—had no feminist emphasis. Their effect on their members was, rather, to reenforce the traditional views of women's roles. Other women's organizations, particularly the suffrage associations and the independent and nonsectarian clubs, had a more unsettling effect on their members. In the 1860s and 1870s, novelist Gertrude Atherton remembered, women's only topics of conversation were dress, servants, children, and,

49

above all, gossip, which, according to Atherton, meant "tearing reputations to pieces."[1] The women's clubs, however, wrought a remarkable change in broadening women's concerns.

At the same time, organized women in their clubs and societies frequently leveled the charge that men had made egregious errors in their use of power, and they claimed that women could rectify these mistakes. It was woman's job, one representative figure felt, to organize as the "consumer and preserver" of humanity, to "correct the defects of man's activities."[2] At women's meetings, men were often portrayed as antagonists. One observer wrote that women's rights meetings in particular were pervaded with "bitterness, contempt, and positive enmity against men."[3] Such rhetoric could only serve to put additional pressure on the woman who chafed at the restrictions of her marriage.

At the very least, such forces were leading a sizable number of well-to-do women to demand more from their marriages than the older standards would allow. Some of them, like women throughout history, turned their drives inward on their families to become the shrews and matriarchs who have long been stock characters of fact and fiction. The wealthy and pampered Mrs. Hurstwood in Theodore Dreiser's *Sister Carrie*, who waits for her husband's first pecadillo so that she might destroy him, could exist in any age. Other women displayed symptoms of neurosis, which, according to historian Carroll Smith-Rosenberg, had been a frequent pattern of behavior in the nineteenth century among discontented wives.[4] In the early twentieth century, physicians consistently reported that most of the patients they treated for nervous disorders were women.[5] In many ways, the lot of wives had improved by the early twentieth century, but with their new freedoms came new frustrations. For example, women were no longer told to cultivate submission to their husbands as a matter of course: by 1909 the word *obey* was no longer included in civil marriage vows, and many churches had dropped it from their marriage ceremonies. Observers commented that companionship was the new standard in marriage.[6]

But companionship was difficult to achieve in a culture that expected men to achieve material success no matter what the cost. In pursuit of success, according to many accounts, men were rarely at home. "The habit and fury of work," wrote one critic, "is a masculine disease in this

31 A middle-class family and servants: the Drummonds on the back porch of their house on West 22nd Street, New York, circa 1910.

country."[7] Left to their own devices, many wives were drawn to shopping as sublimation: among them, according to one observer, bargain hunting had become a "mania." Or they turned to social climbing. And, according to sociologists Helen and Robert Lynd, "the coinage in this social market is much more subtle than that with which their husbands deal."[8] Middle-class women, not their husbands, resorted to the divorce courts with increasing frequency. According to one conservative critic, fashionable young matrons were drinking, smoking, using make-up, playing bridge for money, and demanding an "absolute independence of any power in heaven or in earth."[9] As a general summary of middle-class behavior in the 1900s, such judgments were overstated, but they nevertheless identified an important trend in fashion and life style that became dominant by the 1920s.

The discontent and confusion of many middle-class women—their difficulty in coping with increased leisure, the breakdown of old standards, and the rise of a new code of freedom for women that could easily be used to justify self-indulgence—were particularly evident in the way they treated their servants (and in the decades before the First World War, status considerations plus the still-demanding nature of housework dictated that every family of means have a servant). In the 1900s and 1910s there was an outpouring of writings on the so-called servant problem—the shortage of women willing to work as maids and cooks. This literature made clear that female employers, and not just working conditions, were driving servants away. It was not simply that servants were expected to work long hours and were not well paid; they were also subject to the whims and status anxieties of their mistresses. One analyst of domestic service concluded that middle-class women did not want intelligent, responsible servants. Rather, they wanted employees to whom they could feel superior and whose lives they could control.[10] So empty were the lives of many of these well-to-do women, wrote one observer in exasperation, that the "3 D's" occupied their time: "dress, disease, and domestics."[11]

Some women were able to find fulfillment by joining voluntary associations. Many obviously found contentment in home and family: one could argue that as the older functions of the family were eroded, new ones were found to take their place. As families grew smaller, for example, children became increasingly important, and the concerned mother took great care with her children's upbringing and education. The growth of publishing and the development of the domestic science movement brought no end of books of advice to wives on home management, and their ultimate message re-enforced women's traditional roles. Magazines like the *Ladies' Home Journal* (first published in 1889) glorified the home and motherhood. While many also portrayed the career woman in an attractive light and gave guarded support to feminist goals, the implication was that there was no conflict between the careerist and the homemaker, and that the housewife should not feel threatened by the successful working woman.

The majority of women probably adhered to traditional views about woman's nature. Novelist Frances Parkinson Keyes expressed the prevailing point of view when she wrote that marriage and motherhood were a woman's destiny. Speaking eloquently from the experiences of her own life, Keyes wrote that love was a woman's "whole existence." In the sex act, according to Keyes, the woman "surrendered" to the man, while the birth of a child produced a sense of "blinding glory."[12] Finally, Keyes extolled the emotional experience of nursing, which she viewed, in addition to marriage, as one of the two closest relationships a human being could have.[13]

Yet despite her belief in the centrality of marriage and motherhood to a woman's life, Keyes herself was both a wife and a careerist, although she took up writing in large part because her husband's salary as governor and later senator of Vermont was insufficient to support their family. Other women, too, were able to combine marriage and a career. Among them were the significant number of women lawyers and doctors married to men in the same profession. For many, however, it was not easy. Margaret Sanger, leader of the birth-control movement, suffered a nervous breakdown because she felt stagnant in a seemingly happy marriage. She had to leave her husband and children and embark on her own career before she completely recovered. Charlotte Perkins Gilman, the most important feminist writer of the decades preceding the First World War, had a similar experience. (Later in life, both Sanger and Gilman remarried.) Carrie Chapman Catt, president of the National American Women's Suffrage Association, felt it necessary before marriage to draw up a contract with her fiancé that stipulated that she would be guaranteed freedom from the responsibilities of marriage for three months a year in order to fulfill her duties as president of the NAWSA.

In the early decades of the twentieth century there were obvious problems involved for women who tried to combine marriage and a career. Senator Keyes opposed his wife's career because he thought it was degrading to his position as head of the household. It took an exceptional man to tolerate a working wife in an era that regarded such an arrangement as a clear sign of a man's inability to provide and lack of masculinity. One woman doctor married to a colleague catalogued further difficulties. Intellectually her husband accepted her career; emotionally he wanted her to stay at home. As she saw it, his attitudes about women were set by his mother when he was a child. He wanted his wife to measure up to the memory of his mother's dependence and dedication to home and husband. In subtle but effective ways he undermined her career. Yet, she concluded, "it can't be so easy being the husband of a 'modern' woman. She is everything his mother wasn't—and nothing she was."[14]

The Rural Wife

Discontent with their marriages was perhaps less evident among women who lived in rural communities, and as late as 1914 the majority of American women still did. By 1900 in most of Western farmlands the frontier era in which women had shared equally with men the burdens of heavy field labor and of family defense had ended. One observer in 1910 did find that families in the far west of Montana and Colorado were still living in isolation in log cabins held together with mud, but these frontier conditions were no longer characteristic of the farmlands

32 Maintaining the farm: a family enterprise.

33 and 34   Two rural families: *(above)* the Walters, Lubert County, Georgia, 1896; *(below)* East Custer County, Nebraska, 1888.

in the Midwest.[15] Yet there, as in New England, women still bore heavy responsibilities in maintaining the farm, which was typically a family enterprise. In addition to housekeeping chores, the farm wife cared for the family's vegetable plot and for its supply of livestock for family use. During harvest time, she cooked round the clock for her family and the farm hands. Among. the majority of farm families who were not wealthy, daughters typically worked as teachers or as domestic servants in other households to supplement the family income. In the South, the prolonged post-Civil War agricultural depression forced white women as well as black women to join husbands and fathers in the fields, while many daughters of the less well-to-do found employment in the still-rural cotton textile mills.

On the surface, the life of the rural woman appears busy and uneventful. Enmeshed in the traditionalist attitudes of rural culture, herself the mainstay of a conservative Protestant ministry, and isolated by geography from urban sophistication, her adjustment to her role seems foreordained. Yet farm life, no less than city life, could be volatile. The fluctuation in income that was characteristic of farming introduced an

35   Suffragists work on farms as part of the war effort, 1917.

elementary uncertainty, as did the steady movement of the farm population to the city (and sometimes back again). There were also conflicts
between the generations within farm families, particularly as daughters
and sons came to attend public elementary and high schools. Widows
and spinsters who could not make their way in a farming community
and sought a livelihood in the city were not uncommon. Furthermore,
by the 1890s small towns dotted the rural landscape, and the isolated
farm was increasingly a rarity. Women on farms and in small towns
dominated the Women's Christian Temperance Union, and they were
not absent from the ranks of the suffrage movement. Moreover, rates
of divorce were consistently higher in the West than in the East, although this was partly because divorce laws were less stringent in many
Western states. As the twentieth century progressed, elements in the life
of the town-dweller and the city-dweller were fast coming to resemble
one another.

Prototypes of the Period

For a graphic picture of the frustrations and satisfactions of the average middle-class woman in these years—whether in country or city—
perhaps the best source is Sinclair Lewis' novel *Main Street*, which is
set in a small town in the years before the First World War. A variety
of types are limned: the spinsterish schoolmarm; the embittered widow;
the prim, proper, but sexually starved matron, doting on doctors and
Christian Science. All are somewhat influenced by the new currents of
the age, such as the automobile and the movies. But only the heroine
of the novel, Carol Kennicott, is profoundly moved by them. She is a
radical, a skeptic, a feminist. Yet as discontented as she is with her marriage because of her beliefs, she cannot find the strength either to end
her marriage, to give up her beliefs, or to seek a different life by flee-
ing with the passionate romantic who differs substantially from her
stolid husband. She becomes a dilettante, embarking on one unsuccessful crusade after another. Her one lengthy attempt at independence
ends with her return to her husband and the subsequent birth of a
child. She, like many other women, found the new ideas she had
learned at college, from books, or from friends profoundly disturbing
but difficult to apply in her own life.

The Working-Class Woman

Middle-class women faced a problem characteristic of modernizing societies: how to reconcile freedom with responsibility, how to combine in some satisfactory way the traditional role of wife and mother with the new possibilities of freer sexual expression and of professional commitment. The difficulties for working-class women were no less profound. For them, subsistence was the first problem. Many were peasant immigrants who had fled economic upheaval and political tyranny in Europe, and who flooded American shores from the 1880s on. Without funds and without experience in an industrial, urban society, they and their families became prey to industry's demand for cheap labor. They jammed into the decaying city districts of cheap tenement flats and crowded the company towns of the New England mills and the Pennsylvania mining fields.

36 Immigrants arriving in the United States, circa 1910.

37   An immigrant woman and her children doing piecework at home.

At base, the mores of working-class culture were determined by their ethnic identification. Italian women were different from Jewish women and these from Irish women. But there were certain similarities. The most important was that among all these groups, married women did not usually work away from their homes. Middle-class women and working-class women alike tried to respect the dictate that wives ought not to take on remunerative labor in the same way as their husbands. Therefore, the typical married woman of the working class worked at home, taking in wash, boarders, or piecework from a factory, while her middle-class peer took up volunteer work.

Among the working class, however, black women were an exception. Among them, 25 percent of married women worked in 1900 as against 5 percent of married white women. All working women were subject to the charge that they were not ladies, and each ethnic group was subject to specific nativist slurs, but such allegations were heightened when it came to black women. The descendants of slaves of Southern plantation owners, they were still identified in the white mind either as "mammies"—the simple-minded, carefree domestics happy to do the whites' menial labor—or as naturally promiscuous temptresses, the Eve

38   A cottonfield in Georgia.

figure incarnate. Such mythology about the nature of black women was used as a rationalization to exploit them and to keep them out of sought-after factory jobs. At a time when 25 percent of white laboring women worked in factories, only 3 percent of black women did so. Most still eked out a narrow existence on farms in the rural South. But the growing number who migrated to the cities of the South and North found work, for the most part, as laundresses or as domestic servants—the form of labor lowest in status. Often they had to take such jobs because their husbands, who faced similar discrimination, could not find work.

Among the working class as a whole, primarily widows, spinsters, and unmarried daughters worked. For the women classified by the census as immigrants, the percentages were high: in 1900 approximately 66 percent of unmarried immigrant women worked, as did nearly 100 percent of unmarried black women. From census data we can glean what kinds of work they did. According to the census of 1910, for example, 25 percent of employed women worked on farms (a figure that indicated the continued importance of farming in the economy). Twenty-five percent were employed in manufacturing; 31 percent in domestic service; 8 percent in the professions, mostly as teachers and nurses; 4 percent in clerical occupations; 4 percent in trade, mostly as clerks and saleswomen; and a small number were classified in transportation and in public service, mostly as telephone and telegraph operators.

Among employed women, there was a definite status hierarchy, and it often worked itself out along ethnic lines. White native-born women monopolized clerical work and predominated in sales work and in semi-skilled factory labor. Immigrant women of Polish and Slavic background found their place in unskilled factory labor and in domestic work, although Jewish women entered the garment industry in significant numbers and were even employed in skilled positions. Italian women were often exempt from such categorizations, but because of the

39 Female domestic servants pose for their portrait outside their Massachusetts boarding house.

extreme patriarchism of Italian society, in which a woman's virtue was under constant guard by father, brothers, and husband, the percentage of Italian women who worked was smaller than among other nationalities.

Such differentiations often masked very real sexual and racial discrimination. For example, both black and white men and women had been employed in Southern tobacco factories since before the Civil War. In these factories, white males were the supervisors and the skilled laborers; white women, the weighers and counters; black men made containers and did the sweeping and cleaning; and black women did the hand work of shredding and blending. Each type of worker occupied a special building, and each had a separate pay scale—with black women at the bottom.

Working Conditions In all the occupations, conditions were difficult. Without strong unions to represent the workers' interests, wages were low, and employers were able to violate state safety and sanitary laws with impunity. Women employed as cooks and housekeepers, even in private homes, were required to be available at all hours of the day and night, and their wages, although sometimes better than factory rates, were still minimal. Domestic workers complained about the loneliness of their occupation and about the irrationality of their employers. Waitresses often worked under unsanitary conditions, and they were dependent on tips for a living. Even in the relatively desirable working-class position of department store clerk, there were often no vacations, no rest breaks, and no chairs on which to sit (store owners wanted saleswomen to appear busy even when the store was empty). Moreover, workers were required to work evenings and Saturdays during the Christmas shopping rush.

Similar exploitative conditions characterized factory labor for women—as they did for men. This is well-illustrated in the ladies' garment industry, a large employer of factory women in the early twentieth century. Centered in the cities, the industry was organized around a system that included both factory and home labor. Major firms often sent finishing work to individual subcontractors who set up small workshops in tenement apartments, where rents were low and where

40 and 41   Long hours
and low wages were the lot
of working-class women,
from waitresses in New
Hampshire *(above)* to
pieceworkers in New
York's lower East Side
(below).

42 A sweatshop, 1888.

they could hire laborers—particularly women who lived nearby—for a pittance. It was a cheap method of production, but the "sweatshops," as these workrooms came to be known, became a national scandal because of their unsafe and unsanitary conditions.

Women who worked in a garment factory could expect to labor at least a ten-hour day and a half-day on Saturday, to be paid little, and to be required to buy their own equipment. Finally, they would be relegated to tasks less prestigious and less well-paid than those the male factory workers performed. They suffered other indignities as well. At the Triangle Shirtwaist Company in New York City, eventually to become notorious in 1911 as the scene of a major industrial fire, doors were locked so that employees could not abscond with company merchandise, and a guard at the one open door searched each woman's pocketbook as she left the factory. Given the conditions of work for these women, it is not surprising that pilferage became a form of protest.

Under such circumstances, why did working-class women work? Most Americans at the time believed that they did so to accumulate a dowry and to buy clothes and other frivolities. Some native daughters of Anglo-Saxon parentage may have worked for this reason; indeed, more than 50 percent of this group did not work at all in 1900. Yet, studies by private foundations and government agencies proved that the pin money theory was a myth. Daughters of the working class worked because they had to, because their fathers and brothers did not earn sufficient money to support their families. The large number of working women who lived with their families did so, not to save money to spend on themselves, as the pin money theorists argued, but because there was insufficient housing in American cities for unmarried working women; because in many immigrant cultures it was considered a disgrace for an unmarried daughter to live separately from her family; and, finally and most important, because many working women were not paid enough money to be able to support themselves in a private apartment or a boarding house. A 1910 Women's Trade Union League survey of Chicago department store saleswomen showed that as many as 30 percent of these workers earned little more than a subsistence wage.

Strikes and Unions Why, then, did working women not rebel against their lot? They often did. Leaders of the labor movement in-

43 Working conditions show little improvement as women make Army uniforms in 1917.

cluded women as well as men: heroines like the nonagenarian Mary "Mother" Jones, who devoted her long life to organizing laborers among the most oppressive industries in the nation—coal, Western mining, and Southern cotton mills; and Elizabeth Gurley Flynn, whose fiery oratory brought her to public prominence at the age of seventeen. Women also participated in local strikes and local labor organizations. Layoffs or wage cuts could arouse the anger of women workers as well as men. In 1898 women glovemakers in Chicago went on strike when new assembly-line techniques were introduced. They had tolerated piecework wages, tyrannical male foremen, and having to buy their own equipment, but an increase in the monotony of their work and a probable decline in wages were more than they could bear. In 1905 in Troy, New York, eight thousand women laundry workers went on strike because of the introduction of fines for talking and lateness, irregular work assignments, and a new machine, all of which substantially cut wages. In 1909, twenty thousand women shirtwaist workers in New York City and Philadelphia took to the streets in the most famous

44 Shirtwaist workers on strike.

45 The bodies of workers killed in the 1911 Triangle Shirtwaist Company fire.

strike of women workers of the century. And in 1912 the determination of striking women textile workers in Lawrence, Massachusetts, was central to the success of one of the decade's most violent confrontations between industry and labor.

The evidence of the strikes in Chicago, Troy, New York City, Philadelphia, and Lawrence demonstrates that it is incorrect to assume that working women in the early twentieth century did not have the capacity for labor militancy or for organization. Some observers at the time were convinced that women made better strikers than men—whether because of a "characteristic feminine tenacity," as one analyst put it, or because, without husbands and children dependent on them, they felt freer in their response.[16] However, it was almost impossible for the strikes to succeed, for employers had the power to use the courts, the police, and the organs of public opinion to break up such protests. The success of the 1909 shirtwaist workers' strike was due, more than anything else, to the fact that a number of well-to-do female philanthropists joined the pickets and provided bail money. Their participation brought public sympathy to the strikers and forced the owners to settle. But not all the workers even in this strike were successful. Women at the Triangle Shirtwaist Company, who had been among the organizers of the strike, gained no concessions from their employers. Instead, many of them were killed in the fire that destroyed the Triangle Company building in 1911. Their deaths could have been prevented had the owners installed proper safety equipment.

Despite their capacity for organization during strikes, women workers were reluctant to unionize. The first act of labor leader Mary Anderson on coming to the United States from Sweden was to seek out a union for companionship,[17] while Jane Addams at Hull House recounted the story of the Chicago scrubwoman who found that unionization brought job security, regular pay, and a sense of comradeship with fellow workers whom she previously had feared as rivals.[18] But they were the exceptions, not the rule. Dorothy Richardson, who wrote a perceptive account of working women in New York City in the 1900s, provided the simplest explanation of the lack of unionization among women workers: "The lot of the working girl is hard, but she has grown used to it; for, being a woman, she is patient and long suffering."[19]

But there were other reasons as well. Employers often hired women

46   Shutters buckled, fire escapes collapsed in the Triangle fire.

from various immigrant backgrounds, and the resulting suspicion and language barriers among the workers made organization difficult. The female labor force was unstable: many women did seasonal work and were laid off in slack periods. Young women, who made up the majority of the female work force, looked on work as a temporary occupation before marriage. Nor did all women respond negatively to difficult working conditions. Women of peasant stock were used to long hours of labor on farms. Rose Schneiderman, reminiscing after approximately forty years as a labor leader, was proud of her experience as a shirtwaist worker, proud of her honest toil. Theodore Dreiser in his novel *Sister Carrie* sketched a brilliant portrait of a sensitive and selfish woman who could not tolerate factory labor, but he also described her co-workers who were not discontented with their lot. There were, in addition, positive aspects to working in a factory. It provided a world outside the sometimes stifling immigrant homelife, a place where young men and women could socialize. Women formed firm friendships in the factories; they often met their husbands there.

Also, working-class women had their pride and self-respect to consider. They were sensitive to the allegation that women who participated in strikes and in labor unions, or even in work outside the home, were no better than prostitutes. The allegations were not uncommon. As a result of the mass immigration of the late nineteenth and early twentieth centuries, nativism was rampant in the United States, and the nativist and antifeminist points of view easily merged into the argument that since the majority of prostitutes came from working-class and immigrant families, all female members of these groups were potential recruits to prostitution. The only exceptions to this generalization were white Anglo-Saxon women, who did not yet work in large numbers.

Working women even took steps themselves to protect their respectability. In Perry, New York, a typical mill town, women who failed to keep to a strict moral standard were called "bums" and were forced to quit by their co-workers.[20] Lillian Wald at the Henry Street settlement recounted that neighborhood working women solicited her aid in unionizing because her support would lend respectability to the venture. The 1909 shirtwaist strikers in New York City were particularly pleased, for the same reason, to have upper-class allies.[21]

Finally, women failed to unionize because existing labor unions were hesitant to organize them. The Knights of Labor, which flourished in the 1880s, had welcomed women as members, had supported their strikes, and had carried out active recruiting campaigns among them. But violence and economic depression destroyed the Knights of Labor in the 1890s, and the American Federation of Labor (AFL), founded in 1886, came to dominate organized labor. The AFL was then composed almost exclusively of skilled craftsmen. Intent on bettering their own position in an industrial world where the owners of industry had the support of the police and the courts, these workers had little interest in taking on the problems of the unskilled trades in which women clustered. (Blacks and most immigrant males were also excluded from the craft-organized AFL.) Nor did AFL members desire the competition of women, always a cheap supply of labor, for their own jobs. The AFL constitution officially outlawed sex discrimination among member unions, and most unions nominally complied. But since in many industries women performed different tasks from men, even when this work might be considered skilled labor, union leaders simply excluded women's work in defining the crafts included in their union. One official of the International Association of Machinists told a labor investigator that "there are few real machinists. A machinist is born and not made. One must have a feeling for machines and women haven't got that."[22] Such beliefs about women dominated many skilled crafts. Even in those few AFL unions in which women members predominated, like the International Ladies' Garment Workers' Union, the officers were invariably men, except for the secretary, who was frequently a woman.

There were other reasons for the exclusion of women. For a man, the union was also a club, a refuge from the family, a place where he could socialize and escape from the difficulties of everyday life. Unions generally met in saloons, bastions of male camaraderie that the presence of women would destroy. Moreover, many wives of working men were probably opposed to allowing other women to fraternize with their husbands. Even many women workers viewed unions as "male" institutions.

The sex discrimination of the AFL was not so true of the more radical

47 Rose Schneiderman, who helped organize the WTUL, later became its first national president.

unions. Like the Knights of Labor before them, the Industrial Workers of the World (IWW), for example, did not exclude women from positions of leadership, while they made the organizing of mass-production industries, without regard to sex, their primary goal. Yet even they were not entirely free of sex bias. Women members of the IWW local in Lawrence, Massachusetts, charged that the men in their union would no more elect them to office than would men in the AFL.[23]

When women workers did protest against their working conditions, they often turned not to the radical unions or to the AFL, but to well-to-do women reformers. From this alliance grew two major organizations of the Progressive years. The first, the Consumers' League, was formed in 1890 for the purpose of improving working conditions for saleswomen in department stores through consumer boycotts. The second, the Women's Trade Union League (WTUL) was founded in 1903 at a convention of the AFL; its goals were to educate and organize both middle-class and working-class women in the cause of women's labor. The Consumers' League rapidly became a primarily middle-class organization. But the Women's Trade Union League consistently remained an amalgam of the workers and the well-to-do. Among its early state and national presidents, for example, were Alice Henrotin, a former president of the General Federation of Women's Clubs; Margaret Dreier

71

Robins, a wealthy New York philanthropist; and Mary Anderson, a daughter of Swedish immigrants who began her career working in a shoe factory.* The WTUL has been the only women's organization in the twentieth century in which women have been able to cross class barriers in a common cause.

The WTUL, even with some funding from the AFL, was always short of money, and its success was limited. Some supporters contended that the AFL purposely kept its membership small. Middle-class members in local chapters were often much too eager to stress cultural uplift rather than union organization. Above all, the social, cultural, and economic realities already described probably precluded the successful unionization of women at this time. Whatever sense of feminism existed among working-class women, it was for the most part unfocused. Too many of these women were products of peasant and immigrant cultures, which viewed women's work in the fields with equanimity while holding that a woman's proper role was to be subordinate to men. One of the reasons for the militancy of women shirtwaist workers, for example, was that some of them came from Russian and Polish Jewish immigrant families with revolutionary leanings. Most immigrant women, however, like most immigrant men, were not so inclined. In the late nineteenth century in Cohoes, New York, for example, female immigrant workers feared more than anything else the loss of the modest economic advance they had achieved, and they directed their anger not against their employer but against the unemployed who might take over their jobs.

Married Life In any case the paramount goal of the young working woman was not improved working conditions, but marriage. The acceptance of premarital sexual relations characteristic of some peasant societies, which was re-enforced by the free-and-easy society of the factory and the dance hall, may have made some working women less protective of their chastity. But casual attitudes toward sex made the supposed security and romance of marriage no less desirable. Films,

*As director of the Women's Bureau in the Department of Labor between 1919 and 1944, Anderson became one of the few women to hold a major federal appointment in this century.

72

plays, and novels hammered the theme home. The message of popular culture supported both the traditional goals of parents anxious to make good matches for their daughters and the rebelliousness of those daughters for whom marriage seemed the only way of ending their status as perpetual dependents, supplementing their elders' income.

Yet marriage among the working class had its own stresses. Particular conditions varied among the different cultures, regions, income levels, and age groups. Still, some general conclusions can be made.

Life was not easy for working-class families. With the exception of artisans and skilled laborers, the majority had incomes so small that the wives and daughters had to work to supplement them. Men left the responsibility for contraception to their wives, who were expected to be sexually available at their husbands' behest. But information about birth control was not easy to come by. One commentator noted that many mothers tried to prolong the nursing of their infants in the mistaken belief that lactating women could not conceive.[24]

48 A visiting nurse calls on a family in a city slum, circa 1890.

According to many sociologists, the patriarchal family has remained the model in the working class much longer than in the middle class. One observer at the time wrote that "the conventions of the working class are more rigid than any other class. They are the last to be affected by changing psychology or institutions."[25] The idea of companionship in marriage differentiated middle-class values from working-class values. Given economic pressures, the patriarchal ideal often served as a justification for harsh treatment: of husbands against wives, of parents against children. Under these circumstances, many marriages became strained, with husbands and wives living, according to one observer, with "little affection" and "little spiritual comradeship."[26] Husbands generally gave wages to wives to distribute; thus working-class women gained power within their families. But then each characteristically retreated to his or her own territory: husbands to newspapers, saloons, or sporting events; wives to homes or children. For the working class, divorce was difficult: it was expensive, it required knowing how to find a lawyer, and among Catholics and Jews it was a disgrace. This is not to imply, however, that discontented couples always remained together. Cases of desertion were numerous among the working class, and by the 1920s the divorce rate had begun to equal and even surpass that of the middle class. Poverty, ignorance, the shock of American culture and the city, and traditional views about the nature of male–female relationships made marriage as difficult, if not more difficult, among the working class as among the well-to-do.

Yet, like women of the middle class, working-class women often found respite from their marriages by joining an organization. Immigrant groups founded churches and ethnic societies, which nurtured traditional values and helped offset a sense of insecurity and isolation in an indifferent environment. Local chapters of the American Federation of Labor formed women's auxiliaries, where wives could meet congenial friends and gain some sense of partnership with their husbands' work. And for some, there was relief from constant child-bearing: studies showed that knowledge and use of contraceptives grew as income rose and length of residence in the United States increased.

But what they all had was hope: hope for the future of their children. That was the promise of American life. It was a viable hope, for their daughters as well as their sons. The young woman factory worker might become a secretary or a nurse, with the promise of greater status and a higher salary; she might even marry a businessman or a doctor. For society in general, such possibilities—and, more important, the belief in them—acted as a powerful safety valve. That women took advantage of these opportunities is shown by statistical studies. In 1900 almost all women who worked were domestics, farm laborers, or unskilled factory workers. By 1910, however, stenography and typing employed 7 percent of all women workers. By 1920 the figure had risen to 16 percent, and by 1930 to almost 19 percent. By 1940 clerical work was the largest single field of women's employment. The transition from domestic to factory to office work was rarely made in the same generation. But for the immigrant mother whose sons became lawyers and doctors and whose daughters became secretaries, nurses, and the wives of lawyers and doctors, the American promise was fulfilled.

THE OTHER WAY: PROSTITUTION

Not all American women in the early twentieth century—whether black or white, immigrant or native—played the socially approved female roles of wife and mother or of volunteer worker or paid employee. A few turned to prostitution—the occupation that particularly challenged Victorian notions of female purity and propriety.

It is difficult to determine the number of prostitutes in the United States in the 1900s. Since the occupation was illegal, few women would willingly reveal their participation. In any event, prostitution seems to have been on the increase in the late nineteenth century.

Its Growth

Its expansion was largely due to the explosive growth of cities in that period. Among the shifting and anonymous urban population, prostitution could flourish as it never had in rural, tradition-bound communities. Moreover, because polite society was unwilling to recognize that prostitution existed, little public pressure was exerted to suppress it. For sailors in port, for unmarried men, for traveling businessmen, for husbands bored at home, the prostitute became a real or imagined necessity, readily available, knowledgeable about sex techniques, and willing to accommodate practices that would horrify Victorian wives.

During the late nineteenth century, public officials were aware of the existence of prostitution, but with a characteristic Victorian attitude, they looked on it as a "necessary evil" to protect the virtue of pure women. In most cities the police had driven prostitution, at least as practiced in brothels, into so-called red light districts, far from the middle class who might be offended by it. Thus gathered together, prostitutes provided revenue to the city and to individual policemen who threatened arrest unless regular payments were made. In some cities, a system approaching the European practice of licensing, under which prostitutes paid fees to the state and were required to have regular medical examinations for venereal disease, had come into being. Among the red light districts, which also functioned as havens for criminals, the French Quarter in New Orleans and the Barbary Coast in San Francisco were best known, but their replicas existed in large and small cities throughout the nation. Even in the city of Muncie, Indiana, with a population of about eleven thousand, there were twenty to twenty-five brothels in the 1890s, with four to eight women per house.[27]

Its Practitioners

Why did women become prostitutes? Some observers at that time were convinced that all prostitutes were forced into a "life of vice" by male procurers who were employed by national and international syndicates. For a time around 1910 concern about the "white slave" trade reached the level of a national hysteria, pervaded by rumors that men with hypodermic needles traveled crowded streetcars and haunted amusement parks seeking likely victims to drug and abduct. Contributing factors to this hysteria were reactions against the new feminism and against the concerted efforts by reformers to force Americans to discuss taboo subjects like prostitution and venereal disease. Also it was difficult for the typical Victorian to believe that a woman could embark on a life of prostitution unless she was attacked and drugged. For reasons of health and social welfare, Americans could approve the creation of vice commissions in most major cities after 1900, but it was difficult

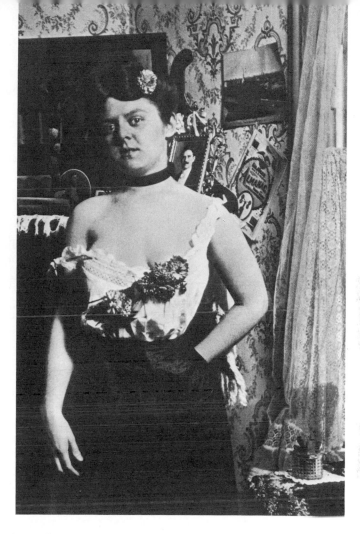

49 Prostitution: innate depravity or just another kind of work?

for a society still shot through with repressive attitudes about sex to digest their findings that poverty lay at the bottom of prostitution and that many prostitutes were not repelled by their life. The white slave story was more shocking, more thrilling, and easier to accept.

This paranoia was given currency by some well-documented cases of women who actually were drugged and awakened in brothels. There were men who hung around dance halls, trying to strike up an acquaintance that might turn into a seduction. These men were well aware of the prevailing notion that a woman, once "fallen," might just as well take to the streets. Among some immigrant groups—the Italians and the Orthodox Jews, for example—a fall from viture, if discovered, could result in ostracism from the family. But there was little evidence that any large syndicates lurked behind the recruitment to prostitution.

Most surveys of prostitution played down the white slave story and looked elsewhere for an explanation of why women became prostitutes. They found that the most common factor was economic need. Most prostitutes came from the working class. Studies made in Eastern cities indicated that prostitutes were drawn primarily from among second-generation immigrant women. In the Midwest, the majority seemed to be women of native Anglo-Saxon stock who had recently moved to cities from farm communities. In the South, the majority of prostitutes were probably black women. Among all these groups, many reported that they had turned to prostitution as a last resort, either because they had a family to support or because they could earn much more money as a prostitute than as a seamstress or even a salesclerk. "Poverty causes prostitution," concluded the writers of the Illinois Vice Commission Report of 1916,[28] and the investigations of other vice commissions invariably agreed. In addition, most studies singled out domestic work as the most common previous occupation of prostitutes.

The argument that poverty caused prostitution, however satisfying to a society still ambivalent about female sexuality, provided only a partial explanation. Perceptive observers, despite a middle-class orientation, could not fail to note that many prostitutes disclosed that they had entered the occupation because of "personal inclination." As early as 1858, in the first detailed investigation of prostitution in the United States, Dr. William Sanger of New York found that approximately 25 percent of his sample of two thousand women said that they had become prostitutes simply because they wanted to. Despite Sanger's medical orientation, he could not accept this explanation. To this Victorian, "personal inclination" indicated "an innate depravity, a want of true womanly feeling, which is actually incredible."[29] He reasoned that liquor or drugs must have produced the sexual arousal these women reported. It did not occur to him that they might have come from a world in which sexuality was open and prostitution just another kind of work. Some fifty years after Sanger, Jane Addams in *A New Con-*

science and an Ancient Evil (1913) came to a conclusion similar to Sanger's. Chaste women, she thought, were defiled and then "degraded morally" by "horrible devices" so that they would willingly become prostitutes.[30] Like Sanger, Addams seemed to admit that women had some sensuality, but only under unnatural conditions. She could not believe that they might willingly become promiscuous.

Other investigators were more objective about the causes and conditions of prostitution. From their observations and hints (for few individuals in that age dared condone free sexuality) we can construct a fairly complete picture, not only of prostitution itself, but of the culture out of which it grew.

Its Operation

Many prostitutes, although far from the majority, worked in brothels. Streetwalking was sometimes dangerous, and there is an indication that in some cities streetwalkers were primarily older women who had been edged out of brothels by younger competitors. Brothels were run by madams, who took responsibility for protection, solicitation, and accommodations. They were often resourceful and innovative business-women. Because the vice commission and police drives of the early twentieth century often concentrated on their easily identifiable houses, madams devised new methods of carrying on their trade. They reopened their houses under the guise of private dance studios and massage parlors. They invented clever call-girl systems, in which the madam simply kept a list of women, whom she could telephone to arrange a meeting with a client at a convenient hotel. If police surveillance was suspected, the location could always be changed.

Many prostitutes were connected with male pimps—or "cadets" as they were then called—to whom they gave most of their earnings and from whom they received spending money. If the prostitute did not work in a brothel, the pimp sometimes would serve as her procurer. The 1916 Kneeland investigation in New York City, for example, suggested that the pimp–prostitute relationship there had grown out of friend-ships among boys and girls in street gangs in slum districts and that in this case the pimps solicited for their women. Frequently, however, the pimp lived a life of leisure, supported by his woman. Often a pimp

50 "Parlor House" occupied by Bob Ford's girls in Creede, Colorado, during the 1890s.

would have more than one prostitute working for him, and the women would vie for his affection.*

Not all prostitutes worked for madams or for pimps. Both demanded sizable percentages of a prostitute's fees. A prostitute's connection with a brothel was hard to conceal from family, friends, and the police. Moreover, in many cities the prostitute could make her own assignations with relative safety in dance halls and saloons, while there were always hotels that catered to the prostitute and her clientele. Such conditions made independent prostitution attractive to some women

* It is difficult to determine why this relationship came into being. There is some indication that it first developed in France and was imported to the United States. Psychologists argue that it may express a deep self-hatred on the part of prostitutes; sociologists contend that, like marriage among the middle class, it may simply be a norm within the culture of prostitution that many prostitutes follow.

unable to find work or anxious to supplement inadequate wages. There was, as one observer described it, a certain amount of "semi-prostitution" among working women.[31]

This was not the case with all working-class women of course. Different women reacted in different ways to their new roles as workers outside of the home. To many who aspired to higher status it was clear that virtue was a valued possession of middle-class women, and they enforced on themselves and their daughters the strict standards that seemed at the heart of middle-class life. Other working-class women took an opposite direction. Work had brought them into contact with young men, while responsibility had given them the nerve to scorn parental restraints. They expected to go to dance halls and to meet men. For some, sex was the next step. The investigators for the Massachusetts Vice Commission reported in 1914 that in every Massachusetts city sizable numbers of young women loitered around cafés and dance halls, waiting to be picked up by men. "To the total stranger," the investigators reported, "they talk willingly about themselves, their desire to 'see life,' to 'get out of this dead hole,' to go to Boston, or to New York." Many of these women, the investigators found, were willing to have sexual relations with them.[32] Assuredly, this was sexual license, but it was not prostitution, as the Massachusetts reporters were quick to point out. For most of these women were incensed by the offer of direct payment for an assignation. They drew a fine line between their own definitions of virtue and vice: payment meant prostitution, and they were not prostitutes.

It seems evident that prostitutes were, to a large extent, recruited from the sexually experienced, some probably from the very group of women that the Massachusetts investigators described. What was it that made a woman turn from casual sex to prostitution? The most reasonable explanation is that for most, it was an unthinking decision. All studies showed that the average prostitute had had her first sexual experience before she became a full-fledged prostitute and that her partner usually was a man she knew well. After this encounter she drifted into casual relations with other men, until finally it seemed reasonable to accept money, especially when it was obvious that a successful prostitute could earn double or triple the wages of a salesgirl or a domestic servant.

The actual category of prostitution remained ambiguous. Many investigators were aware that beyond those women actually committed to prostitution, who for the most part were their subjects, lay a shadowy world in which women worked as part-time prostitutes or took up the trade between jobs or between husbands. These women successfully avoided both the law and the vice commission investigators. Sometimes, almost by accident, reporters stumbled into this world.

One such reporter was Frances Donovan, who for several months in 1920 donned a uniform to study the occupation of the waitress. There were a number of such studies of working women in the early twentieth century: many educated young women eager to advance themselves and the cause of women found it challenging to enter the working-class world and record their experiences. Few, however, investigated their subjects with as much candor, or were so challenged by their findings, as was Donovan.

At first Donovan was shocked as she plumbed the world of the waitress. Here sexuality was always present. In their spare time her new acquaintances boasted of their affairs and openly discussed their abortions. Her sheltered upbringing had not prepared her for this nor for the women's constant use of obscenities and profanities. Nor could she reconcile herself to their penchant for retelling off-color jokes heard from patrons or for pointing out to each other men who supposedly were sexual perverts.

But slowly Donovan came to respect these women. She began to believe that their way of life represented a negative appraisal of middle-class culture. Their behavior went far beyond a simple openness about sexual relations. They had lived, Donovan judged, in a way that no middle-class woman, bound to convention, could. Many of them had married and had left their husbands, and that fact, plus their economic independence, lay at the heart of the matter, according to Donovan. They were free of the dominance of men. "With economic independence the waitress has achieved a man's independence in her relations with men; she doesn't have to get married and she doesn't have to stay married very long." "She is a free soul," wrote Donovan.[33]

Doubtless Donovan romanticized the life of the waitress, with its long hours, hard work, and subservient status. Like many feminists, she allowed her suspicion of men to color her interpretation. Yet there was more than a grain of truth in what she had to say. Were not these waitresses more honest about life and work than their middle-class peers? "To go out into the world and grab from it the right to live in spite of the competition of youth is vastly more interesting than to make weekly pilgrimages to the beauty parlor in the vain attempt to get rid of the symbols of old age that bear witness to the fact that you have never lived." "Here," Donovan concluded, "we have the feminist movement and ideals embodied in a class."[34]

To a certain extent, Donovan was correct: without sexual liberation, women could never be free. But was sexual liberation enough? And did women not have other responsibilities—to themselves, to their families, to society? Should marriage and the nuclear family so easily be assumed oppressive? And if women left the home, as Donovan's waitresses did, who would raise their children? (Curiously, any mention of children is absent from Donovan's narrative.) These were some of the basic questions facing American women of all classes in the early years of this century, and the increased freedom of expression and action that the transition to the new century brought only served to make more difficult women's attempts to work out the answers in their own lives.

Notes

[1] Gertrude Atherton, *Can Women Be Gentlemen?* (Boston: Houghton Mifflin, 1938), p. 39.

[2] Mary I. Wood, *The History of the General Federation of Women's Clubs* (New York: General Federation of Women's Clubs, 1912), p. 65.

[3] Annie Nathan Meyer, "Woman's Assumption of Sex Superiority," *North American Review*, CLXVIII (January 1904), 108.

[4] Carroll Smith-Rosenberg, "The Hysterical Woman: Sex Roles and Role Conflict in Nineteenth-Century America," *Social Research*, XXXIX (Winter 1972), 652–78.

[5] American Sociological Society, *Papers and Proceedings of the Third Annual Meeting of the American Sociological Society: The Family* (Chicago: University of Chicago Press, 1908), p. 132.

[6] Anna A. Rogers, *Why American Marriages Fail and Other Papers* (Boston: Houghton Mifflin, 1909), p. 62.

[7] Katherine G. Busby, *Home Life in America* (New York: Macmillan, 1910), p. 149.

[8] Helen Merrell Lynd and Robert S. Lynd, *Middletown in Transition: A Study in Cultural Conflicts* (New York: Harcourt Brace Jovanovich, 1937), p. 95.

[9] Rogers, *Why American Marriages Fail and Other Papers*, pp. 174–75.

[10] Mary R. Smith, "Domestic Service: The Responsibility of Employers," *Forum*, XXVII (August 1899), 678–89.

[11] Lucy Maynard Salmon, *Progress in the Household* (Boston: Houghton Mifflin, 1906), p. 95.

[12] Frances Parkinson Keyes, *All Flags Flying: Reminiscences of Frances Parkinson Keyes* (New York: McGraw-Hill, 1972), p. 13.

[13] *Ibid.*, p. 31.

[14] Mabel S. Ulrich, "A Doctor's Diary, 1904–1932," *Scribner's* (June 1933). Reprinted in *Ms.*, I (July 1972), 11–14.

[15] Busby, *Home Life in America*, p. 283.

[16] Helen Marot, *American Labor Unions, by a Member* (New York: Henry Holt, 1914), p. 74.

[17] Alice Henry, *Memoirs of Alice Henry*, ed. Nettie Palmer, typescript (Melbourne, 1944), p. 71.

[18] Jane Addams, *Twenty Years at Hull House* (New York: Macmillan, 1910), p. 166.

[19] Dorothy Richardson, *The Long Day: The Story of a New York Working Girl as Told by Herself* (New York: Century, 1905), p. 303.

[20] Mrs. John Van Vorst and Marie Van Vorst, *The Woman Who Toils: Being the Experiences of Two Gentlewomen as Factory Girls* (New York: Doubleday, Page, and Co., 1904), p. 92.

[21] Lillian Wald, *The House on Henry Street* (New York: Henry Holt, 1915), p. 203.

[22] Theresa Wolfson, *The Woman Worker and the Trade Unions* (New York: International, 1926), p. 110.

[23] Marot, *American Labor Unions, by a Member*, p. 68.

[24] Frank Hatch Streightoff, *The Standard of Living Among the Industrial People of America* (Boston: Houghton Mifflin, 1911), p. 138.

[25] Wolfson, *The Woman Worker and the Trade Unions*, p. 43.

[26] Streightoff, *The Standard of Living Among the Industrial People of America*, pp. 138–64.

[27] Lynd and Lynd, *Middletown in Transition: A Study in Cultural Conflicts*, p. 113.

[28] State of Illinois, *Report of the Senate Vice Committee* (Chicago, 1911), p. 203.

[29] William Sanger, *The History of Prostitution: Its Extent, Causes, and Effects Throughout the World* (New York: Medical, 1927), p. 488.

[30] Jane Addams, *A New Conscience and an Ancient Evil* (New York: Macmillan, 1914), p. 22.

[31] Frances Donovan, *The Woman Who Waits* (Boston: Richard Badger, 1920), p. 224.

[32] Massachusetts Commission for the Investigation of the White Slave Traffic, *Report of the Commission for the Investigation of the White Slave Traffic, so-called* (Boston, 1914), p. 43.

[33] Donovan, *The Woman Who Waits*, p. 224.

[34] *Ibid.*, p. 226.

Bibliography

A wealth of material is available to reconstruct a profile of the middle-class woman in any period of her history. For the early twentieth century, one can consult newspapers and journals, diaries and biographies, contemporary analyses and novels.

On the history of the family, Arthur Calhoun, *Social History of the American Family*, 3 vols. (Cleveland: Arthur Clark, 1918) is the standard (and just about the only) history. For divorce, see William O'Neill, *Divorce in the Progressive Era* (New Haven: Yale University Press, 1967). Also useful are Sidney Ditzion, *Marriage, Morals, and Sex in America: A History of Ideas* (1953; reprint ed., New York: Octagon, 1970); Nelson Blake, *The Road to Reno: A History of Divorce in the United States* (New York: Macmillan, 1962); and several studies by sociologists, including John Sirjamaki, *The American Family in the Twentieth Century* (Cambridge, Mass.: Harvard University Press, 1953); Hugh Carter and Paul Glick, *Marriage and Divorce: A Social and Economic Study* (Cambridge, Mass.: Harvard University Press, 1970); Ruth Shonle Cavan, *The American Family*, 4th ed. (New York: Crowell, 1969); Sophonisba P. Breckinridge, *The Family and the State: Select Documents* (1934; reprint ed., New York: Arno Press, 1972); and Ernest Mowrer, *Family Disorganization: An Introduction to a Sociological Analysis* (Chicago: University of Chicago Press, 1927). Useful analyses by contemporaries include Lydia Commander, *The American Idea* (1907; reprint ed., New York: Arno Press, 1972); Anna A. Rogers, *Why American Marriages Fail and Other Papers* (Boston: Houghton Mifflin, 1909); and the American Sociological Society, *Papers and Proceedings of the Third Annual Meeting of the American Sociological Society: The Family* (Chicago: University of Chicago Press, 1908).

To get a sense of the life of the working-class woman, one can proceed in a variety of ways, although here the autobiographical material is more limited than for middle-class women. There are, for example, innumerable studies of ethnic cultures, and recently some of them have begun to pay specific attention to women. See, for example, Virginia Yans McLaughlin, "Patterns of Work and Family Organization: Buffalo's Italians," *Journal of Interdisciplinary History*, II (Autumn 1971), 299–314, and Daniel Walkowitz, "Working-Class Women in the Gilded Age," *Journal of Social History*, V (Summer 1972), 464–90. On black women, the secondary literature is especially thin. A recent and extremely useful compilation of primary source material is Gerda Lerner, *Black Women in White America* (New York: Pantheon, 1972). On the conditions of women's work, Robert Smuts, *Women and Work in America*, 2nd ed. (New York: Schocken, 1971), and Elizabeth Faulkner Baker, *Technology and Woman's Work* (New York: Columbia University Press, 1964), in particular, provide useful information. One can also profitably consult studies of individual industries and labor unions, such as Benjamin Stolberg, *Tailor's Progress: The Story of a Famous Union and the Men Who Made It* (New York: Doubleday and Company, 1944), and Leon Stein, *The Triangle Fire* (Philadelphia: Lippincott, 1962). The most extensive contemporary survey of working conditions is the United States Bureau of Labor, *Report on the Conditions of Woman and Child Wage Earners in the United States*, 19 vols. (Washington D.C., 1910). On women in the labor movement, see vol. X of the Bureau of Labor survey; Helen Marot, *American Labor Unions, by a Member* (New York: Henry Holt, 1914); Theresa Wolfson, *The Woman Worker and the Trade Unions* (New York: International, 1926); Gladys Boone, *The Women's Trade Union Leagues in Great Britain and the United States of America* (New York: Columbia University Press, 1942); and Alice Henry, *The Trade Union Woman* (1915; reprint ed., New York: Burt Franklin).

Progressive reformers conducted numerous surveys and exposés of the conditions of work for women. Among the most revealing are Elizabeth Butler, *Women and the Trades: Pittsburgh, 1907–1908* (New York: Charities Publication Committee, 1909); Helen Campbell, *Prisoners of Poverty: Women Wage-Workers, Their Trades and Their Lives* (Boston: Roberts Brothers, 1890); and Mrs. John Van Vorst and Marie Van Vorst, *The Woman Who Toils: Being the Experiences of Two Gentlewomen* as *Factory Girls* (New York: Doubleday, Page, and Co., 1904). Several interesting autobiographies of workers are also available, including Dorothy Richardson, *The Long Day: The Story of a New York Working Girl as Told by Herself* (New York: Century, 1905); Agnes Nestor, *Woman's Labor Leader: Autobiography of Agnes Nestor* (Rockford, Ill.: Bellevue Books, 1954); and Rose Schneiderman (with Lucy Goldthwaite), *All for One* (New York: Paul S. Eriksson, 1967).

The subject of women in radical movements awaits its historian. James Weinstein, *The Decline of Socialism in America* (New York: Monthly Review Press, 1967) gives some information, but most of the standard works on socialism, anarchism, and the IWW fail to deal with women. Mary Jones, *Autobiography of Mother Jones*, ed. Mary Field Parton (Chicago: C. H. Kerr, 1925), and Elizabeth Gurley Flynn, *I Speak My Own Piece* (New York: Masses and Mainstream, 1955) are interesting, as is Ella Reeve Bloor, *We Are Many: An Autobiography by Ella Reeve Bloor* (New York: International Publishers, 1940). On Emma Goldman, discussed in Chapter 3, see Emma Goldman, *Living My Life*, 2 vols. (New York: Alfred A. Knopf, 1931); Richard Drinnon, *Rebel in Paradise: A Biography of Emma Goldman* (Chicago: University of Chicago Press, 1961); and Alix Kates Shulman, *To the Barricades: The Anarchist Life of Emma Goldman* (New York: Crowell, 1971).

On the working-class woman in the family, one can consult the general works mentioned above. For comparison with later periods, one might consult Mirra Komarovsky, *Blue-Collar Marriage* (New York: Random House, 1962).

Progressive vice reformers and middle-class attitudes toward prostitution have not lacked their historians. See, for example, Egal Feldman, "Prostitution, the Alien Woman, and the Progressive Imagination, 1910–1915," *American Quarterly* (Summer 1967), 192–206, and Robert Riegel, "Changing American Attitudes Towards Prostitution," *Journal of the History of Ideas*, XXIX (July–September 1968), 437–52. There is no study, however, of the culture of prostitution itself, although the vice commission reports and other surveys conducted in a number of cities early in this century provide a wealth of information. On prostitution in more recent decades, there is an extensive literature. See, for example, Charles Winick and Paul M. Kinsie, *The Lively Commerce: Prostitution in the United States* (New York: Quadrangle, 1971).

Women as Organizers and Innovators: Suffrage, Reform, and Feminism, 1890–1920

Between 1890 and the First World War, the feminist movement was vigorous and active. Historians have often interpreted these years as an era when the women's suffrage movement held a virtual monopoly over organized women. But it was in fact a period when a variety of innovative feminist studies appeared, and women's organizations proliferated. Feminists and reformers were aware of a wide range of problems that women encountered in a modernizing America, and they moved in many ways to confront them. Never before or since have so many women belonged to so many women's organizations; not until the 1960s was feminism again so vigorous. Most organized women were social feminists. But there were radical women, too: some were involved with political causes; some concentrated their efforts on women's causes. By 1914 all the segments of the women's movement had come together around a commitment to suffrage as their main goal. But before that time feminism looked in many directions.

SUFFRAGISM ON THE WANE

In the first decade of the twentieth century, the suffrage movement fell on hard times. The suffrage crusade had followed a difficult path since Reconstruction (1867–1877), when Congress and the nation enfranchised blacks but would not give the vote to women. In 1868 its force had been weakened by the split in the movement between the more militant wing led by Susan B. Anthony and Elizabeth Cady Stanton, who wanted to pressure Congress into passing a suffrage amendment, and the moderate wing led by Lucy Stone, who wanted to concentrate on passage by the states. In 1875 in *Minor v. Happersett* the Supreme Court had added its stamp of approval to the doctrine of disfranchisement.

But even the reunion of the two factions into the NAWSA in 1893 did not accomplish a great deal. If anything, the NAWSA in the first decades of its existence achieved less than the divided organizations had before. Under the auspices of the Stanton-Anthony organization, for example, the suffrage bill had first been introduced into Congress in 1868. It had reached the floor of both houses each year after that date; and each year hearings were held on it. The NAWSA, which was dominated by the Stone group, decided to abandon the congressional campaign and concentrate on the states. The result was that after 1893, with feminist pressure removed, Congress paid little attention to the amendment. Yet the NAWSA had no better success with its state campaigns. Between 1896 and 1910 referenda on the suffrage were held in only six states, and they were defeated in all six. In 1910 women had equal suffrage in only four states.

These failures were partly due to the vigorous antisuffrage opposition. In the late nineteenth century, local antisuffrage groups, often headed by socially prominent women, had appeared. In 1911 they united to form the National Association Opposed to the Further Extension of Suffrage to Women. The organization gained political support from three powerful groups: the liquor industry, which was afraid that suffrage for women would bring prohibition; the political bosses, who were fearful that women would vote for reform politicians; and the Catholic Church, which staunchly believed that a woman's place was in the home.

SUFFRAGETTE VOTE-GETTING
THE EASIEST WAY.

51   A turn-of-the-century post card
poking fun at suffragists.

The arguments of the antisuffragists also spoke powerfully to American men and women who upheld traditional values. Politics, they believed, was no place for a woman. It was, and should be, a special male preserve. It meant exhausting activity and long periods of time spent away from home and had the unsavory aura of barroom deals and underhanded practices. Politics was, as suffrage leader Abigail Scott Duniway put it in the 1900s, "sacred to the aristocracy of the [male] sex."[1] The antisuffrage argument played on all the standard fears: if women voted, they would hold office; if women held office, they would leave the home, break up the family, and take power away from men. Woman, wrote one representative antisuffragist,

> has not incorporated in her nature those qualities as mystical and as holy as the life which she transmits to the world; she has not become an inspiration and the very savior of our life, in order that she may turn traitor to herself and her ideal for a paltry bit of paper, and the boast that, from being man's superior she has now become his equal.[2]

52 Antisuffrage leaders presenting their case to legislators.

"O SAVE US, SENATORS, FROM OURSELVES!"

Suffrage, according to the more hysterical antisuffragists, was a revolt against "nature." Pregnant women might lose their babies, nursing mothers their milk, and women in general might grow beards or else be raped at the polls.*

Yet the more rational antisuffragists were not necessarily conservative on issues other than women's voting. Many of them were social feminists, active in reform organizations. They added a further argument to the common objections to suffrage for women. They reasoned that without the vote and without party affiliations, women could have a greater influence on legislators because their motives could not be questioned. However naive this view of political reality, the argument had a sizable impact on women's organizations like the General Federation of Women's Clubs, which refused to endorse suffrage until 1914.

*Most polls in this period were set up in saloons and barber shops, which partly explains the hysteria of the extreme antisuffragists. After 1920, when women could vote, polling places were moved to schools, churches, and firehouses.

The appeal of the antisuffrage argument, however, does not entirely explain the failures of the suffrage movement in the first decade of the twentieth century. Indeed, there were problems within the leadership of the movement. Decades of unsuccessful campaigning had inevitably produced ennui and discontent. By the turn of the century, leadership had passed from the founders to a generation of more moderate women. In 1892 at the age of seventy-six, Elizabeth Cady Stanton relinquished the presidency of the NAWSA to Susan B. Anthony, who remained in the office until 1900 when, at the age of eighty, she, too, retired from active work. In 1893 Lucy Stone died at the age of seventy-five. Among the moderates, Anna Howard Shaw, who had been Anthony's trusted lieutenant, assumed a dominant role. In 1904 she became president of the NAWSA, a post she held until 1915. She was an unfortunate choice.

53 An antisuffrage meeting of the General Federation of Women's Clubs at the Hotel Astor, New York.

Although a brilliant orator, Shaw had limited administrative skill. She was censorious and dictatorial as president and did not inspire the confidence of her associates. Backbiting and pettiness began to emerge among the NAWSA leadership, and much time was spent in internal conflict and intrigue.

Shaw and her associates wanted primarily to maintain a moderate profile, to appear as sober seekers after justice. They held conventions each year; they circulated petitions; they issued instructions to state organizations. But rather than spurring the membership on to new kinds of action, they took the traditional path of trying to educate women through reasoned pamphlets and genteel meetings. They would have nothing to do with the kind of militancy that might associate them in the public eye with radical groups, like the anarchists, or the early axe-wielding, saloon-destroying members of the WCTU whom the press so derided. Nor did the moderates attempt to form alliances with working-class groups that ought to have been their allies, especially in helping them counteract the opposition of political bosses and the Catholic Church. Harriot Stanton Blatch, daughter of Elizabeth Cady Stanton and herself a skilled suffragist in New York, judged that "the old order of suffragists had kept youngsters 'in their place,'" "had left working women alone," and had not "'bothered' with men bent on politics."[3]

The position of the middle generation of suffragists was not entirely wrong-headed. Their very conservatism of action, which was matched by equally conservative arguments in their speeches and writings, played a large role in defusing American fears about giving women the vote. Stanton and Anthony had argued that women deserved the vote because, like men, they had a "natural right" to it. The next generation contended that women as mothers needed the vote to protect the home and that the nation needed the votes of native Anglo-Saxon women to counteract the supposedly pernicious effects of immigrant and black males' votes. The argument from natural right implied a challenge to conventional male–female roles. The new "argument from expediency," as historian Aileen Kraditor has called it, suggested no such direct threat. President M. Carey Thomas of Bryn Mawr College wrote that in 1908, when she was instrumental in founding the National College Equal Suffrage League, the subject of suffrage was still so inflammatory that even college students hesitated to discuss it, while conventions of the Association of Collegiate Alumnae regularly barred the subject from their agendas. Within a few years these reservations had vanished, and suffrage had become respectable among the academic community. Thomas suggested that the change had occurred to a large extent because the old arguments based on women's right to the vote were replaced by the argument that women needed the vote to protect the home and to become effective reformers.[4]

In any case, between 1890 and the First World War, the suffrage movement was only one woman's cause among many, and the majority of organized women probably did not support it. Before 1912, wrote Rheta Childe Dorr, the suffrage movement was dead. "No newspaper or magazine editor would have printed an article on the subject. No politician gave it a thought."[5] She may have exaggerated, but her comment underscores the fact that other issues besides suffrage held the attention of organized women in the early years of this century.

FEMINISM AND PROGRESSIVISM: A CASE OF GIVE AND TAKE

Central among these concerns was a renewed interest in social justice for women and the disadvantaged. This social feminism was a natural outgrowth of the new freedoms for women under the law and new opportunities in education and the professions. It also stemmed from the general climate of social reform, in which people were widely questioning the benefits of unregulated industrialization and urbanization. Membership in voluntary associations to promote social welfare was flourishing. The debate over the nature of the American democratic order was vigorous and penetrating. Both Progressives and reformers to the left of them could not help but add women's oppression to their list of social injustices in America. Moreover, like women in the abolition movement of the early nineteenth century and women in the civil rights movement of the 1960s, socialist and Progressive women came to see their own condition partly reflected in the problems of the disadvantaged whom they worked to help. Muckraking journals, too, were eager to print feminist exposés of the lives of working women, of prostitutes, and of the general oppression of women. The subject was fresh and vital and itself a stimulus to the reform impulse.

As much as Progressivism sparked feminism, feminism itself played an important role in the Progressive movement. Only recently has the participation of women in Progressivism begun to be explored. In the past, historians have viewed Progressivism in many ways: as a movement of status-conscious professionals attempting to re-create an older, simpler society; or as an attempt on the part of certain business interests to gain favorable legislation. But from the work of historians like David Thelen, on Wisconsin Progressivism, and Allen Davis, on the settlement houses, a new interpretation of the period is emerging. This interpretation stresses reform aspects such as conservation, pure food and drug acts, child-welfare legislation, kindergartens and educational innovation and finds a main source of the reform impulse in women's interest in expanding their roles and providing viable lives for their families in an increasingly industrial and urban America.

The Organizations: Growth and Changing Goals

Since the early nineteenth century, and especially after the Civil War, women had been organizing in associations concerned with social-welfare issues. The Women's Christian Temperance Union, for example, headed between 1878 and 1896 by the charismatic Frances Willard, put reform causes at the forefront of its program. In addition to its better known campaigns for the prohibition of alcohol and for stricter moral codes, its leadership publicized the benefits of exercise and of rational dress for women and agitated for kindergartens in the public schools, for police matrons to serve women prisoners, and for child-labor laws. Willard secured WCTU support for the Knights of Labor and for the peace movement, while she herself was influential in the reform-minded Prohibition party. In 1896 Willard's conservative opponents gained control of the WCTU and made temperance its main concern. But during Willard's years of leadership, the WCTU educated many home-bound, rural and small town women to a sense of social responsibility. Women often joined the WCTU and from there became involved in women's suffrage and progressive reform causes. As Willard herself put it, their "consciousness" of themselves and of their society was raised.[6]

Similarly, the women's clubs that flourished in the late nineteenth and early twentieth centuries often had both reform platforms and a feminist stance. Established in the 1870s as lecture and discussion clubs with an emphasis on art, literature, and travel, women's clubs were slowly drawn into social reform. This had partly to do with the influence of the widely read journalist Jane Croly, who wrote under the pseudonym Jennie June. Croly is credited with having founded the first women's club, Sorosis, in New York City in 1868, after women journalists had been excluded from a banquet in honor of the visiting English author Charles Dickens. Like Frances Willard, she was able to interest many women's clubs in feminism and reform. In other cases, clubs adopted social-welfare causes in response to local conditions. In numerous clubs, a similar pattern was repeated: lectures on art and beauty stimulated drives to beautify cities by planting flowers and grass; these drives in turn generated an interest in public parks and playgrounds and ultimately in a variety of municipal agencies and functions bearing on the health and happiness of the family. One mother's concern over her children's schooling might lead to an investigation of the local school system or to the introduction of kindergartens

54 A kindergarten class, 1914.

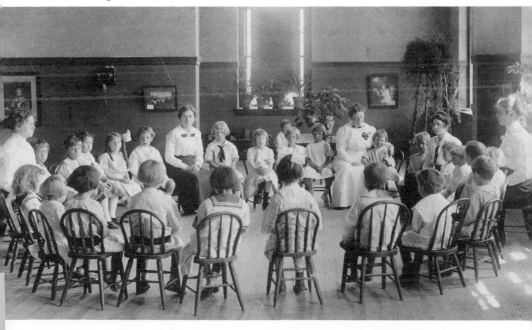

—the German innovation that promised more effective education for young children and more free time for their mothers. Or, as one observer, explaining women's advocation of improved street cleaning, commented, "It is their dresses which must sweep up the debris."[7] In 1892 Jane Croly, among others, organized the General Federation of Women's Clubs, and the national organization increased the pressure on local clubs to undertake reform causes.

Women's clubs made headway in many areas of reform between the 1890s and the First World War. The Chicago Civic Club and the Boston Women's Municipal League led successful drives in their cities to raise investment capital to buy and improve tenement houses in order to show that landlords could improve slum conditions and still make a profit. In New York, as elsewhere, the Women's Municipal League acted as a watchdog group to make certain that existing laws about tenement housing were enforced. They also lobbied for the extension and tightening of these laws. Pressure exerted on state legislatures by federations of women's clubs in Iowa, Ohio, Pennsylvania, and Michigan was largely responsible for the creation of systems of juvenile courts. In most states, club federations worked for improvements in penal systems. Many observers credited the passage of the federal Pure Food and Drug Act of 1906 to a letter-writing campaign coordinated by women's organizations throughout the nation.

White Anglo-Saxon women were not the only ones to organize for community improvement. Within the Jewish community, the National Council of Jewish Women, founded in 1893, encouraged the adoption of social service as a goal of American Jewish organizations. By the 1900s, Zionism, the movement to establish a separate Jewish state, was strong among American Jews. In 1912 Hadassah, the women's Zionist organization, was formed. It centered its energies on providing funds for medical services for the Jewish community in Palestine. After the Civil War, black women, too, founded local clubs, and in 1895 these clubs federated into the National Association of Colored Women. Even more than among the white women's clubs (which generally excluded blacks), the primary purpose of the black organization was social welfare. For blacks, the association was the first social-service agency in the nation. It was founded nearly fifteen years before the better-known, male-dominated organizations, the National Association for the Advancement of Colored People and the Urban League.

That black women would take such a leadership role in social welfare was natural, for they had often played key roles in black churches and other voluntary organizations. Local black women's clubs established day nurseries, kindergartens, playgrounds, old people's homes, and homes for female juvenile delinquents, while they worked for better housing, schools, and employment opportunities for black women. When one critic charged the Illinois chapter members with being "butterflies on dress parade," the president retorted that the members were rather "self-sacrificing women, ever on the alert to relieve suffering humanity."[8] NAACP leader Mary White Ovington pointed out that black women were often appointed to organize the programs of the NAACP in its early years, for they had learned to be leaders through their work within their churches and their clubs.[9]

The broad spectrum of women's groups in the Progressive period included a number of associations with a variety of programs. The YWCA

55 A meeting of the National Board of the YWCA, 1914.

spent its funds on recreation and housing for working women. The Association of Collegiate Alumnae worked for municipal reform and supported the efforts of settlement-house workers. Even the Daughters of the American Revolution undertook letter-writing campaigns on behalf of conservation and child-labor reform. Voluntarism was characteristic of America's years of unsettling urbanization, immigration, and industrialization. But what was unique about the new women's organizations was the commitment of so many of them to social reform. According to one observer in 1906, this interest in the public welfare was not characteristic of men's clubs.[10]

Women not only supported the Progressive movement in their clubs, but they also took on leadership roles individually. For example, Albion Fellows Bacon of Indiana, who was married and the mother of four children, began her reform career as a volunteer member of the sanitation committee of Evansville's Civic Improvement Society and then worked as a "friendly visitor" (the predecessor of the modern social worker) for Evansville's associated charities. Like many Progressives, she decided that inadequate housing lay at the heart of poverty. She singlehandedly launched a statewide campaign of publicity and organization for the regulation of housing, a goal she achieved in 1913. Katherine Bemont Davis, a Vassar graduate with a doctorate in sociology, for some years headed a Philadelphia settlement house before she became, in 1901, superintendent of the new Women's Reformatory in Bedford Hills, New York. Under her superintendency, according to historian Blake McKelvey, the Bedford Hills institution was "the most active penal experiment station in America."[11] In 1914 she became Commissioner of Corrections in New York City, and three years later she took the job of general secretary of the Bureau of Social Hygiene of the Rockefeller Foundation, in which position she authored studies of prostitution, narcotics addiction, and general sexual behavior.

That women like Bacon and Davis were able to pursue careers in reform is perhaps not as surprising in the long run as it might seem. Dr. Alice Hamilton, a pioneer in the field of industrial medicine, which focused on industrial pollution as the presumed source of many illnesses of workers, contended that her sex was a distinct advantage in her work. She explained that to most Americans it seemed natural that a woman should put the health of the workman ahead of the value of his product. Such impulses in a man, she contended, would have been interpreted as indications of an unmanly sentimentalism or of radicalism.[12]

Women also began to take on leadership roles in male-dominated Progressive organizations. At first, men did not accept women easily into their midst. In 1894 Lillian Wald, prominent among women Progressives for founding the Henry Street Settlement in New York City and for her attempts to improve the status of the nursing profession to which she belonged, reported that she had been dropped from the list of potential members of a New York mayoral commission on industrial safety because of the objections of the male members. They feared that if a woman were present, proper etiquette would not permit them to take off their coats and roll up their shirt sleeves.[13] Within a few years such attitudes had weakened, and women of the prominence of Wald were often appointed to reform commissions. Even the vice commissions, dealing with the delicate question of prostitution, included at least one woman in their membership, as if the presence of a woman would legitimate their reform endeavor and give them credibility before women's organizations.

The Settlement Houses

Within the Progressive movement, women were often innovators. Nowhere is this more apparent than their leadership in settlement houses. Jane Addams at Hull House and Lillian Wald at Henry Street were only the two most famous women settlement workers. There were hundreds more. For the most part they were recent college graduates who were fired with a sense of dedication to women and to humanity. In many instances they were among the first generation of women college graduates. They were pioneers, determined to prove to a skeptical world that educating women was not socially wasteful, that women could be as forceful and as innovative as men. Faced after college with a choice between marrying, making their way in professional and graduate schools that still discriminated against women, or taking low-status positions as schoolteachers or nurses, they responded with typical American ingenuity: they invented their own profession by founding

56 and 57 *(left)* Jane Addams, founder of Hull House in the slums of Chicago. *(below)* Addams works with some of the neighborhood children.

houses in the midst of urban slums where they would live and provide social services to the poor. Almost immediately settlement work became respectable and, unlike ordinary social work, even glamorous. It perfectly fitted women's traditional role of service. And men did not control it.

For many young women and men, settlement work was an interlude between college and marriage. Like the Peace Corps of the 1960s, it was for some a brief experiment in idealism. Some women married male co-workers and adopted more conventional styles of life. Others became regular social workers or entered a profession. A few, like Jane Addams and Lillian Wald, remained throughout their lives at the institutions they had founded, and from this power base they reached out to influence mayors, legislators, and the general public. Other settlement-house workers, like Florence Kelley, spent some time in settlement houses before moving into positions with other reform organizations. A few were appointed to middle-level government positions. Jane Addams' Hull House in Chicago easily held the record for such appointments. Whether inspired by Addams' example or by their own ambition and sense of mission, many of her close associates became prominent Progressive reformers. Julia Lathrop became the first woman member of the Illinois State Board of Charities and the first director of the Children's Bureau of the federal government, established in 1912. In this position she was followed by Grace Abbott. Sophonisba Breckinridge became dean of the University of Chicago's pioneer School of Civics and Philanthropy, while Mary McDowall was elected the first president of the Chicago branch of the Women's Trade Union League. Florence Kelley was appointed head of the national Consumers' League. All these women served originally at Hull House.

A Measure of Success

Women settlement-house workers and social feminists were particularly concerned about women, children, and the home. They were instrumental in the formation of the Children's Bureau and in the drafting of child-labor laws. The settlements in particular provided special services for women, including homemaking and visiting nurse services, instruction in domestic skills, and nurseries and kindergartens for children of working mothers. Settlement workers, social workers, and women's clubs investigated employment agencies, tried to help newly arrived immigrants, fought for better treatment of servants, and in some cities established legal agencies to help women enforce payment of wages, prevent violations of contracts, and procure divorces. They worked with the vice commissions to investigate prostitution and campaigned for an open discussion of sex as a way of ending prostitution and venereal disease. Particularly through the Consumers' League and the Women's Trade Union League, they tried to improve working conditions for women.

To what extent social feminists succeeded in the overall area of social reform is debatable. The most recent study of Progressivism in Wisconsin gives the impression that women revolutionized the social services of the state. However, a detailed 1909 study of services for working women in Pittsburgh, where there were numerous clubs, settlements, and YWCAs, showed that only about 2 percent of working women were being reached.[14] The most recent study of kindergartens in Massachusetts contends that relatively few were actually opened and that they offered little more than part-time preparation for the rigid discipline of the elementary grades.[15] Yet changing the status quo is never easy. Describing her frustration at not accomplishing more, Lillian Wald in her autobiography detailed the years of painstaking effort it took even to get some New York City streets closed to traffic during a few hours of the day so that children could play safely.[16]

How one interprets the Progressive movement and the achievements of social feminists in it depends very much on one's own political orientation. If in the final analysis their work for municipal reform, for prison relief, for pure food and drug acts, for public assistance to mothers who were heads of households be judged minor, these social feminists nevertheless left an important legacy: the proof that women could be leaders and innovators in society.

THE RADICALS

The social feminists took the path of trying to achieve reform within existing political and social institutions. The radical feminists, while advocating many of the same causes, were more militant in their orientation, their ideas, and their actions. Their outspoken statements added much to the flavor of the age.

A Ferment of New Ideas

Crusaders like Margaret Sanger, who demanded birth control, and Charlotte Perkins Gilman, who called for the building of large apartment complexes with general kitchens, cleaning services, and nurseries staffed by professionals to relieve housewives' burdens, were continually in the public eye. Their demands were supported by other, less well-known but no less vocal men and women who argued for the opening of every occupation to women, for the equalization of men's and women's wages, for unrestricted divorce, for the retention of maid-

58   Volunteers selling copies of the *Birth Control Review,* Margaret Sanger's pioneering publication that first appeared in 1917.

en names in marriage, and for the adoption of simple, uniform clothing that would end fashion's tyranny over women.[17] A few radicals even called for the communalization of social institutions and espoused the notion of free sexual relations. For example, men and women in the anarchist movement would not marry on principle, but rather lived in monogamous unions in which both partners preserved the freedom to have sexual relations with whomever they chose. In print and in public lectures Emma Goldman broadcast their ideas.

The feminist movement, then as in the 1960s, was international in scope. Major foreign writers lent their weight to the native arguments. Swedish feminist Ellen Key suggested that mothers raise their own children alone and that the state pay them to do so. English feminist Cicely Hamilton fulminated against the structure of marriage, which she viewed as an economic arrangement for women, a trade that they entered for lack of any other choice. Olive Schreiner of South Africa in her influential *Women and Labor* (1911) turned Darwinian emphases upside down by arguing that only strong and self-reliant women could bear healthy children and that the race was destroying itself by giving middle-class women nothing to do. Schreiner coined the much-used term *sex-parasitism* to describe the position of married women.

This ferment of feminist ideas was re-enforced in the public mind by plays and novels that explored the relationship of women to men and to marriage. The realist novel was in vogue, and as presented in the novels of Susan Glaspell, Neith Boyce, and Charlotte Perkins Gilman, the message was openly feminist. Among plays, Henrik Ibsen's *A Doll's House* (1879), the portrait of a woman who slowly gains awareness of her oppression in a traditional marriage, had a striking impact on audiences in the United States and in Europe. George Bernard Shaw's plays about the conflicts of strong-minded men and women—*Man and Superman, Saint Joan, Pygmalion*—were also produced and discussed throughout the United States. Sometimes, as in the case of *Mrs. Warren's Profession* (which portrayed prostitution sympathetically) they were suppressed. Many lesser playwrights imitated Ibsen and Shaw. Author and journalist Ben Hecht, no particular feminist sympathizer, complained that "novelists and playwrights were knocking the wind out of the public by presenting radical heroines who had been to bed

59 A scene from a 1937
production of Henrik Ibsen's
A Doll's House, starring
Ruth Gordon and Dennis
King.

with some man before their marriage."[18] One of these plays—a minor
vehicle entitled *Hindle Wakes*—was a hit on Broadway. The plot turned
on a standard seduction theme. A girl spent a weekend in the country
with the son of her father's employer. When discovered, the boy in
time-honored fashion offered to marry her "to save her honor." She
refused, and all were amazed. "Why did you go on the weekend?" she
asked her paramour. "I'm a man," he replied. "It was just my fancy of
the moment." "Well," she countered, in a statement that must have
shocked audiences only one step removed from Victorian prejudices,
"I'm a woman. It was just my fancy of the moment."[19]

A New Breed of Scholars

Feminist scholars added their contribution to the battle for women's
emancipation. Much like feminists in the 1970s, they scanned the past

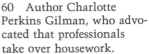

60   Author Charlotte Perkins Gilman, who advocated that professionals take over housework.

and the present for evidence of female superiority. They focused on eras, like the Middle Ages and the Renaissance, when women played an influential social role. Emily Putnam, who was allowed to retain her position as dean of Barnard College when she married but was forced to resign after she had a child, produced the prototype of such works in *The Lady* (1910), an historical analysis of the upper-class female role over the ages. Putnam explored the subtle stages of power and oppression through which woman as cultural heroine had passed: from Greek orientalism to medieval chivalry; from the chatelaine of the manor to the intellectual and voluptuary of the eighteenth-century European salon. Putnam ended her book with a discussion of the eighteenth-century English "bluestocking," the originator of modern feminism, and with her oppressed contemporary, the lady of the Southern antebellum slave plantation. The former, according to Putnam, presaged the future; the latter was an ominous reminder of the extent to which women could be the victims of a caste system.

Other feminist scholars looked beyond the discipline of history. Some authorities in the field of science argued that men, too, underwent periodic emotional disturbances based on bodily changes similar to those that occur during the menstrual cycle. On the basis of new medical and biological evidence that women were better able to resist pain and disease than men, that they lived longer and had greater powers of endurance, some feminists theorized that in a number of ways women were, in fact, superior to men. It was only because of men's superior physical strength that they, rather than women, had become the world's leaders and conquerors. New anthropological knowledge about primitive societies likewise gave some women scholars the data for a new, feminist interpretation of history. They speculated that the earliest societies had been matriarchal, and it was not the evolutionary inferiority of women that led to the creation of patriarchal societies, but rather men's irrational and inherent drives for power and conquest. Charlotte Perkins Gilman was critical of female passivity, but she judged the male-dominated world to be a regrettable evolutionary deviation that had produced a host of ills, not the least of which was warfare. In war wrote Gilman, "we find maleness in its absurdest extremes. Here is to be studied the whole gamut of basic masculinity, from the initial instinct of combat, through every form of glorious ostentation, with the loudest possible accompaniment of noise."[20]

Feminist Action Groups: A Faint Voice

Despite their literary and scholarly endeavors, the militant feminists did not translate ideology into action. There was no National Organization for Women; there were few local feminist action groups. In New York City several groups did emerge, but they did not spread to other areas of the nation. One of these was formed by Henrietta Rodman, a schoolteacher who was associated with the Greenwich Village leftists of the prewar years. Her group, the Feminist Alliance, secured the repeal of the prohibition against married schoolteachers in New York City. They also formed committees of doctors and lawyers who wrote leading law and medical schools to demand an end to restrictions on the admission of women. They discussed, but never carried out, the possibility of constructing one of Charlotte Perkins Gilman's apartment houses. For the most part their actions were piecemeal. But their membership was small, many were career women with limited leisure time, and many ultimately were drawn to the suffrage movement, persuaded that it ought to take priority.

A second New York group was called Heterodoxy. It was even less inclined toward activism than the Feminist Alliance. Its members included many of the leading women of the day, such as Charlotte Perkins Gilman, Rheta Childe Dorr, and Elizabeth Gurley Flynn. They met to discuss their common problems and to give and gain mutual support. One observer, after attending a meeting of Heterodoxy, wrote that they seemed to be "in church, that they were worshipping at some holy shrine, their voices and their eyes were full of religious excitement."[21]

Yet many of these women were divided in their political and professional loyalties. Elizabeth Gurley Flynn was a socialist, Rheta

61 Elizabeth Gurley Flynn addressing striking textile workers in Lawrence, Massachusetts, 1912.

Childe Dorr a professional journalist active in women's suffrage. Charlotte Perkins Gilman had a limited capacity for leadership. She never entirely recovered from the effects of the nervous breakdown she had suffered, and although she was moderately active in the suffrage movement, it was to writing and to feminist scholarship that she devoted her professional career. Nor were other prominent radicals any more likely to emerge as leaders of a unified feminist left. Margaret Sanger and Emma Goldman were both difficult personalities, uncompromising women with whom subordinates and other women leaders easily clashed. Goldman, too, was suspicious of the women's movement, partly because her anarchist principles led her to focus on society and not on women and partly because she did not approve of the feminists' antimale rhetoric and their arguments about women's superiority. In the end, leadership to unify women around a common cause came not from the radicals but from the suffragists.

In general, though, militant feminism was a threat to most Americans. They could accept most Progressive women reformers because, as one analyst put it, for the most part these women were "good wives and mothers" who had "personally deserved public esteem," and who had not taken up "eccentricities of base quality," such as free love.[22] But Americans were suspicious of behavior and ideology that deviated from the middle-class norm. Charlotte Perkins Gilman was vilified by the press for divorcing her husband and later for sending their daughter to live with him; and Margaret Sanger, who went through a similar experience, did not fare much better. Playwright Margaret Anderson had Emma Goldman to dinner at her Chicago apartment, and the next day the manager of the building sternly informed her of numerous complaints from other tenants. "Emma Goldman has been here. We can't allow such a thing," he admonished. "By the public," commented Anderson, Goldman "was considered a monster, an exponent of free love and bombs."[23]

The support of the militant feminists added strength to the coalition of women that achieved women's suffrage. They also gave moral support to the women and men who were trying to establish new roles and relationships in their own lives. But the opposition to fundamental reform for women was strong. It took Margaret Sanger, for example, twenty years of determined agitation just to achieve the legalization of birth control. Besides, as so often has been true in the history of American feminism, there were other issues that seemed more pressing than the achievement of immediate equality for women.

SHAKY GROUNDS FOR ARGUMENT

Seen in retrospect, there were serious weaknesses within the ideology and actions of both the social feminists and the radical feminists. In their own day, these deficiencies were not readily apparent. But they are important in understanding the decline of feminism in the 1920s. Most of these weaknesses stemmed from the fact that both groups were enmeshed in certain ingrained sexual and cultural attitudes. At the time, these women seemed innovators and radicals; to a different generation after the First World War their message was not so obvious.

Women's Frailty and Special Legislation

The attachment of many organized women of this age to the campaign for special legislation for working women gives insight into their underlying conservatism. For example, at the same time the Women's Trade Union League worked to organize women into unions, it lobbied for the passage by state legislatures of maximum-hour and minimum-wage laws that would apply only to women workers.* Behind this campaign lay certain pragmatic arguments: first, women were difficult to organize; second, special legislation for women might force employers to improve conditions for male workers, too; third, the courts had overruled special legislation for men on the grounds that it violated the common law doctrine of "freedom of contract" between worker and employer, but they might be willing to validate it for women.

But behind the special legislation campaign also lay some very conservative reasoning. Those who supported it usually argued that the difficulties of factory labor were greater for women than for men not only because women were physically weaker but also because of their special position as potential mothers. In 1908 officials of the Consumers'

---

*Special legislation was the exact opposite of the Equal Rights Amendment, which most feminists in the 1970s support.

League prepared the brief for lawyer Louis Brandeis on the basis of which the Supreme Court rendered its first decision upholding a minimum-wage law *(Muller v. Oregon)*. They declared that "besides anatomical and physiological differences, physicians are agreed that women are in general weaker than men in muscular strength and in nervous energy."[24] Overlooking the contradictory conclusions of feminist scholars, the Consumers' League cited contemporary medical literature that indicated that women who worked strained nerves and bodies and bore unhealthy children. The Court agreed with them. Yet in so arguing, they implied that men did not need such legislation, at a time when the conditions of work were abysmal for both men and women. They also gave added weight to the arguments of those antifeminists who were convinced that women's anatomy was her destiny. One participant unknowingly pointed to what was both the greatest strength and the greatest weakness in their position: "Another chivalry is coming into the world beside that felt by a strong man for a beautiful woman. It is that felt by strong women for their weaker and less fortunate sisters."[25]

Most feminists probably supported special legislation. Even socialist Elizabeth Gurley Flynn thought that working women needed special legislation and that an equal rights amendment would be against their best interests. It is ironic that in an age of enlightenment about women, an age that in its best moments tried to see women as independent human beings, special legislation campaigns were waged on behalf of two groups within the population: women and children. It had been a favorite theme of Victorian thought that in their gentleness and purity, women resembled no others as much as children. Now once again, they were classified along with children as requiring special treatment. Moreover, conservative rhetoric was easily used in other ways to justify the entire campaign to organize working women. Women in labor unions, wrote one analyst, were making the factory safe and secure like the home. They were fulfilling the historic mission of their sex — "the nurturing and uplifting of the family."[26]

Housekeepers in Government—and Out

The social feminist rationale for the participation of women in reform and in government was similarly antifeminist in implication. Social feminists generally argued that women had a special interest in legislation for education or clean streets or public parks because these issues were intimately related to successful family life. This was a central theme in the thought of Jane Addams. "As society grows more complicated," she wrote, "it is necessary that woman shall extend her sense of responsibility to many things outside of her home if she would continue to preserve the home in its entirety."[27] She contended that "city housekeeping has failed partly because women, the traditional housekeepers, have not been consulted as to its multiform activities."[28]

The problem with this argument was not that it was ineffective or even untrue but that, as in the campaign for special legislation, it was based on the traditional image of the woman. Moreover, there was a counteractive side to this view of women as competent housekeepers. The belief was growing that because of mechanization and new scientific knowledge about, for example, child-rearing and the effective utilization of time, homemaking itself had become so complex that women needed extensive training to be able to manage it properly. The unorganized domestic science movement of the nineteenth century was becoming the highly organized home economics movement of the twentieth century. In the 1900s social feminists regarded it with great favor. It laid claim to being scientific in an age that celebrated science; its advocates in universities and in cities throughout the nation were important women who were often friends with the social feminists; and it was true that most American women did not know much about proper nutrition, clothing, or time-saving housekeeping procedures.

Nor were its practitioners in those early years without a feminist rationale. Ellen Richards, the first woman graduate of the Massachusetts Institute of Technology and a founder in 1908 and an early president of the American Home Economics Association, believed, according to her biographer, that "because women had clung to antiquated ways of doing housework . . . and had failed to take hold of their own problems in a masterful way, they were handicapped when they tried to do systematic work outside the home."[29] Yet seen in retrospect, the ultimate message of training in home economics as read by the general public was not that women would become so highly trained in the home that they could leave it for public affairs, but that the job of running a home

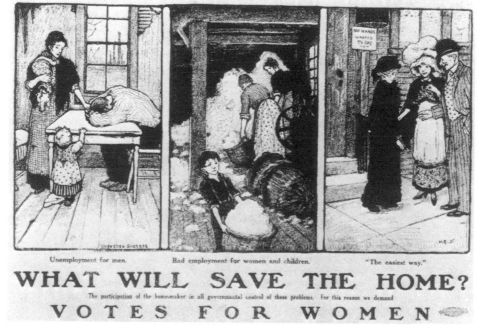

62 A poster issued by NAWSA to gain support of working-class women for suffrage.

was so all-encompassing that it could be mastered over a lifetime only with difficulty. The conservative argument of the social feminists underscored this point.

Suffrage as a Cure-All

Similar ideological weaknesses were to be found in the central arguments for women's suffrage. The argument that women needed the vote to protect the home was undoubtedly effective in making suffrage respectable, just as it was helpful in disarming the opposition to women's participation in reform or to the special legislation campaign. It nonetheless implied that women's real place was in the home. Even Inez Milholland, a beautiful young lawyer and Vassar graduate who gained widespread attention in 1912 when she rode a horse at the head of a New York City suffrage parade, inviting comparisons to Joan of Arc and Helen of Troy, subscribed to this idea. In that year she declared, 113

63 Inez Milholland, lawyer and journalist, leading a suffragist parade.

"Women are the mothers of the race, and as such are admittedly more concerned than any one else with all that goes to protect life." For this reason, she argued, women should have the vote. However, according to suffragist Winifred Scott Cooley, younger suffragists like Milholland used these conservative arguments because they were effective, not because the younger women necessarily believed them. These women, according to Cooley, wanted the vote as the means to an end, and that end was not to protect traditional social institutions. They wanted to effect a feminist revolution.[30]

There were problems within the notion that women would use the vote to effect social change. A central theme in the suffrage argument of both older and younger suffragists was that once women could vote, a social reformation of some sort would ensue. What was on one level a practical argument, designed both to attract social feminists to suffragism and to express the understanding of realistic feminists that suffrage was only a beginning step toward the emancipation of women, at times took on inflated utopian dimensions. Thus suffragists argued that women as voters would inevitably stop corruption and vice, end all discrimination against women, and prevent wars. The argument

THE POISON AND THE ANTIDOTE

Drawn by CALVERT SMITH

64   A drawing in *Judge* magazine, 1920, predicts the downfall of political corruption.

itself reflected the positions of both the militant feminists and the conservative antisuffragists. Both had argued that women were superior to men in their greater gentleness and compassion. The antifeminists used this belief as an argument that women's place was in the home, while the feminists turned the argument the other way. But it still enshrined the same assumptions.

The danger with the militant assumption that women were natural reformers lay not only in its proximity to the conservative position but also that if it proved incorrect in a concrete situation, it would make the feminists appear to be fools, victims of typically irrational "feminine" logic. And insofar as feminism in general was identified with the suffrage movement—and by 1920 the identification was strong—the entire feminist movement would appear to be composed of cranks and dreamers. To a degree, this is exactly what happened. It was apparent after the passage of the suffrage amendment in 1920 that women did not vote as a bloc, that they seemed to vote for the same party and candidates that their husbands and fathers did, and that the suffragists had been incorrect. This failure of women to follow the feminist prediction was no small blow to feminism itself.

Sex versus Soul

Feminists in the prewar years were also contradictory on the issue of free sexuality and of the woman's responsibility to her own physiology. Emma Goldman and the anarchists called for an end to monogomy and marriage, but most feminists were not so inclined. "We are learning to be frank about sex," wrote Inez Milholland in 1913 with seeming forthrightness. "And through all this frankness runs a definite tendency toward an assault on the dual standard of morality and an assertion of sex rights on the part of the woman."[31] But what exactly did this assertion mean? To Margaret Sanger, for example, it meant women's recognition of their own sensuality, of their own ability to enjoy sex. Sanger was, according to Mabel Dodge Luhan—wealthy literary patron and friend of many radicals—"the first person I ever knew who was openly an ardent propagandist for the joys of the flesh."[32]

Other feminists were not so certain that sensuality was a key to women's happiness. Living in an age before Freudian theories made of sex a perceived human necessity, many feminists found the idea of celibacy not disagreeable. Many unmarried women in particular found emotional fulfillment in friendships with men and particularly with other women—friendships that heretofore had been restricted, according to one feminist, because women had traditionally been separated from each other "not only class by class but individual by individual and house by house." Now, she wrote, women in their organizations felt a sense of comradeship and community, a true "sisterhood," which men had always had in their colleges, labor unions, and clubs.[33] When many professional women who had never married reminisced about their lives, they felt little regret. For romantic love and family devotion, they had substituted devotion to a cause and the close friendship of other women. Heterosexuality was not the key to their lives.

Many feminists were suspicious of sensuality on other grounds. A major theme in the thought of nineteenth-century reformers—from free-love advocates to members of the WCTU—had been that excessive male sensuality lay at the heart of female oppression, that man's inability to control his sexual urges had produced both extensive prostitution and widespread venereal disease. Such attitudes continued into the twentieth century. Charlotte Perkins Gilman wrote about the dangers of "excessive sex indulgence,"[34] and social feminists like Jane Addams and Florence Kelley campaigned to make men sexually continent rather than make women sexually free. They wanted what they called a "single standard" of morality. It was not monogamous marriage that they wanted to destroy or sensuality that they wanted to promote; they wished to make of marriage a spiritual union. On this matter of sexuality, Winifred Scott Cooley contended that there was, as in other feminist concerns, a difference between the older activists, who were Victorian in attitude, and the younger generation, which was more liberal. Yet even Cooley was far from subscribing to the idea of free sexuality. She defined the "single standard of morality" as meaning to the younger feminists neither a "strictly puritannical standard" nor "an objectionable loose standard."[35] The idea of morality, seen in terms of constancy of relationships, still influenced her point of view.

Romantic Love and Motherhood

As much as feminists may have disagreed about sensuality, they were almost all romantics at heart. "No one," wrote Inez Milholland, "least of all the advanced feminist thinkers, questions the imperative beauty and value of romantic love. Indeed, the hope is that marriage, far from being undermined or destroyed, can be made real and lasting."[36] Rheta Childe Dorr envisioned a time when marriage would become a matter of "soul selection" and would approach the "sacredness of a sacrament."*[37] While preaching what seemed to them a revolutionary message, the feminists were in reality resurrecting the ideal of passionate attachment to personal relationships that had formed the core of women's romantic longings throughout the nineteenth century. Women once had married for economic security, now they were to marry for

*In his autobiography, journalist Hutchins Hapgood, the husband of feminist novelist Neith Boyce, makes graphically clear the ambivalence that the prewar spiritualists felt about sexual pleasure itself. In criticizing the sensuality of the 1920s, which aimed at sexual satisfaction for women, he wrote: "To us Victorians, sex did not need a skillful prolongation, nor the exploitation of one by the other, to his or her ultimate possibilities of sensation. To us the merely animal act produced the spiritual emotion. To do that, it had to be very simple, a strong instinct, a simple satisfaction, and a lingering gratitude." (Hutchins Hapgood, *A Victorian in the Modern World* [New York: Harcourt Brace Jovanovich, 1939], p. 588.)

117

THE LADIES' HOME JOURNAL

ROMANCE NUMBER

65   What more can a woman want?

love. As the feminists described that emotion in their writings, its epic and ennobling qualities become clear; but when translated into popular terms, the feminists' vision served only to re-enforce the version of sexuality found in magazines and movies, which predicated every relationship on physical longing and saw woman's life as incomplete without a man's love.

Feminists of all persuasions likewise agreed that the chief fulfillment of a woman's life was motherhood. According to Ellen Key, "Women's best qualities . . . are inseparably bound up with the motherhood in her nature."[38] Emma Goldman wrote, "Motherhood is the highest fulfillment of woman's nature."[39] And Charlotte Perkins Gilman echoed her: woman must "understand that, in the line of physical evolution, motherhood is the highest process."[40]

Whether or not such emotions were true is beside the point. The expression of such sentiments was damaging to the entire feminist position, for it adhered to the same sex stereotype that had plagued women's reforms from the start. Many radical feminists realized, as did Inez Milholland, that the woman's movement implied the most genuinely "radical revolution . . . of all history; for the relation of the sexes are the very material out of which the fabric of life is spun and woven."[41] Yet if such a revolution was to be waged, one which, contended Ellen Key, "will finally surpass in fanaticism any war of religion or race,"[42] feminists had to break out of the bondage of traditional concepts of women. They could not, as did Key herself, choose the solution of a communal society and then counsel that in such a society women would not only care for their own children, but they would also be trained for nursing and other service professions related to child care. For this meant, in fact, to "liberate" women to be what they had always been.

SUFFRAGE ACHIEVED

Such ideological weaknesses were hardly apparent as the twentieth century approached its third decade. For the suffrage crusade was emerging from the doldrums, and the women's movement appeared to be stronger and more unified than ever before. Three factors were largely responsible. First, a generation of new suffrage leaders, many of whom had lived in England and had observed the militant suffragist tactics there, began to bring new ideas and new energy to the organization. Second, social feminists who had believed that reform ought to receive priority found conservative suffrage rhetoric appealing, while they had learned that it was votes, not arguments, that swayed politicians. Third, by the second decade of the twentieth century, Progressives increasingly came to regard women's suffrage as part of their program, and the suffrage movement gained strength from its identification with the popular reform movement. Between 1910 and 1914 six additional states—Illinois, Washington, California, Arizona, Kansas, and Oregon—gave the vote to women.

A United Front

By 1914 most activist women had united around suffrage as the central common concern. The women's committee of the Socialist party, for example, came to devote the bulk of its time to women's suffrage. In 1914 the General Federation of Women's Clubs, a last holdout, endorsed the measure. The suffrage coalition was extensive: it included women from a multitude of groups and backgrounds. Jane Addams, who for some years was active in the NAWSA, has given a vivid picture of the variety of its supporters and the reasons for their support. The NAWSA, she wrote, was joined by

> a church society of hundreds of Lutheran women . . . by organizations of working women who had keenly felt the need of the municipal franchise in order to secure for their workshops the most rudimentary sanitation and the consideration which the vote alone obtains for workingmen; by federations of mothers' meetings, who were interested in clean milk and the extension of kindergartens; by property-owning women, who had been powerless against taxation; by organizations of professional women, of university students, and of collegiate alumnae; and by women's clubs interested in municipal reforms.[43]

Tactics and Techniques

The new group of suffragist leaders appeared first in New York state in about 1910. There they revived flagging local organizations, introduced new lobbying techniques, standardized membership lists, and established a state headquarters. They actively sought out contacts with working-class groups. Above all, they introduced the suffrage parade—

66 and 67   Suffragists ride in a parade in New York, 1912 *(above)* and march to the Capitol in Washington, D.C., 1913 *(below)*.

68   Alice Paul, founder of the Woman's Party (left) with Helen Gardener, feminist author and first woman member of the United States Civil Service Commission, 1912.

a striking innovation that gained national attention. Americans were accustomed to political parades and to solidarity marches of ethnic, fraternal, and religious groups. But rarely had a protest organization taken to the streets in a controlled demonstration.

In addition to the New York group, which included Rheta Childe Dorr and Harriot Stanton Blatch, Carrie Chapman Catt and Alice Paul were crucial to the new suffrage strategy. Catt was an older woman who had been president of the NAWSA between 1900 and 1904. She had resigned from the post to move to England because of ill health, leadership tensions in the organization, and an invitation to become president of the new International Woman Suffrage Association. By 1915 Catt had returned to the United States, and she was again elected president of the NAWSA. Alice Paul had also been in England, as a student and an active participant in the British suffrage movement. A woman of strong will and ambition, Paul found it difficult to play a subordinate role in the NAWSA. She was also more militant in her views than Catt, and she disagreed with NAWSA tactics. Paul therefore spurned the existing suffrage organization, and in 1913 she founded her own group, the Congressional Union, in Washington, D.C.

Both Catt and Paul were women of considerable ability. Under Catt, the NAWSA adopted the new tactics of parades, rallies, and tight administrative coordination. Paul used them too; but in contrast to the NAWSA, which had always concentrated on the state legislatures, Paul focused her efforts on Congress, where the suffrage amendment had lain dormant in both houses since 1893. Within one year of the formation of the Congressional Union, her group was able to pressure the Senate into voting on the amendment, although the measure was defeated in this initial attempt.

Six more years of agitation followed. Despite their differences, the NAWSA and the Congressional Union were able to work together effectively during those years, even though in the election of 1916 the Congressional Union broadened its efforts to the state level and regrouped itself into a political party, the Woman's Party. As tension mounted and Congress repeatedly failed to pass the amendment, Alice Paul and the Woman's Party took extreme measures. In 1917 they organized round-the-clock picketing of the White House. President Wil-

69 Picketing the White House: an innovative strategy.

son's administration played into their hands by having them arrested and jailed. They received national press coverage that embarrassed the administration by exposing the harshness of their treatment, including force feeding the women when they refused to eat. Even this action did not bring an immediate victory in Congress. Not until 1919 was passage of the amendment successful, after numerous additional state victories seemed to provide the ultimate necessary pressure. Finally, on August 18, 1920, with its passage by the state of Tennessee, the Nineteenth Amendment giving women the right to vote became law.

The Aftermath of Victory

To what extent the militant tactics—or, indeed, the entire revived campaign after 1914—contributed to the suffrage victory is difficult to determine. Eleanor Flexner in her study of the suffrage movement split the difference: she gave her plaudits equally to the NAWSA and to the Woman's Party. Jane Addams, a close observer of the events of those years, entirely discounted the efforts of the suffrage leaders. She thought

70   The end of a long struggle.

Left; Vice President Thomas B. Marshall signing the suffrage resolution which had just passed the Senate, by a 56 to 25 vote. At his right stands Maud Wood Park at his left Helen Gardener. As this bill had passed the House it now goes to the state June 5th 1919.

Right:- Speaker Gillette signing the Suffrage Amendment, June 4th 1919, with gold-pen "the Victory Pen" now in Smithsonian.

women were given the vote because they had performed so admirably during the First World War in keeping the economy going at home while men were at war. Woman's suffrage, according to Addams, was "a direct result of the war psychology."[44] After all, in 1917 America was at war, and the nation was not sympathetic to dissent. Aliens and political radicals were regularly incarcerated, and no great public outcry was heard. It may well be that Paul's militant tactics produced a substantial reaction against feminism among an American public that by the 1920s no longer responded to the Progressive impulse.

The split between the NAWSA and the Woman's Party was to have grave repercussions for the future. While in seeming agreement on goals, the two groups came to differ substantially on tactics: in 1919 Catt openly disavowed Paul's militancy. Once suffrage was achieved, the disagreement over tactics almost inevitably widened into a disagreement over goals.

Yet in 1920 activist women were euphoric. Not only had women been enfranchised, but during the First World War, as the economy expanded and men left their jobs for battle, women were promoted to the skilled-labor and administrative positions that previously had been reserved for men. Large-scale wars have always had the effect of increasing employment for women. But coming at a time of extensive feminist agitation, the expansion of women's employment during the First World War seemed especially significant. Women were proving that they were capable of performing jobs commonly believed to be impossible for them: they were working as street-car conductors, as engineers on trains, as construction workers, and in steel factories. On the job they were meeting men more and more as equals, or so it seemed then. Furthermore, in 1917 the federal government formed the Women's Committee of the Council for National Defense to mobilize women behind the war effort. Both Anna Howard Shaw and Carrie Chapman Catt served with distinction on it. In 1919 the prohibition amendment, long the goal of the WCTU and of rural Protestant women, many of whom were allied with the suffrage movement, became law. It, too, gave the impression that women had the power to reform society. Viewing the scene in 1920, socialist Elizabeth Gurley Flynn was optimistic. Never before, she wrote, had women been so

71 Broadway chorus girls being trained as Home Guards during the First World War.

well organized, so unified.[45] The future looked bright.

Her optimism proved to be ill-advised. In the 1920s the feminist movement broke into factions, while the interest of American women turned in a different direction, away from feminism and even from social-reform causes. Looking back from the vantage point of the late 1920s, when feminism was passé and conservatism dominant, one analyst of prewar feminism could write as if the movement had hardly existed. With little understanding of the scope of feminism early in the century, she passed it off as the work of "women quite remote in purpose from the millions of census breadwinners," who wanted to show that "they were as good and better than men." The growth of industrialism, she contended, had been the real reason for the changes in women's social, economic, and political position; feminism before the First World War had been only a "little wave" on the broader flow of events.[46] Her point of view was not at all unique.

126

Notes

[1] Abigail Scott Duniway, *Path Breaking: An Autobiographical History of the Equal Suffrage Amendment in the Pacific Coast States* (1914; reprint ed., New York: Source Book Press, 1970), p. 60.

[2] Joseph Gilpin Pyle, "Should Women Vote?" in *Anti-Suffrage Pamphlets*, miscellaneous collection, Princeton University Library, p. 19.

[3] Harriot Stanton Blatch and Alma Lutz, *Challenging Years: The Memoirs of Harriot Stanton Blatch* (New York: G. P. Putnam's Sons, 1940), p. 109.

[4] Edith Finch, *Carey Thomas of Bryn Mawr* (New York: Harper's, 1947), pp. 249–50.

[5] Rheta Childe Dorr, *A Woman of Fifty* (New York: Funk and Wagnalls, 1924), p. 148.

[6] Mary Earhart, *Frances Willard: From Prayers to Politics* (Chicago: University of Chicago Press, 1944), p. 194.

[7] Ida A. Harper, "Women in Municipal Governments," in May Wright Sewall, ed., *The World's Congress of Representative Women; A Historical Resumé for Popular Circulation of the World's Congress of Representative Women, Convened in Chicago on May 15, and Adjourned on May 22, 1893* (Chicago: Rand, McNally, 1894), vol. 2, p. 453.

[8] W. E. B. Du Bois, *Efforts for Social Betterment Among Negro Americans* (Atlanta: Atlanta University Press, 1909), pp. 47, 51.

[9] Mary White Ovington, *The Walls Came Tumbling Down* (New York: Harcourt Brace Jovanovich, 1947), p. 125.

[10] "Men's Views of Women's Clubs," *Annals of the American Academy of Political and Social Science*, XXVIII (July–December 1906), 289.

[11] Blake McKelvey, *American Prisons: A Study in American Social History Prior to 1915* (Chicago: University of Chicago Press, 1936), p. 214.

[12] Alice Hamilton, *Exploring the Dangerous Trades: The Autobiography of Alice Hamilton* (Boston: Little, Brown, 1943), p. 269.

[13] Robert L. Duffus, *Lillian Wald, Neighbor and Crusader* (New York: Macmillan, 1939), p. 71.

[14] Elizabeth Butler, *Women and the Trades: Pittsburgh, 1907–1908* (New York: Charities Publication Committee, 1909), p. 332.

[15] Marvin Lazerson, *Origins of the Urban School: Public Education in Massachusetts, 1870–1915* (Cambridge, Mass.: Harvard University Press, 1971), pp. 36–73.

[16] Lillian Wald, *The House on Henry Street* (New York: Henry Holt, 1915), p. 222.

[17] W. L. George, "Feminist Intentions," *Atlantic*, CXII (December 1913), 731.

[18] Ben Hecht, *A Child of the Century* (New York: Simon and Schuster, 1954), p. 48.

[19] Inez Milholland, "The Liberation of a Sex," *McClure's*, XL (February 1913), 185–88.

[20] Charlotte Perkins Gilman, *The Man-Made World: or, Our Androcentric Culture* (New York: Charlton, 1911), p. 211.

[21] Hutchins Hapgood, *A Victorian in the Modern World* (New York: Harcourt Brace Jovanovich, 1939), p. 377.

[22] Marie Theresa Blanc, *The Condition of Women in the United States: A Traveller's Notes*, trans. Abby Langdon Alger (1895; reprint ed., Freeport, N.Y.: Books for Libraries Press, 1972), p. 88.

23 Margaret Anderson, *My Thirty Years' War: An Autobiography* (New York: Covici, Friede, 1930), pp. 55, 74.

24 Josephine Goldmark, "The World's Experience Upon Which Legislation Limiting the Hours of Labor for Women is Based," in Josephine Goldmark, *Fatigue and Efficiency: A Study in Industry* (New York, 1912), p. 1.

25 Catherine Waugh McCulloch, "Response," in Elizabeth Cady Stanton *et al.*, *History of Woman Suffrage*, 6 vols. (New York, 1881, 1922), vol. 5, p. 312.

26 Lydia Commander, "The Self-Supporting Woman and the Family," in American Sociological Society, *Papers and Proceedings of the Third Annual Meeting of the American Sociological Society: The Family* (Chicago: University of Chicago Press, 1908), p. 149.

27 Christopher Lasch, ed., *The Social Thought of Jane Addams* (Indianapolis: Bobbs-Merrill, 1965), p. 144.

28 *Jane Addams: A Centennial Reader* (New York: Macmillan, 1960), p. 115.

29 Caroline Hunt, *The Life of Ellen Richards* (Washington, D.C.: American Home Economics Association, 1958), p. 160.

30 Winifred Scott Cooley, "The Younger Suffragists," *Harper's Weekly*, LVIII (September 27, 1913), 6–7.

31 Milholland, "The Liberation of a Sex," p. 185.

32 Mabel Dodge Luhan, *Intimate Memories* (New York: Harcourt Brace Jovanovich, 1936), vol. 3: *Movers and Shakers*, p. 69.

33 Alice Duer Miller, "The Sisterhood of Women," in Stanton *et al.*, *History of Woman Suffrage*, vol. 5, p. 283.

34 Charlotte Perkins Gilman, *Women and Economics* (1898; reprint ed., New York, 1966), p. 30.

35 Cooley, "The Younger Suffragists," p. 7.

36 Inez Milholland, "The Changing Home," *McClure's*, XL (March 1913), 214.

37 Dorr, *A Woman of Fifty*, pp. 450–51.

38 Ellen Key, *Love and Marriage* (New York: G. P. Putnam's Sons, 1911), p. 124.

39 Emma Goldman, "Marriage and Love," in Miriam Schneir, ed., *Feminism: The Essential Historical Writings* (New York: Vintage, 1972), p. 322.

40 Gilman, *The Man-Made World: or, Our Androcentric Culture*, p. 245.

41 Milholland, "The Changing Home," p. 208.

42 Key, *Love and Marriage*, p. 214.

43 Jane Addams, *Twenty Years at Hull House* (New York: Macmillan, 1910), p. 237.

44 Jane Addams, *The Second Twenty Years at Hull House* (New York: Macmillan, 1930), p. 103.

45 Elizabeth Gurley Flynn, *I Speak My Own Piece* (New York: Masses and Mainstream, 1955), p. 267.

46 Mary Ross, "The New Status of Women in America," in Samuel D. Schmalhausen and V. F. Calverton, eds., *Woman's Coming of Age, A Symposium* (New York: H. Liveright, 1931), pp. 545–48.

Bibliography

Although historians have long focused on the women's suffrage movement—to the exclusion of other areas of women's experience—there is still need for a comprehensive study of its origins and development. Alan P. Grimes, *The Puritan Ethic and Woman Suffrage* (New York: Oxford University Press, 1967) argues that the need for order in Western states brought the early vote for women there, although he pays insufficient attention to organized suffragist activity. Aileen S. Kraditor, *The Ideas of the Woman Suffrage Movement, 1890–1920* (New York: Columbia University Press, 1965) was the first historian to explore the flaws in the suffrage argument, although she slights its positive elements. The most recent study of the last years of the movement is David Morgan, *Suffragists and Democrats: The Politics of Woman Suffrage in America* (East Lansing, Mich.: Michigan State University Press, 1972). Morgan should be supplemented by some of the many works by participants, including Elizabeth Cady Stanton *et al., History of Woman Suffrage,* 6 vols. (New York, 1881, 1922); Harriot Stanton Blatch and Alma Lutz, *Challenging Years: The Memoirs of Harriot Stanton Blatch* (New York: G. P. Putnam's Sons, 1940); Carrie Chapman Catt and Nettie Rogers Shuler, *Woman Suffrage and Politics: The Inner Story of the Suffrage Movement* (New York: Charles Scribner's Sons, 1926); and Maud Wood Park, *Front Door Lobby,* ed. Edna Lamprey Stentiel (Boston: Beacon, 1960). There is yet no study of the extensive antisuffrage movement or of its rhetoric.

Of the many women's organizations, few have been subjected to scholarly scrutiny. There is no recent study of the YWCA or of the women's clubs white or black. On the Daughters of the American Revolution, see Margaret Gibbs, *The Daughters of the American Revolution* (New York: Holt, Rinehart & Winston, 1969). The most insightful account thus far of the WCTU is found in Mary Earhart, *Frances Willard: From Prayers to Politics* (Chicago: University of Chicago Press, 1944). On the Consumers' League, see Maud Nathan, *The Story of an Epoch-Making Movement* (Garden City, N.Y.: Doubleday, Page, 1926).

Material on women in the Progressive movement is scattered throughout the literature on the period. The most useful recent works are Allen Davis, *Spearheads for Reform: The Social Settlements and the Progressive Movement, 1890–1914* (New York: Oxford University Press, 1967), and David P. Thelen, *The New Citizenship: Origins of Progressivism in Wisconsin* (Columbus, Mo.: University of Missouri Press, 1972). For a fascinating account of the relationship between college culture and settlement house involvement, see John P. Rousmanière, "Cultural Hybrid in the Slums: The College Woman and the Settlement House, 1889–1894," *American Quarterly,* XXII (Spring 1970), 45–66. Biographies and autobiographies are available for most major women Progressives, who themselves wrote extensively on their work. See, in particular, Lillian Wald, *The House on Henry Street* (New York: Henry Holt, 1915), and Jane Addams, *Twenty Years at Hull House* (New York: Macmillan, 1910). For an interesting, although flawed, critique of the motives of Jane Addams— and, by implication, the motives of other reformers like her—see Christopher Lasch, *The New Radicalism in America, 1889–1963: The Intellectual as a Social Type* (New York: Knopf, 1965). Jill Conway, "Women Reformers and American Culture, 1870–1930," *Journal of Social History,* V (Winter 1971–72), 164–77, although critical, gives a more balanced argument. One should also consult Mary R. Beard, *Women's Work in Municipalities* (New York: D. Appleton, 1915); Sophonisba Breckinridge, *Women in the Twentieth Century: A Study of Their Political, Social, and Economic Activities* (New York: McGraw-Hill, 1933); and Rheta Childe Dorr, *What Eight Million Women Want* (1910; reprint ed., Boston: Kraus, 1971).

There has been little investigation of militant feminism in the early twentieth century. June Sochen, *The New Woman: Feminism in Greenwich Village, 1910–1920* (New York: Quadrangle, 1972) provides an introduction to some of the New

York activists. On Margaret Sanger, David Kennedy has written the most recent—although hostile—biography. To supplement his *Birth Control in America: The Career of Margaret Sanger* (New Haven: Yale University Press, 1970), Sanger's own *Margaret Sanger: An Autobiography* (1938; reprint ed., New York: Dover, 1971) ought to be read. There is no biography of Charlotte Perkins Gilman, but her *The Living of Charlotte Perkins Gilman: An Autobiography* (New York: Appleton Century, 1935) is well worth consulting. Floyd Dell, *Women as World Builders: Studies in Modern Feminism* (Chicago: Forbes, 1913) is also interesting.

For a discussion of new biological and sociological views of women, see Avrom Bennett, *Foundations of Feminism: A Critique* (New York: Robert McBride, 1920). Two important treatises are Anna Garlin Spencer, *Woman's Share in Social Culture* (New York: Mitchell Kennerly, 1913), and Scott Nearing and Nellie Nearing, *Woman and Social Progress* (New York: Macmillan, 1912).

The 1920s: Freedom 4
or Disillusionment?

What characterized the woman's movement of the 1920s more than anything else was its splintering into a number of groups, each involved with a separate concern. True, most established women's organizations continued to function, and several major new ones were organized as the war ended and suffrage was achieved. The formation in 1919 of the National Federation of Business and Professional Women's Clubs (BPW) and of the Women's Bureau in the federal Department of Labor as well as the Women's Joint Congressional Committee (WJCC) and the League of Women Voters in 1920 seemed to promise further striking progress for women. But such was not to be. Soon after the passage of the suffrage amendment, Anna Howard Shaw remarked to Emily Newell Blair, then a young suffragist and later vice president of the National Committee of the Democratic party, "I am sorry for you young women who have to carry on the work for the next ten years, for suffrage was a symbol, and now you have lost your symbol."[1] Shaw could not foresee that political conservatism and an emphasis on personal gratification would come to characterize the decade of the 1920s. But she realized the potential for a breakup into factions within the united woman's movement. Essentially there were four groups: social feminists, pacifists, professional women, and feminists.

WOMEN'S ORGANIZATIONS IN TRANSITION

The largest faction of women was clustered around social feminism. With suffrage won, the NAWSA disbanded. Instead of Alice Paul's Woman's Party being designated as its successor, however, a new organization, the League of Women Voters, was formed. During the 1920s, the League came to concentrate on three goals: general social reform; the elimination of state laws that discriminated against women; and the education of women to their responsibilities as citizens.

As an agency of reform, the League was not without effect. Its efforts at local, state, and national levels on behalf of municipal reform, conservation, tighter consumer laws, a Child Labor Amendment, and public support of indigent mothers have earned for it the accolade of historian Stanley Lemons. In his study of social feminism in the 1920s, he argues that women's organizations, and particularly the League, were primarily responsible for whatever Progressive impulse still existed in an essentially conservative decade. State chapters of the League were successful, too, in whittling down the number of discriminatory marriage and property laws still on the books. They also successfully fought for the repeal of laws that prohibited women from serving on juries or holding office—laws that a number of state legislatures passed after ratification of the suffrage amendment. The League often served as a training ground for women interested in politics. The career of Lavinia Engle was not exceptional. After serving seven years as a field secretary for the NAWSA, she became director of the Maryland League in 1920. Later she was elected to the Maryland legislature, and in 1936 she became an official in the federal Social Security Administration.

In function and approach, however, the League has always been a conservative organization. Not only was this apparent in its commitment to social reform but also in its emphasis on education. True, its early history, in many ways traumatic, determined its destiny. As former suffragists who had expected the vote to produce a national reformation, League leaders were shaken when the elections of the early 1920s revealed that the turnout of eligible women voters was light and that their voting patterns did not differ from those of men. Moreover, the League retained no more than a small percentage of the NAWSA's

72 At a suffrage headquarters, newly enfranchised women learn how to vote.

sizable membership. In reaction to this turn of events, League leaders decided that the education of women for responsible citizenship, rather than their mobilization to reform the political system, must be one of their primary functions.

As this concept of education was worked out, it took on conservative and nonpartisan overtones that influenced the entire League approach. Instead of using education as a means of proselytizing for feminist or social-reform goals, as the suffragists and the Progressives had done, the League came to view education in its classic sense, as study to arrive at truth. In the typical local League, women met to study the problems of government in an objective manner. The state and national organizations were no less cautious. The League attempted, wrote one analyst, "to bring to politics the aloof detachment of the scientific method. . . . Inquiry is centered upon some definite, limited problem. Data are assembled and studied objectively. Conclusions and new ideas are tentatively held, are tested, and are revised."[2]

Behind this notion of nonpartisan study lay the idealistic hope that

133

73 "Ma" Ferguson (seated), elected governor of Texas in 1935, one of the first women to hold the office.

the entire political system might follow the League's example. But the problem was that lengthy inquiry delayed taking a firm stand on any issue. It also re-enforced the belief that women were insecure in the political world and ignorant about politics. In the male world of politics it was dangerous to project a female image and expect to be taken seriously. But, committed to social welfare and education, the League accepted the fiction that the political parties were open to women, even though representation on party governing committees was token, and few women actually ran for political office. Indeed, members of the League who became candidates for political office were required to resign from the League so as not to jeopardize its nonpartisan stance. Moreover, although the League used the political techniques of lobbying and letter writing in its social feminist campaigns, its approach was genteel. The League method was "wooing our legislators in a dignified and league-like [ladylike] manner."[3]

That another approach might have been more effective in challenging the political system is apparent in the striking campaigns of Florence Allen for the Ohio State Supreme Court in 1922 and 1928.* In both elections, Allen won the judgeship without party support. Instead she formed an organization made up of women activists. The plan was simple. Her managers contacted women in every county who had been suffragists, and these women handled publicity, arranged meetings, and distributed campaign literature. But it was difficult to form an effective coalition of women around any issue in the 1920s. Many former activists were exhausted from their exertions as suffragists before the war. One former Connecticut suffragist explained: "After we got the vote, the crusade was over. It was peacetime and we went back to a hundred different causes and tasks that we'd been putting off all those years. We just demobilized."4 Indeed, membership in women's organizations in general dropped off, and the national leadership of the League complained of a dearth of able women willing to take leadership positions in local chapters.

A number of organizations active in the Progressive coalition before the war turned away from activism. Most important, local women's clubs, which before the war had led the social-welfare coalition, often developed in the 1920s into social organizations in which women played bridge or discussed fashions, gardening, and cooking. One ex-president of a formerly flourishing suburban club in the Midwest bemoaned the fact that her clubhouse had once echoed with brilliant speeches, while "now it rings with such terms as 'no trump' and 'grand slam'".5 Only with difficulty did the national leadership of these clubs arouse the members' interest in reform legislation. This change in the character of women's clubs was partly due to the general conservatism of the decade; but also, other organizations with a social feminist emphasis, such as the League of Women Voters, were drawing away their reform-minded members, while professional women were more and more deserting them to join professional organizations.

Social workers and settlement-house workers, too, were dropping away from the social activist coalition. To postwar college graduates, themselves influenced by the conservative and individualist tenor of

---

*In 1934 Franklin Roosevelt appointed Allen to the Circuit Court of Appeals, the highest court below the Supreme Court.

the decade, settlement work, by now in its fourth decade of existence, no longer held out the same appeal as it had to the first generation of settlement workers. Public and private sources of funding similarly fell off, while the movement of blacks into the formerly Jewish, Italian, and Slavic neighborhoods that the settlements served made the challenge of living in the midst of their clientele ever more difficult. Moreover, settlement workers themselves were influenced by general trends within the profession of social work. After several decades of more or less uncontrolled growth, the calling had entered a time of rationalization, of concern with issues of professional standards, training, and pay. At the same time, the influence of Freudian psychology made the individual client and not the social environment seem important to the caseworker.

Organizations like the Women's Trade Union League and the Consumers' League, still headed by Florence Kelley, remained in existence. The prewar activists in these groups were joined by vigorous lieutenants like Frances Perkins, a former Hull House resident who worked for the Consumers' League in the 1920s before becoming head of the New York State Department of Labor under Governor Franklin Roosevelt, and in the 1930s Secretary of Labor in the federal government (the first woman to hold a cabinet position) under President Franklin Roosevelt. Like the League of Women Voters, settlement and social-welfare groups lobbied for a Child Labor Amendment, for special legislation for working women, for federal relief for indigent mothers, among other social-welfare goals. But in the 1920s their support and successes were limited. The old issues of Progressivism no longer prevailed.

At the same time, many former influential suffragists took up pacifism rather than domestic welfare as their primary concern. Carrie Chapman Catt established the National Conference on the Cause and Cure of War, while Jane Addams became involved in the Women's International League for Peace and Freedom (WILPF). For some longtime suffragists, like Rheta Childe Dorr, internationalism promised a new and exciting crusade: their change of heart was in the nature of a "conversion." With the onset of the First World War, Dorr found herself no longer interested in the woman's movement, but rather in "humanity." She resigned from Heterodoxy, of which she had been a devoted

74 The first United States congresswoman: Jeanette Rankin of Montana, elected in 1917.

member, because "alternate Saturday lunches had no more attractions for me." World events took precedence.[6]

For others, pacifism was a logical extension of their feminism. Organized women were outraged by the outbreak of the First World War, which they saw as the most menacing example possible of male aggressiveness. At the very time that the suffragists and the social feminists were working for a national reformation, men were threatening to destroy the social order. Women as mothers, pacifist rhetoric stressed, had a "peculiar moral passion against both the cruelty and the want of war." To Jane Addams, pacifism meant "the replacement of the war virtues by virtues which sublimate the heroic but anachronistic energies of the soldier into aspirations towards harmony and justice in society."[7] Pacifist leaders, too, criticized preexisting antiwar societies, dominated by men, for their failure to respond quickly to the war's outbreak. By 1916 most women's organizations advocated peace.

In the 1920s the efforts of women pacifists were not without success. The WILPF, for example, was an important pressure group behind the various disarmament and peace conferences that national governments

75 Delegates of a peace mission to end the First World War. Second from left is Jane Addams.

and pacifist groups held throughout the decade. They played no small part in pressuring the United States and foreign governments into signing the Kellogg-Briand Pact of 1927, which outlawed war as national policy. It is perhaps only in retrospect that their actions appear somewhat futile. Yet one inevitable byproduct of their praiseworthy campaign for peace was a further scattering of the feminist effort at home.

Professional women, too, were becoming an increasingly difficult group to activate behind goals other than equal pay and equal employment opportunities. During the war the absence of men had offered greater advancement possibilities to them, while the government, as part of its general program of bolstering citizen morale, had encouraged them to organize. These experiences had heightened their consciousness of their role as professionals and of discrimination within their professions. With the ending of the war, new professional women's associations appeared in many fields, including dentistry, architecture, and journalism. In 1919, under the sponsorship of the YWCA, to which many women professionals had previously belonged, representatives of these groups founded the National Federation of Business and Professional Women's Clubs. Its focus was on the attainment of equal rights for women within the professions, although on occasion it supported social feminist causes.

In the 1920s the inheritors of the prewar feminist mantle split off from their sometime associates in the suffragist coalition. The Woman's Party, founded by Alice Paul in 1916, refused to endorse the League of Women Voters' program of social feminism and education for women. Instead, the Woman's Party centered its efforts on attaining an Equal Rights Amendment (ERA), which would, they believed, be the surest way of ending the many state and national laws that discriminated against women. In 1916 and after, Paul's technique of pressuring Congress for the suffrage amendment had seemed fruitful; now she and her associates decided to follow the same course. The amendment—which read simply that "men and women shall have equal rights throughout the United States and every place subject to its jurisdiction"—was first introduced in Congress in 1923. The League, as well as most women's organizations, opposed the ERA. They did want to eliminate the legal strictures against women in areas like marriage and property holding, but they judged that factory women still required special legislation.

The membership of the Woman's Party was small, but it contained numerous women of wealth and professional eminence. It was not a radical group. Crystal Eastman—socialist, pacifist, and an associate of Henrietta Rodman in the prewar Feminist Alliance and of Alice Paul in the prewar Woman's Party—charged that when she presented Paul with a list of militant demands, including the legalization of birth control, Paul refused to consider them.[8] The concern of the Woman's Party was to be the ERA. The strategy was not without effect. Even though Congress consistently refused to vote on the ERA, all commentators were impressed by the lobbying skill of Woman's Party members—a skill that may have stemmed from experience and from the fact that they were working for just one measure.

For many women who were concerned specifically about women's rights, an equal rights amendment was too broad a concept. Some young New York professional women, led by journalists Jane Grant and Ruth Hale, wife of newsman Heywood Broun, formed the Lucy Stone League after Hale was unable to obtain a passport under her maiden name. The purpose of the organization was to persuade married professional women, following Lucy Stone's nineteenth-century example, to use their maiden names and to pressure the government to make this usage legal. In support of this limited reform, the women wrote editorials, held rallies, and lobbied. For a number of years even the BPW did not support the ERA. It was a signal triumph when, in 1928, through the efforts of members influential in professional groups, the Woman's Party secured the support of the BPW, which was convinced by the argument that the ERA was essential to advancing the position of women within the professions.

If any strong sense of common purpose existed among women in the 1920s, that common purpose was social feminism. In 1919 a number of women's organizations formed the Women's Joint Congressional Committee to work as a common lobby. At one time or another, the League of Women Voters, the BPW, and the General Federation of Women's Clubs were members of the committee, as were the National Congress of Parents and Teachers, the WCTU, the American Association of University Women (AAUW), and the National Council of Jewish Women. In many states similar legislative councils emerged. The national committee worked for improved education, maternal and infant health care, the Child Labor Amendment, the World Court, and increased funding for the Children's Bureau and the Women's Bureau. Its successes, however, were limited. Even its major triumph, the 1921 Sheppard-Towner Act, which provided matching federal grants to set up maternity and pediatric clinics, was to all intents and purposes overturned in 1929. Part of the difficulty lay in the ambivalence of the members of many of these organizations about social welfare; part lay in the evident fact that a woman's voting bloc—which might have forced Congress to pay more heed to social-welfare and feminist campaigns—had not emerged.

In addition to the WJCC, the Women's Bureau in the Department of Labor, established as the result of women's work during wartime and the vigorous lobbying of women's organizations, might have served as an agency to unify women's organizations. But more than anything else in its early years, the Women's Bureau played the role of a fact-finding and publication service. It concerned itself almost exclusively with women's employment. Its first and long-term president, Mary Anderson, had come from the ranks of the Women's Trade Union League. For the first few decades of its existence, the bureau was a firm supporter of special legislation for women.

Although one can discern a certain united spirit among women in the 1920s around social feminism, the prewar suffrage coalition had largely disintegrated. Organizations like the League of Women Voters tried to keep faith with the Progressive spirit, and some historians think that, especially on the state level, their efforts were not insubstantial. But the very lack of unity among women's organizations made further progress on the feminist front difficult.

ANTIFEMINIST UNDERCURRENTS

Unity or no unity, the general mood of the country was not receptive to feminist reform. Americans in the 1920s were tired of reform causes and dazzled by seeming prosperity and mass-produced consumer goods: automobiles, radios, and, for women in particular, washing machines, vacuum cleaners, and electric kitchens. What need was there for social service when industry was apparently fulfilling its promise of providing material prosperity to all Americans? What concerned Americans—at least of the middle class—were their cars, the availability of illicit liquor, the opportunities for stock-market and land speculation, the radio serials and the latest movie, the exploits of sports stars and cultural heroes, and the pursuit of beauty and youth. The women's clubs, which turned from social service to bridge, were indicative of the general mood of the middle class. Vida Scudder, a Wellesley College professor active in Boston settlements and in the Women's Trade Union League, concluded that "those ten exhausted years [the 1920s] were the worst I have ever known."[9]

By the mid-1920s it had become a matter of belief, proclaimed by press and radio, businessmen and politicians, that women had in fact

141

achieved liberation. Suffrage had been won. The number of women's organizations had not diminished. Women had been employed in large numbers during the First World War in positions of responsibility; they had become men's comrades in the office and factory, or so it seemed. Legions of Vassar and Smith graduates descended on New York City every year to become secretaries, copy editors, and management trainees in department stores. Women were smoking in public, wearing short skirts, and demanding and gaining entry into saloons, speakeasies, men's clubs, and golf courses. Female sports stars, like Helen Wills in tennis and Gertrude Ederle in swimming, were challenging any remaining notions that women could not excel in athletics. And sports promoters were promoting them as vigorously as any male athlete. Even Suzanne LaFollette, author of one of the few militant feminist treatises of the decade, wrote in 1926 that the woman's struggle "is very largely won."[10]

The premise that women had achieved liberation gave rise to a new antifeminism, although it was never stated as such. In essence, it involved the creation of a new female image, certainly more modern than before but no less a stereotype and still based on traditional female functions. It was subtle in argument and compelling to a generation tired of reform causes and anxious to enjoy itself. By the late 1920s numerous articles appeared in popular journals contending that in gaining their "rights," women had given up their "privileges." What these privileges amounted to in this literature were self-indulgence, leisure, and freedom from working. The new antifeminists did not openly question women's right to work. They simply made it clear that they did not think women were capable of combining marriage and a career. Women's world in the home was pictured as exotic and self-gratifying. One representative writer contended that working women simply did not have the strange and delightful experience of taking "an hour to dress," of "spending the day in strictly feminine pursuits," of "actually making the kind of cake that [now] comes from the bakery."[11]

The proponents of this new antifeminism not only borrowed the rhetoric of the prewar feminists but claimed that they were the real feminists of the 1920s. "It [the return to the home] is going to be almost as long and hard a struggle . . . as the struggle for women's rights."[12] Prewar feminists were attacked as unfeminine and asexual. In 1927 writer Dorothy Dunbar Bromley defined a "feminist—new style." She bore no relationship to "the old school of fighting feminists who wore flat heels and had very little feminine charm, or the current species who antagonize men with their constant clamor about maiden names, equal rights, women's place in the world." The "new-style feminist" was well-dressed, admitted that she liked men, did not care for women in groups, and was convinced that "a full life calls for marriage and children as well as a career," with the stress on the former.[13]

Other molders of public opinion spread the message far and wide. Advertising, which doubled in volume in the 1920s, found its major market in women, who spent the bulk of the family income. To sell dishwashers, refrigerators, and cleaning products, advertisers pictured the woman as the model consumer whose existence was devoted to the improvement of family life through the purchase of new products. As the clothing and cosmetic industries began their phenomenal growth in the 1920s (a growth that was largely a product of advertising), women were shown as beings for whom fashion, beauty, and sex appeal were the most important concerns in life.

76 In the 1920s the woman who stayed at home was glamorized almost beyond recognition.

New writings on the nature of women's sexuality drove the message home. Before the First World War, a few bold feminists and doctors had suggested that women could enjoy sex; now marriage manuals advocating sexual pleasure for women and spelling out erotic techniques were readily available. Their message was underlined by the scientific theories of Sigmund Freud, who had argued as early as the 1890s that unconscious drives, and especially sex, were central forces in human behavior. A small number of doctors and Greenwich Village intellectuals had known of Freud's work before the war, but it was not until the 1920s—an age preoccupied with the notion of pleasure—that Freudian theories became popular. Yet Freud's ideas were as confining for women as they were liberating. While Freud gave the final scientific refutation to the old belief that sex was an unpleasant duty for women, he also argued that women were prey to a particular disability besides the basic human irrationality. The crucial factor in female personality formation, according to him, was the female child's envy for the male sex organ—an envy that produced a lifelong dissatisfaction with being a woman. The only way to overcome this discontent, according to Freud, was through motherhood.

However, the influence of Freudian theories in the 1920s must not be overemphasized. In the later years of the decade, the behaviorist ideas of John B. Watson were in vogue. Watson played down the importance of suppressed drives as factors controlling human actions and stressed that, through will power, the individual could control his or her behavior. His message to women was nonetheless ambiguous. In his *Psychological Care of Infant and Child* (1928), the standard reference on child-rearing for a decade or more, Watson argued that most women were failures as mothers and that they should decide either not to have children or to realize that child-rearing was a skill so complex that it required extensive training and complete dedication. Unlike Freud, Watson did not view motherhood as the natural role for all women, but his prescriptions for child-rearing, which centered around the conscious withholding of parental affection and the establishment of fixed schedules of activity for the child in order to nurture self-reliance, placed heavy demands on the mother who wanted to seek employment outside the home.

144

Yet the theories of Freud and Watson were secondary to the fact that the notion of the pleasures of sexuality, in which woman was alternately seen as temptress and slave, permeated the culture. Women's magazines were full of it. The films and the radio made it a stock device. Sex-story magazines like *True Confessions* exploited it and quadrupled their sales. Mabel Dodge Luhan, whose psychoanalysis in 1915 set the example for many of her wealthy and intellectual friends, laid clear the ultimate meaning of the new ideas about sexuality. "The sex act," she wrote, is "the cornerstone of any life, and its chief reality," especially for women. "It is indeed the happy woman who has no history," because she has lived for erotic gratification, for her husband or lover, and for her children.[14]

To these ideas the feminist rebuttal was weak. The arguments of those feminists who had wanted a "single standard" of sexuality and who had attacked male sex drives seemed antiquated: Charlotte Perkins Gilman, for example, found it almost impossible in the 1920s to secure speaking engagements or to get her books published.[15] The arguments of those feminists who had preached a doctrine of the erotic or who had upheld motherhood did not really seem to disagree with the new ideas. Nor were the two schools of thought necessarily antagonistic. The new sexuality did represent new freedom for women. Feminists themselves were taking an interest in the new theories. Gilman reported that by the mid-1920s Heterodoxy was devoting discussions to sex psychology, a topic that, she admitted, did not particularly interest her.[16] The Greenwich Village feminists who before the war had formed the Feminist Alliance were dispirited as a result of the war experience, and they left New York City. The next generation of women in Greenwich Village in the 1920s were primarily interested in the pursuit of pleasure, according to historian June Sochen. It was the experience of bohemia, not the hope of a reorganized society, that captivated them.

Finally, antifeminism was aided by extraordinary accusations of communism lodged against many feminist leaders by organizations like the American Legion and the Daughters of the American Revolution (which had evolved from a sometime advocate of social feminism into a right-wing supporter of military preparedness). Jane Addams was charged with being a communist because of her involvement in pacifist causes; Florence Kelley was similarly accused because of her socialist past and her support for the Child Labor Amendment, which the extreme right saw as a socialist measure. Such charges did not create a major stir in the 1920s, but they contributed to the popular belief that feminism was foreign and dangerous.

"FLAMING YOUTH": NEW LIBERTIES, OLD ATTITUDES

Feminism also failed to take roots in the 1920s because by and large it did not appeal to the young women of that generation. No movement can long prosper without attracting younger members to its ranks. In 1910 the suffrage campaign had been reactivated by a group of younger women, including Alice Paul and Rheta Childe Dorr. Such was not the case with the feminist cause in the 1920s, nor, indeed, until the 1960s.

Rarely before or since the 1920s has a generation of youths been so conscious of its own identity or of its perceived difference from an older generation. Their attitude was cavalier to the concerns and achievements of their elders, including the hard-won gains in women's rights. Lillian Hellman, playwright and member of this generation, has described their feelings:

> By the time I grew up the fight for the emancipation of women, their rights under the law, in the office, in bed, was stale stuff. My generation didn't think much about the place or the problems of women, were not conscious that the designs we saw around us had so recently been formed or that we were still part of that formation.[17]

Young people had other preoccupations. Foremost was their rebellion against Victorian culture, its mores and especially its sex taboos. They set the tone of the 1920s. They were the leaders in fashion, in dance, in the introduction of a freer morality. Young women were "flappers," and they lived for fun and freedom, which they saw in terms of short skirts, cigarettes, automobiles, dancing, sports, and speakeasies. The cult of the young had been a muted theme before the First World War. Some among the well-to-do had owned automobiles and had affairs; some young working-class women had been free and easy in their behavior; daring young women had smoked cigarettes and danced new dances like the bunny hug and the turkey trot; and hems had risen as

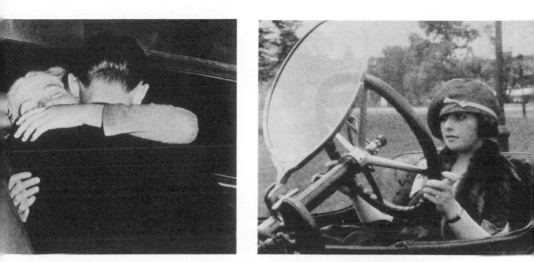

77 and 78   The automobile: in the back seat or front, it meant fun and freedom.

79   Flappers compete in a Charleston dance contest.

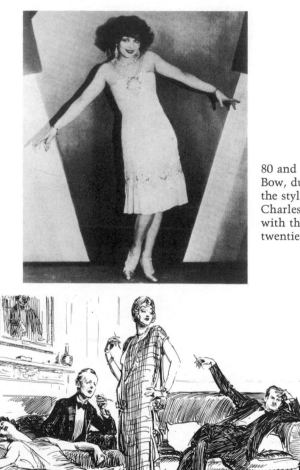

80 and 81 *(left)* Film star Clara Bow, dubbed the "It" girl, sets the style for flappers. *(below)* Charles Dana Gibson catches up with the new attitudes of the twenties.

82   John Held's answer to the Gibson girl. From *Life* magazine, 1926.

1896   1926

Thirty Years of "Progress"!

early as 1910. But in about 1920 these qualitative changes took a quantitative jump, and the age of "flaming youth" was on.

In 1921 the conservative *Ladies' Home Journal* first recognized the existence of a "rebellion of the young," moved to do so by letters from frantic mothers throughout the country. "It would be a fine thing for this generation," said the *Journal*, "if the word 'flapper' could be abolished." Before the war (and the *Journal* held the war responsible for the changed attitudes of the young) the word *flapper* meant "'a sprightly and knowing miss in her early teens.'" Since the war, its "morbid" side had emerged, under which rubric was included cigarette smoking, short skirts, obscene dancing, one-piece bathing suits, jazz, psychoanalysis, birth control, and Bolshevism.[18]

In the 1920s, artist John Held, Jr., captured the "flapper" for *The New Yorker* magazine in a series of drawings that were widely reprinted. Like the Gibson girl of the 1890s, the Held flapper became the symbol of her generation: with her short, straight skirt, her lean torso and her cropped hair, the rouge on her cheeks and the cigarette in her mouth, she was the epitome of youth, adventure, and healthy sex.

149

To what extent such behavior constituted a true sexual revolution is debatable. Some rudimentary surveys of sex attitudes were attempted during the 1920s, but what they pointed to was a limited, rather than an extensive, change in behavior. Among her sample of about two thousand older, middle-class women, Katherine B. Davis found that 7 percent of the married women had had sexual relations before marriage, while 14 percent of the unmarried women had had sexual relations. Among the latter group 80 percent saw no justification for premarital sex.[19] In Denver, Judge Ben Lindsey, whose work among teenagers through the Juvenile Court there gained him a national reputation, judged that before the war, young men in sizable numbers commonly had had sexual relations with prostitutes, while after the war it was their schoolmates who were their partners—a change produced by the vice commission's success in breaking up the red light district, by the war experience, and by the new permissiveness among young women. Yet he was reluctant to estimate that more than 10 percent of Denver's young women were permissive when it came to sex.[20] Left-wing writer and editor V. F. Calverton, who like Lindsey applauded the indications of a new morality and hoped that the young might be the vanguard of a new, liberated ideal of human relationships, had to admit that the new morality was still "embryonic in form." "Although it has had widespread social expression," he wrote, "it, unhappily, still remains a revolt of individuals rather than groups."[21] Indeed, surveys of the incidence of premarital sex among college students in the 1930s indicated that no more than 25 percent of women students engaged in sex before marriage.[22]

Far from all young women adopted the new standards of behavior. If they had, the "sexual revolution" would have emancipated their own generation, and their daughters and granddaughters in the generations to come would not have reported conflicts with their parents over their own desires for sexual freedom. Novelist Mary McCarthy, raised in the 1920s in a strict Catholic family, was forbidden to date until she was eighteen; instead, she daydreamed about men. In one wild and secret flight with female friends to a distant state, she had a passionate, although unconsummated, affair with a married man who gallantly preserved her "virtue."[23] Author Anne Morrow Lindbergh has reported that she spent her time at Smith College and afterward in the classic manner of the bright college student: working hard at her studies, hoping to win the poetry prize, seeing numerous men, and fretting whether she would ever marry.[24]

The path that Anne Lindbergh followed was, more often than not, a characteristic one. Sexual emancipation, if it led anywhere, led to marriage. Divorce statistics continued to rise, as they had throughout the previous decade. But the number of marriages remained equally high, and the median age of first marriage remained relatively constant. For women the vaunted sexual revolution was as disturbing as it was fulfilling. Premarital or extramarital sex was potentially dangerous: it violated mores learned in childhood, and it could result in pregnancy or, as public health officials made clear, in venereal disease. In the 1920s, birth-control devices were still difficult to obtain. In all states they were illegal. A sympathetic doctor or druggist willing to violate the law had to be found, or the woman had to take her chances or use a douche.

Whether fearful or bold, young women could not help but be influenced by the currents of the age. One analyst of women undergraduates wrote that "freedom" was their primary goal. It meant, on the one hand, attending countless college proms and weekends; on the other, an aversion to any rules, even to compulsory bed and meal times.[25] Many commentators agreed that the crusading spirit that had motivated the first generation of women college students had dissipated. Now, women often chose to attend college because they could not think of anything better to do.[26] A similar attitude existed about going to work. One observer wrote that "working has lost the glamour which surrounded it in the days when women had to struggle against odds for this means of self-expression." "Freedom," defined in sexual and personal terms, was the new value.[27] If young women wanted power and influence over men, they could get it by playing standard female roles: by being a temptress on the dance floor or a companion on the golf course. They could drink, they could smoke, they could enjoy sex. Why chose the difficult paths that Susan Anthony or Alice Paul had followed?

Seen in retrospect, however, this generation of young women often did not know what to do with the freedom it had achieved. Its rebellion

151

83 A page from the 1927 *Vassarion*, showing sophomore students.

was a typically adolescent one: it came from the heart and spirit, not from the mind. When it had played itself out, its adherents fell back on the standards that their parents and their culture had set for them — marriage and motherhood. In no way had this generation overcome women's greatest difficulty: the profound sex-role conditioning that was an integral part of their upbringing.

Then, as before and after, little girls played with dolls, their brothers with cars. Boys were encouraged to run, jump, and suppress their emotions; girls were encouraged to be ladylike and were expected to show their emotions. Girls who stepped out of line were known as tomboys. Pilot Amelia Earhart's husband, in his biography of her, emphasized that Earhart's childhood had been strikingly different from that of most girls of her age: along with her brothers, she was permitted, even encouraged, to experiment, to build, to explore the out-of-doors. He traced her later "masculine" spirit of adventure to this deviant upbringing. Psychologist Floyd Allport, writing in 1929, called for an end to the subtle indoctrination of sex roles in home and school. Woman, he wrote, "not through nature but by early training . . . becomes a reflection of a feminine image which men carry about in their heads."[28]

Progressive women had risen above such conditioning because to do so was new and challenging and because they and their culture had played down the importance of sex in people's lives. But the generation of the 1920s was overwhelmed by it. Writing in the early 1930s, one participant in the youth culture of the 1920s remembered that they had debated free love and companionate marriage, that they had bobbed their hair and carried hip flasks, but there the rebellion stopped. Ten years later these women were respectable citizens, "worried about the interest on the mortgage; making poor Aunt Ida feel she really isn't a burden; and fervently hoping Junior will escape the epidemic of measles ravaging the fourth grade."[29]

Those women who did try to combine marriage and a career still found it difficult. True, the number of married women in the work force was rising. Five percent of married women had worked in 1900; by 1910 the figure stood at 11 percent, and it remained as high as 9 percent in 1920. In the latter year, married women constituted 23 percent of the female work force. Most, analysts believed, were of the working class.

They worked not because they wanted to, but because of economic necessity. Moreover, most professional women were still unmarried — a fact that one analyst explained was due to the isolation of cities, where most of them lived, to their own high standards for a potential husband, and to the fact that many middle-class men still considered it degrading if their wives worked.[30]

Yet writers like John Watson were giving some encouragement to women who wanted to pursue careers as well as marriage, while new mechanical contrivances were lessening the burden of housework. Some observers believed that a new consumerism, stimulated by advertising, was eroding the old belief that wives must stay at home. Noting a trend that would not become widespread until after the Second World War, economist Lorine Pruette wrote that "the two-car family . . . demands the two-wage family."[31] Moreover, at least one study of wives with professional careers reported that ninety women among its sample of one hundred were able easily to find full-time servants to care for their homes and children.[32]

For others it was not so easy. Late in the decade and early in the 1930s popular journals featured a number of revealing "autobiographies" and "confessions" by self-styled "ex-feminists." The revelations were all similar: how even "liberated" women found it impossible both to work and to have a family. All began marriage with their husbands' agreement that family responsibilities were to be shared. But faced with reality and given their upbringings, husband and wife reverted to the conventional roles. One woman realized that the problem was partly her own lack of strength, yet she also held her husband to blame. "He has given lip-service to my aspirations," she wrote, "but when it has come to the difficulty of putting them into practice, he has not helped me."[33] Another woman who married a socialist she met while working at Norman Thomas's office had the same problem: lack of support from her husband. Bitterly she wrote, "Feminism as a personal religion was as interesting to him as Mr. Thomas's socialism," but not when it interfered with his own aspirations and comfort. For the many women who wanted, as one "ex-feminist" admitted, "the rich domestic life of husband, home, and babies that my mother's generation enjoyed" and a career as well, the problem was indeed profound.[34]

WOMEN AT WORK: PROGRESS AND SETBACKS

The popular evidence of women's emancipation in the 1920s—the numbers of women at work, the new sexuality, the new clothing styles—masked the discrimination against women that still existed. At the height of women's employment during the First World War, for example, only 5 percent of women workers had not been in the labor force before the war. What seemed to reflect new employment reflected instead the fact that women already in the work force were promoted during the war to higher-paying, higher-skilled jobs. In some cases this meant a permanent transfer into clerical work. In other cases, women who had replaced men were demoted or fired when the war ended. In Cleveland, Ohio, the women who became street-car operators for a time were cultural heroines, but they were laid off when returning male operators went on strike against the women's continued employment. In some industries—like automobiles or iron and steel—women had registered permanent gains by 1920. But, according to Women's Bureau analysts, the opening of some new industries to women and the advancement of a few to skilled positions were offset by the wage discrimination that existed in every category of women's employment. [36]

Similarly, the common assumption that the proportion of women who worked increased during the 1920s is fallacious. It is true that an additional 2 million women had jobs, but this was primarily a reflection of the general population growth. In fact, whereas 23 percent of American women were employed in 1920, 24 percent were employed in 1930—an increase of only 1 percent. This stability in employment figures was probably due to the fact that the immigration restriction acts of the early 1920s had largely cut off the flow of poverty stricken Eastern European families into the nation.

Furthermore, with the exception of their movement into clerical work, women did not substantially improve their position in the labor force in the 1920s. Although the number of women increased in most professions, women still held jobs that were less prestigious and lower-paid than those of men. For example, although women received about one-third of the graduate degrees awarded annually, only 4 percent of the full professors in American colleges were women. Few colleges would promote women beyond the lower ranks: Mary Ellen Chase, novelist and distinguished scholar of English literature, left the University of Minnesota in 1926 for Smith College because it was clear that Minnesota would not promote a woman beyond the level of assistant professor. Smith, however, preserved enough of its feminist origins to deal more fairly with its female faculty.[36]

In medicine the proportion of women to men actually declined. Dr. Alice Hamilton thought that it had been easier for a woman to become a doctor earlier in the century, when feminism was still a powerful force and "a woman doctor could count on the loyalty of a group of devoted feminists who would choose a woman [doctor] because she was a woman."[37] Few medical or law schools refused admission to women, but most applied quotas on female admission. (Until 1945 the quota at most medical schools was about 5 percent.) Most women lawyers and doctors continued to perform the less lucrative and challenging services in their fields or to minister principally to women and children. The few women who were dentists were primarily children's orthodontists. They predominated in that field only temporarily: by the 1950s the majority of children's orthodontists were men.

Even the expanding fields of business administration and advertising offered limited opportunities for women aside from clerical work. Female Horatio Algers, it is true, could always be found to bolster the nation's success mythology and its belief that feminism had achieved its goals. Often in the 1920s these businesswomen made their money by marketing products designed for women. Industries like fashion and retailing have always been relatively open to determined career women. And in those years shrewd female entrepreneurs recognized the immense potential of the market created by the new sex consciousness. Helena Rubinstein, who parlayed her mother's home beauty cream into a gigantic cosmetics empire, was only one of a number of such women. Another was her competitor, Elizabeth Arden.

Making their way in the masculine world of business was not easy. M. Louise Luckinbill, a secretary at the Schultz-McGregor Advertising Agency in New York City, declined a proferred promotion to a vice presidency. Businessmen, she wrote, "would throw up their hands in horror at the idea of a woman being . . . vice-president of an [advertis-

84   Helena Rubinstein, to whom personal beauty was a source of both power and profit.

ing] agency which served them."[38] Edith Mae Cummings, who built her job as an insurance saleswoman into a firm of her own, contended that any woman could succeed in business through self-reliance and perseverance. Yet, she admitted, businessmen were hostile to businesswomen because of their fear that women so employed would lose their "feminine daintiness."[39] Helena Rubinstein recalled, "It was not easy being a hard-working woman in a man's world." In order to survive in the business world she became a tyrant. Her rages became legendary. She married a count, lived in lavish style, and was known as "madame." For "added courage," she wore elaborate and expensive jewelry. To Rubinstein, the quest for beauty, which was central to her business and her life, did not represent enslavement, but was a "force . . . to make you feel greater than you are."[40]

The situation of the working-class woman was little better. On the surface, the 1920s seemed to be years of economic prosperity, but it was a prosperity in which many workers did not participate. Vast sectors of the economy were in a state of depression: at least one-half of farm and industrial workers earned barely enough to survive. Sizable wage increases went primarily to skilled laborers. The income of many unskilled workers, which included the majority of women workers, rose but little. If anything, the relative position of these women worsened: according to one major study, the differential between the hourly wages paid to unskilled male and female workers rose from 6.3 cents in 1923 to 10.2 cents in 1929.[41]

Working-class mothers who worked away from home faced particular difficulties. For the most part, they left young children with relatives or neighbors, while older children fended for themselves after school.[42] In 1930, one study revealed, there were approximately eight hundred nursery schools in the nation.[43] Despite the fact that most were run by charitable organizations specifically for lower-income working women, most mothers were suspicious of them—a suspicion that stemmed partly from the fact that welfare agencies only too readily placed the children of indigent mothers in asylums and foster homes. Furthermore, many social workers opposed the further establishment of nursery centers, arguing that what was needed was the further extension of county and state programs of direct relief to mothers with children so that they could stay at home. However, such programs, which many states had mandated in the late 1910s and early 1920s, were badly underfunded and poorly administered.[44]

In part, this situation of low pay and little relief for working mothers reflected the fact that the union movement was in disarray in the 1920s. Membership had plummeted, and there was not much significant strike activity. Women workers, as well as men, showed little drive to challenge employers, who promised (but generally did not deliver) a new welfare capitalism under which employers would take responsibility for the welfare of their workers. But workers were constantly threatened by unemployment during the decade and chastened by the defeats that unions suffered in a series of major strikes after the end of the war. By 1919, for example, the telephone operators of New England, primarily women, had finally managed to form a union, but an unsuccessful strike in 1921 proved its undoing. Membership in the union evaporated, and former members were fired and blacklisted by the telephone companies. There were no further attempts at organization or strike activity during the 1920s.

Even the International Ladies' Garment Workers' Union fell on hard days. The rise in demand for ready-to-wear clothing for women was a boon to the garment industry, but individual companies became alarmingly dependent on the caprice of fashion. When a dress style failed, the company that had created it and the workers who had made it suffered accordingly. Such worker insecurity made organization difficult. Even more disastrous for the ILGWU was the appearance of a strong communist faction among its membership in the 1920s. Instead of concentrating on organization and agitation, the union spent the decade in bitter infighting for control. By 1930 the communists were defeated, but the struggle had nearly destroyed the union. Its membership dropped from 250,000 to 40,000; its treasury was over $2 million in debt.

Those progressive organizations that had focused on working women—the Consumers' League and the Women's Trade Union League in particular—continued operations in the 1920s; but they, too, were beset by problems. The WTUL, dependent on the regular unions for its funds, had no greater success than these unions did in organizing workers. Its entire budget was never more than $20,000 yearly; and its officers eventually had to discontinue publication of its official journal. The Consumers' League continued to focus on special legislation for working women, but the 1921 Supreme Court decision in *Adkins v. Children's Hospital*, which outlawed federal minimum-wage laws for women, made advances in special legislation difficult.

Moreover, it was difficult to persuade well-to-do women to support progressive programs for working women. They were busy with other activities and ready to believe businessmen's propaganda. In 1926 Maude Nathan, a wealthy founder of the New York Consumers' League, wrote that over the years there had been a "complete metamorphosis" in the conditions of work for women in urban department stores. Consumers' Leagues, she implied, were no longer necessary, at least not for women in this category. Yet the improvements, as she had to admit, were only relative. Although pay had risen, it was still extremely low. Women worked a twelve- rather than a sixteen-hour day. They had won the right to sit down on occasion and to take a week's vacation a year.

159

All of this, according to Nathan, proved that the merchants were "vying with each other in giving humane attention" to their employees. The problem, in short, had been solved.[45] Nathan's attitude was representative of the popular view that women were achieving equality on a wide variety of fronts and that society need do little more for them.

THE NEW HEROINES

Every age has its heroines, and those chosen by the 1920s generation tell us much about the prevailing attitudes toward women. In the 1910s, Jane Addams had been the national heroine, the secular saint whose deep compassion and forceful personality endeared her to a generation of humanitarian Americans. The heroines of the 1920s were of a different stamp. Among them, the pilot Amelia Earhart, the movie actress Mary Pickford, and the "vamp," a standard film character, stand out as representative. Each was strikingly different; and although their

85 Amelia Earhart, who flew a Lockheed Vega monoplane solo from Newfoundland to Ireland in 1932 and became one of the most celebrated women of her time.

careers seemed to give weight to the notion of women's emancipation, together they signaled the demise of feminism as the prewar generation had known it.

In her way, Amelia Earhart was a feminist *manqué*. Her early career was peripatetic and split between a devotion to social feminism and to flying. A graduate of Barnard College, Earhart tried a number of jobs before she became a settlement worker in Boston. Meanwhile she learned to fly. She searched out women instructors, for she found male pilots insulting, hostile, or overprotective. In 1927 representatives of Amy Phipps Guest, a wealthy New York flying enthusiast, contacted Earhart with the proposition that she make a solo flight across the Atlantic as Lindbergh had done the year before. With Guest's financial backing, Earhart made the flight, was welcomed by impressive crowds, and vaulted to national prominence.

Earhart's life was an eloquent testimony to women's abilities. But in the long run, her fame and her achievements did little to advance the feminist cause. Part of the difficulty was that she was shy and self-effacing, a female counterpart to the boyishly appealing Lindbergh. She was popularly known as "Lady Lindy," for she bore a striking physical resemblance to Lindbergh, and there were those who said that this was the reason she had been chosen for the flight. Despite her membership in the Woman's Party, her feminism was modest. She wrote, "probably my greatest satisfaction was to indicate by example now and then, that women can sometimes do things themselves if given the chance." But it was flying above all that thrilled her and that she publicized; her books described each of her flights in detail and celebrated the dangers and glories of aviation.

Earhart's last flight, on which she disappeared, took place in 1937. After her presumed death, there were other women flyers, but none who captured the public imagination in the same way. As aviation became professionalized, men flyers would come to dominate the career. Finally, in 1931, an innovation was added to commercial air flights that made clear the future position of women in aviation. Airline stewardesses—who were then called "hostesses" and were required to have a nursing degree—made their appearance. Now, as doctors had their nurses and businessmen their secretaries, pilots had their helpers

86　The world's first airline stewardesses, hired in 1930 to fly the Chicago to San Francisco run.

too. Once again women were to perform their traditional role of service.

If the public of prewar America made the social worker the heroine of the 1910s, the public of the 1920s thrilled to individual feats of courage and daring, and these Earhart provided in abundance. Mary Pickford and the "vamp" gave expression to other sides of the American character, both of which were antifeminist in implication. Pickford was the virginal child-woman incarnate, "America's Sweetheart," its "Little Mary"; the vamp was the eternal temptress, the Eve, who led men astray and lived for sex.

Between the First World War and the 1930s, Pickford's triumph was unquestioned. Golden-haired and impish, she played adolescents on the verge of maturity, roles similar to those that Shirley Temple would play at a younger age in the next decade. Pickford was no feminist. Yet she was iron-willed and shrewd: she was the first in her profession to demand and receive the high salaries that have become standard in the movie industry. She had less success in trying to convince the public to accept her as something other than the personification of pure youth—a role she came to hate. Films in which she played other types of women were generally commercial failures, and when, in the late 1920s, she cut off the long blonde curls that had been her trademark, she almost lost her audience. As much as it thrilled to the *femme fatale* and the sex dramas of the 1920s, the movie audience wanted Pickford to show them an idyllic America, where women were graceful and lovely and never grew up.

The opposite type, the vamp, appealed to the nation's new fascination with sexuality. Her origins can be traced to the days of prewar burlesque and vaudeville, to music-hall stars like Lillian Russell and the Floradora girls, who bared shoulder and ankle to beguile the male public. As was often the case, the war simply speeded up a trend that was al-

87 and 88   From "America's Sweetheart" to the *femme fatale: (left)* Mary Pickford in *Rebecca of Sunnybrook Farm; (right)* Marlene Dietrich in *Blonde Venus.*

ready underway. As a type, the vamp went through several transformations during the course of the decade. For a time she was the seductress pure and simple; then with the rise of the youth cult and the appearance of censorship codes that restricted open sexuality on the screen, she was transformed into the flapper. Finally she emerged as the *femme fatale,* which would remain a major screen character into the 1930s, particularly as personified by Greta Garbo and Marlene Dietrich. The history of the vamp was determined largely by the movie directors who, in consultation with scriptwriters and producers, tried to gauge public taste. Cecil B. DeMille, for example, correctly calculated that the public would respond to his brand of sultry and sophisticated sex dramas in the early 1920s, while writer Elinor Glyn is usually credited with having created the screen version of the flapper.

The vamp first appeared in 1915 in a movie entitled *A Fool There Was.* It starred Theda Bara, who became famous overnight for her brand of sultry sexuality. Press agents transmogrified her typical American background into a saga of Egyptian illegitimacy and sexual license:

89   Theda Bara, promoted as the "wickedest force in the world" and the star of *Cleopatra.*

she was the daughter of an Algerian soldier and an Egyptian dancer; she was kidnapped and raised by a band of Egyptian cutthroats; she had occult powers. Bara supposedly played the role in real life as well as on the screen. (Bara was also the first screen personality to wear eye make-up; Helena Rubinstein invented it for her as a way of creating a new cosmetic market.) After the war, the mantle of sex queen passed on to Gloria Swanson. She was more sleek and sophisticated than Bara, but she fulfilled the same role of seductress. In her films, surprisingly, wives were sometimes allowed to philander and to divorce their husbands, and women of easy virtue to go free without punishment. In the beginning, before censorship was imposed, the movie industry endorsed women's new sexual freedom.

The flapper was different: she was the flirt, the sex tease, eternally promising sex play but not mature passion. In her character there were overtones of the Pickford role: the flapper was the virginal, healthy, adolescent grown a bit older and wiser. Although the flapper smoked, danced, and went to petting parties, at heart she was honest and de-

90 Pearl White, the "Pauline" of the film serial who could take care of herself.

165

served the hero's love. The *femme fatale,* however, returned to the tradition of the vamp: whereas the flapper was flighty, the *femme fatale* was sophisticated, ageless, and often tragic. But whereas the vamp had been open and brazen, the *femme fatale* was subtle and mysterious. Whether vamp, flapper, or *femme fatale,* the end in life for all three was a man.

That another screen image for women might have been possible is illus'rated by the popularity of the prewar serials that often starred a woman as the main character. The most famous of these was the *Perils of Pauline,* starring Pearl White. She was capable of finding her own way out of a given predicament without the assistance of the strong and handsome hero. The early Pauline could ride and shoot as well as any man. And in *The Goddess,* made in 1915, the heroine was a modern Joan of Arc, raised on a desert island in the belief that she was a goddess destined to solve the world's ills.

91   A local beauty contest, circa 1905.

92　Miss Washington becomes the nation's first "Miss America," 1921.

Such feminist themes were inappropriate to the decade of the 1920s, which wanted its women soft and pliant and accepted aggressiveness only in sex or sports. The emblem of the change was the beauty queen. In 1920 the hotel owners of Atlantic City, New Jersey, thought up a promotional scheme to lengthen the summer season at the beach. Their idea was to host a beauty contest late in September when most vacationers had gone home—a contest to select America's reigning beauty, its Miss America. They raised the beauty contest to a level of national attention and enshrined it as a typically American institution. And more than anything else, they provided the ultimate symbol of what the American woman in the 1920s was supposed to be.

Notes

[1] Emily Newell Blair, "Wanted—A New Feminism," *Independent Woman* (December 1930), 499.

[2] Sara Barbara Brumbaugh, *Democratic Experience and Education in the National League of Women Voters* (New York: Teachers College Press, 1946), p. 45.

[3] Martin Gruberg, *Women in American Politics: An Assessment and Sourcebook* (Oshkosh, Wis.: Academia Press, 1968), p. 91.

[4] Marion K. Sanders, *The Lady and the Vote* (Boston: Houghton Mifflin, 1956), pp. 141–42.

[5] Anna Steese Richardson, "Is the Women's Club Dying?" *Harper's*, CLIX (October 1929), 607.

[6] Rheta Childe Dorr, *A Woman of Fifty* (New York: Funk and Wagnalls, 1924), pp. 280ff.

[7] Marie Louise Degen, *The History of the Woman's Peace Party* (Baltimore: The Johns Hopkins Press, 1939), p. 20.

[8] June Sochen, *The New Woman: Feminism in Greenwich Village, 1910–1920* (New York: Quadrangle, 1972), pp. 115–16.

[9] Vida Scudder, *On Journey* (New York: E. P. Dutton, 1937), p. 300.

[10] Suzanne LaFollette, *Concerning Women* (New York: Albert and Charles Boni, 1926), p. 10.

[11] Elizabeth Onativia, "Give Us Our Privileges," *Scribner's*, LXXXVII (June 1930), 593–94.

[12] *Ibid.*, p. 597.

[13] Dorothy Dunbar Bromley, "Feminist—New Style," *Harper's*, CLV (October 1927), 552–60.

[14] Mabel Dodge Luhan, *Intimate Memories* (New York: Harcourt Brace Jovanovich, 1936), vol. 3: *Movers and Shakers*, p. 263.

[15] Charlotte Perkins Gilman, *The Living of Charlotte Perkins Gilman: An Autobiography* (New York: Appleton-Century, 1935), pp. 332–33.

[16] *Ibid.*, p. 313.

[17] Lillian Hellman, *An Unfinished Woman: A Memoir* (Boston: Little, Brown, 1969), p. 35.

[18] *Ladies' Home Journal* (October 1922), 30.

[19] Katherine B. Davis, *Factors in the Sex Life of Twenty-Two Hundred Women* (New York: Harper and Brothers, 1929).

[20] Ben B. Lindsey and Evans Wainwright, *The Revolt of Modern Youth* (New York: Boni and Liveright, 1925), pp. 66–67.

[21] V. F. Calverton, *The Bankruptcy of Marriage* (New York: Macaulay, 1928), p. 90.

[22] Dorothy Dunbar Bromley and Florence Britten, *Youth and Sex: A Study of Thirteen-Hundred College Students* (New York: Harper and Brothers, 1938).

[23] Mary McCarthy, *Memories of a Catholic Girlhood* (New York: Harcourt Brace Jovanovich, 1957).

[24] Anne Morrow Lindbergh, *Bring Me a Unicorn: Diaries and Letters of Anne Morrow Lindbergh, 1922–1928* (New York: Harcourt Brace Jovanovich, 1972).

[25] Dorothy Waldo, "College or Not?" in Mabelle Babcock Blake *et al.*, *The Education of the Modern Girl* (Boston: Houghton Mifflin, 1929), pp. 99–118.

26 Jessie Bernard, *Academic Women* (University Park, Pa.: Pennsylvania State University Press, 1964), pp. 36–37.

27 Phyllis Blanchard and Carolyn Manasses, *New Girls for Old* (New York: Macauley, 1937), p. 175.

28 Floyd Allport, "Seeing Women as They Are," *Harper's*, CLVIII (March 1929), 406.

29 Maxine Davis, *The Lost Generation: A Portrait of American Youth Today* (New York: Macmillan, 1936), pp. 25–26.

30 Chase Going Woodhouse, "Married College Women in Business and the Professions," *Annals of the American Academy of Political and Social Science*, CXLIII (May 1929), 341.

31 Lorine Pruette, "The Married Woman and the Part-Time Job," *Annals of the American Academy of Political and Social Science* (1929), 302.

32 Virginia MacMakin Collier, *Marriage and Careers: A Study of One Hundred Women Who Are Wives, Mothers, Homemakers, and Professional Women* (New York: The Channel Bookshop, 1926).

33 "Confessions of an Ex-Feminist," *New Republic*, XXII (April 14, 1926), 218ff.

34 Worth Tuttle, "Autobiography of an Ex-Feminist," *Atlantic*, CLII (December 1933), 645.

35 Alice Rogers Hager, "Occupations and Earnings of Women in Industry," *Annals of the American Academy of Political and Social Science* (1929), 65–73.

36 Mary Ellen Chase, *A Goodly Fellowship* (New York: Macmillan, 1939), p. 285.

37 Alice Hamilton, *Exploring the Dangerous Trades: The Autobiography of Alice Hamilton* (Boston: Little, Brown, 1943), p. 268.

38 *Women of Today* (1926), 235.

39 Edith Mae Cummings, *Pots, Pans, and Millions: A Study of Woman's Right to Be in Business: Her Proclivities and Capacity for Success* (Washington, D.C.: National School of Business Science for Women, 1929).

40 Helena Rubinstein, *My Life for Beauty* (London: Bodley Head, 1964).

41 Irving Bernstein, *The Lean Years: A History of the American Worker, 1920–1933* (Boston: Houghton Mifflin, 1960), p. 69.

42 Gwendolyn Hughes Berry, "Mothers in Industry," *Annals of the American Academy of Political and Social Science* (1929), 315–24.

43 The White House Conference on Child Health and Protection, *Nursery Education* (New York: Century, 1931)

44 Katharine Anthony, *Mothers Who Must Earn* (New York: Survey Associates, 1914).

45 Maude Nathan, *The Story of an Epoch-Making Movement* (Garden City, N.Y.: Doubleday, Page, 1926), pp. 105–09.

Bibliography

The major study of women in the 1920s is J. Stanley Lemons, *The Woman Citizen: Social Feminism in the 1920s* (Urbana, Ill.: University of Illinois Press, 1973). His work contains valuable information on women's organizations, but his thesis that feminism remained strong after the early 1920s is questionable. On the social-work profession and the settlement houses, see Clark A. Chambers, *Seedtime of Reform: American Social Service and Action, 1918–1933* (1963; reprint ed., Ann Arbor: University of Michigan Press, 1967). One might also read with profit Jane Addams, *The Second Twenty Years at Hull House* (New York: Macmillan, 1930), and the 1929 issue of the *Annals of the American Academy of Political and Social Science*, "Women in the Modern World." On cultural attitudes, Frederick Lewis Allen, *Only Yesterday: An Informal History of the 1920s* (New York: Harper, 1931), and Helen Merrell Lynd and Robert S. Lynd, *Middletown: A Study in Contemporary American Culture* (New York: Harcourt Brace Jovanovich, 1929) are still indispensable. Walter Lippmann, *A Preface to Morals* (New York: Macmillan, 1929) is insightful.

There are as yet no comprehensive studies of advertising in the 1920s, of the impact of Freudian ideas, of the participation of women in the peace movement, or of the exact dimensions of the youth "rebellion." On each of these subjects, one might consult Otis Pease, *The Responsibilities of American Advertising: Private Control and Public Influence, 1920–1940* (New Haven: Yale University Press, 1958); Grace Adams, "The Rise and Fall of Psychology," *North American Review*, CLIII (1934), 82–92; Lucille C. Birnbaum, "Behaviorism in the 1920s," *American Quarterly*, VII (Spring 1955), 15–30; and Gertrude Bussey and Margaret Tims, *Women's International League for Peace and Freedom, 1915–1965* (London: Allen and Unwin, 1965).

To what extent the 1920s witnessed a change in sexual attitudes has caused considerable debate. The most important recent article is James R. McGovern, "The American Woman's Pre-World War I Freedom in Manners and Morals," *Journal of American History*, LV (September 1968), 315–18. For contemporary points of view, Ben B. Lindsey and Evans Wainwright, *The Revolt of Modern Youth* (New York: Boni and Liveright, 1925); Phyllis Blanchard and Carolyn Manasses, *New Girls for Old* (New York: Macauley, 1937); and V. F. Calverton, *The Bankruptcy of Marriage* (New York: Macauley, 1928) are insightful. One might also consult Freda Kirchway, ed., *Our Changing Morality: A Symposium* (New York: Albert and Charles Boni, 1924); V. F. Calverton and S. D. Schmalhausen, *Sex in Civilization* (New York: Macauley, 1929); and Floyd Dell, *Love in the Machine Age: A Psychological Study of the Transition from Patriarchal Society* (New York: Farrar and Rinehart, 1930).

On women and work, Irving Bernstein, *The Lean Years: A History of the American Worker, 1920–1933* (Boston: Houghton Mifflin, 1960); William H. Chafe, *The American Woman: Her Changing Social, Economic, and Political Roles, 1920–1970* (New York: Oxford University Press, 1972); and a number of the studies cited in Chapter 2 provide information. On this topic, the studies of the Women's Bureau of the Department of Labor are also indispensable.

On Amelia Earhart, see George Palmer Putnam, *Soaring Wings: A Biography of Amelia Earhart* (New York: Harcourt Brace Jovanovich, 1939). The only general study of women in films is Marjorie Rosen, *Popcorn Venus: Women, Movies, and the American Dream* (New York: Coward, McCann & Geoghegan, 1973). Additional information is provided by Alexander Walker, *The Celluloid Sacrifice: Aspects of Sex in the Movies* (New York: Hawthorn, 1966); Edward Wagenecht, *The Movies in the Age of Innocence* (Norman, Okla.: University of Oklahoma Press, 1962); Maurice Bardèche and Robert Brasillach, *The History of Motion Pictures*, trans. and ed. Iris Barry (New York: Norton, 1938); Bosley Crowther, *The Great Films: Fifty Golden Years of Motion Pictures* (New York: G. P. Putnam's Sons, 1967); William K. Everson, *The American Movie* (New York: Atheneum, 1963) and *The Bad Guys: A Pictorial History of the Movie Villain* (New York: Citadel, 1964); and Jim Harmon and Donald F. Glut, *The Great Movie Serials: Their Sound and Fury* (Garden City, N.Y.: Doubleday, 1972). On Mary Pickford, see her autobiography, *Sunshine and Shadow* (Garden City, N.Y.: Doubleday, 1955). One might also consult Cecil B. DeMille, *Autobiography*, ed. Donald Hayne (Englewood Cliffs, N.J.: Prentice-Hall, 1959).

Women in Depression 5
and War: 1930–1945

The advances women made during the First World War and the 1920s were secondary in importance. Their new freedom to compete in organized sports, to wear comfortable clothes, to expect sexual fulfillment represented no inconsiderable progress. But behind these gains lay the traditional concept: home, husband, and the attainment of beauty were still held to be woman's paramount goals. During the 1930s and 1940s, these basic attitudes about women remained constant. But some countervailing forces appeared. The federal government was coming to concern itself with the plight of working women. Labor unions began to make a genuine commitment to the organization of women workers. Major women's organizations, after a long period of factionalism, began to unite around advocacy of the Equal Rights Amendment. Finally, during the Second World War, as during the First, extensive new employment opportunities opened up to women. Once again it seemed that war might bring women the liberation that peace had been unable to provide.

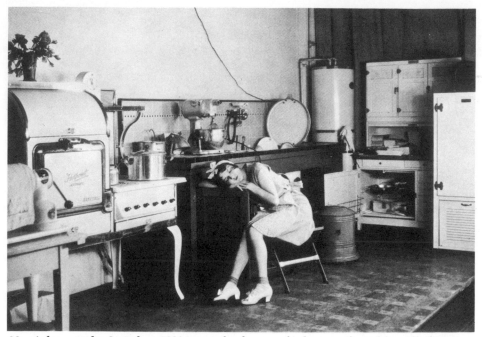

93 *Asleep at the Switch:* a 1933 movie burlesque of a housewife and her all-electric kitchen.

FEMINISM AND WOMEN'S ORGANIZATIONS

On the whole, feminist causes were not the central concern of organized women during these years. Social feminism had dominated the decade of the 1920s; the depression made social welfare seem even more pressing. In addition, the federal government was more than ever before responsive to the social-reform pressures of groups like the Consumers' League, the Women's Trade Union League, settlement and social-work organizations, and the League of Women Voters. According to historian Clark Chambers, these groups were crucial to the formulation and passage of much New Deal legislation, while their leaders were often tapped for positions within the growing social-welfare bureaucracy. Moreover, their abhorrence of war still impelled many activist women to work for groups like the Women's International League for Peace and Freedom. Nor were their efforts without success. For example, the congressional investigation under Senator Gerald Nye between 1934 and

172

1936 into the munitions industry resulted in large part from the effective lobbying of women's pacifist organizations. Finally, the General Federation of Women's Clubs centered on a campaign with domestic feminist overtones. It put its efforts into making the housewife familiar with labor-saving devices and efficient techniques of housework as a way of eliminating waste and conserving human and material resources.

This is not to argue that women's organizations abandoned their feminist efforts entirely. For a time in 1936 it appeared possible that a loose union of the major women's organizations around a charter of women's rights might be achieved. Mary Anderson, head of the Women's Bureau, worked with women leaders, particularly social worker Mary Van Vleeck, to draw up such a charter. Anderson's draft catalogued the standard feminist demands: equal rights for women and men in politics, education, law, and employment. Few women's organizations, however, actually endorsed it. According to Anderson, by the time organizations like the League of Women Voters had finally finished studying the draft, the time for action had passed. Moreover, Anderson had also included a clause stating that when specific exploitation of women workers existed, there should be special legislation to protect them. To this the Woman's Party, with its adamant stand in favor of the ERA, could never agree, and its leaders mounted a vigorous attack that had no little effect in destroying altogether the hope for a united women's charter.[1] Yet the Woman's Party was slowly achieving success in its campaign for the ERA. In the late 1920s the National Federation of Business and Professional Women's Clubs had come to support the ERA. In 1940 the Republican party endorsed the amendment in its platform; in 1943 the General Federation of Women's Clubs announced its support; in 1944 the Democratic party in its platform followed suit.

Women's organizations worked on other fronts to advance women's causes. The BPW continued to work for equal employment for women in the professions, although the declining proportion of women professionals in the depression decade would seem to indicate that its efforts were primarily a holding action. The League of Women Voters, too, took some action on behalf of women. In coalition with the BPW and other women's organizations, the League successfully lobbied for the defeat of many state bills that proposed prohibiting the employment of married women who were not heads of households. Moreover, the League vigorously protested federal legislation that disallowed the employment of both husband and wife in the federal civil service— legislation that resulted in the firing of large numbers of women employees.

But the League continued to give primary allegiance to issues of general social welfare. During the Roosevelt administration, the League was responsible for the passage of state and national laws that extended the merit system within the civil service. The League worked with other organizations to improve public-school education. Many League members served on the various lay panels that advised FDR's National Recovery Administration, established in 1933 to draw up codes for industrial production. The League was a major promoter of the Social Security Act of 1935 and of the Food, Drug, and Cosmetic Act of 1936. The variety of goals it pursued necessarily limited its activities on behalf of women. But it still defined its purpose in social feminist terms. The League's opposition to the nepotism legislation for the federal civil service was based on the argument that it violated the merit system of appointment, not that it discriminated against women. "We of the League are very much for the rights of women," wrote one leader, "but . . . we are not feminists primarily; we are citizens."[2]

ELEANOR ROOSEVELT: EXEMPLAR OF HER ERA

The social-welfare concern of the 1930s, prominent particularly during the New Deal administration of Franklin Delano Roosevelt, did not exclude women. The primary spokesperson for women within the government and outside it was Eleanor Roosevelt. Through her radio broadcasts, newspaper columns, books, and speeches, aided by her position as the president's wife, she molded public opinion at the same time that she reflected it.

Eleanor Roosevelt was a feminist of a traditional sort. Above all, she thought that the focus of women's concerns ought to be on providing the qualities of compassion and self-abnegation that were lacking in male-dominated institutions. Her thinking was influenced by the traditional view that men functioned best as hard-headed patriarchs and professionals, while women were sensitive homemakers and volunteer workers. Women had "understanding hearts," wrote Eleanor Roosevelt, while men had "ability and brains." Still men had the alarming propensity in a crisis situation, to always feel "that they must fight," and the natural pacifism of women was needed to moderate male aggressiveness.[3] Such reasoning resembled that of Jane Addams and other Progressive women of a social feminist point of view. It gained from the same strengths and suffered from the same deficiencies that theirs had. Like Addams, Eleanor Roosevelt accepted the popular belief that a woman's primary responsibility was to her family. Again like Addams, she argued that the complexities of the modern world necessitated that women, with their special gifts, take part in public

94   Eleanor Roosevelt at the age of twenty-three, holding one of her children.

affairs to preserve the home. By appealing to the nation's prejudices, Eleanor Roosevelt offered compelling justifications for the widening of women's sphere. Yet she ran the risk of appearing to give support to those who, arguing from the same premises, would deny women any positions of real responsibility outside the home.

Eleanor Roosevelt's attitudes reflected her Victorian upbringing and early marriage. Although the Roosevelts from whom she descended were a wealthy New York family, her father was a ne'er-do-well. After her mother died at a young age, she was raised by her strict grandmother. She married her cousin Franklin Roosevelt, who in domestic matters was dominated by his own mother. For the first fifteen years of her marriage, Eleanor Roosevelt was a shy and dutiful wife, regularly bearing children, acceding to the wishes of her mother-in-law, and remaining in the background while her husband served as Assistant Secretary of the Navy between 1913 and 1920 and ran for vice president on the unsuccessful Democratic ticket of 1920. As a result of her husband's crippling attack of polio in 1921, however, she found the strength to defy her mother-in-law, to persuade her husband to return to public life, and to play a public role in her own right. She gave up the round of social activities that occupied the leisure time of the typical wealthy matron to become active in the League of Women Voters, the Consumers' League, the Democratic party, and especially the Women's Trade Union League. Through her, many women leaders came to know Franklin Roosevelt and later to counsel him on labor and social-welfare decisions.

The transformation of her life and behavior was not easy for Eleanor Roosevelt. By nature she was retiring. She had a high voice and a nervous giggle. She did not speak well in public. Throughout her life she depreciated her looks. But she was faced with the probability that if she herself did not maintain her husband's position in politics while he was ill, they would permanently retire to his wealthy mother's estate and live under her domination. Eleanor Roosevelt found experts to coach her in public speaking and in politics, and she learned through practical experience. In the end, she developed into a capable speaker and a skilled politician.

Eleanor Roosevelt's problems did not end once her own difficulties

95 Eleanor Roosevelt opens the Grandmothers' War Bond League campaign.

had been conquered and her husband had reentered public life. During FDR's first two terms as president, the press pilloried her for playing an activist role while she was the president's wife. Cartoonists caricatured her prominent teeth, her patrician manner. But managing the household and arranging ceremonial occasions—the standard routine of a president's wife—took only a fraction of her time. Instead, she used her tremendous energy also to lecture, write articles and books, and work for the Democratic party. She was FDR's unofficial adviser on domestic matters and his frequent representative on public business. By the end of the 1930s, Eleanor Roosevelt had ridden out the storm of abuse, and polls began to show that she was very popular among the public. After her husband died in 1945, there was talk of her running for the presidency. But given her own traditional attitudes, her age (sixty-one), and her shrewd political sense, it is doubtful that Eleanor Roosevelt would seriously have considered the idea. Rather, she made internationalism and the United Nations her special concerns, serving as United States representative to the United Nations General Assembly in 1946, and from 1947 to 1952 as United States representative to the United Nations Human Rights Commission and the Economic and 177

Social Council. In thus turning to internationalism, she followed a path typical of many earlier social feminists.

During her years of public life, Eleanor Roosevelt as ideologist stressed women's duty to humanity. It was counsel that she consistently followed in her own work. Aside from her formative role in conceiving government sponsorship for the building of planned communities in rural areas and in planning the Federal Theater project, through which the government undertook its first extensive subsidy to the arts, Eleanor Roosevelt was not involved in the central planning decisions of New Deal programs. Rather, she served as a special lobbyist for those groups—particularly blacks, the poor, and women—whose interests were easily overlooked in a power-oriented Washington. Largely due to Eleanor Roosevelt's influence, FDR appointed a relatively sizable

96 An army redistribution station, where Eleanor Roosevelt confers with officers prior to visiting with returnees.

number of women to important government offices, including the first women as ministers to foreign countries (the rank directly below ambassador) and the first woman judge on the Circuit Court of Appeals (the court directly below the Supreme Court). Ruth Bryan Owen, daughter of William Jennings Bryan, served as minister to Denmark; Florence Jaffray Harriman, widow of the railroad magnate, served as minister to Norway; Florence Allen was elevated from the Ohio Supreme Court to the Circuit Court of Appeals. Women from organizations like the Consumers' League and the Women's Trade Union League—which themselves were strong advocates of social-welfare programs in the 1930s—were found in every New Deal agency.

FDR played only an indirect role in a large number of the appointments of women to his administration. All federal relief agencies—from the Federal Emergency Relief Administration, established in 1933 to channel federal money directly to state relief agencies, to the Resettlement Administration, established in 1935 to aid impoverished farm families—were anxious to implement their mandates as soon as possible. In order to do so, they often hired social workers as administrators, for these individuals were both trained and experienced in social-welfare work. Since social work was a profession dominated by women, it was inevitable that some would find their way into the New Deal bureaucracy. Yet while exulting in the number of women within New Deal agencies, Grace Abbott, historian of New Deal welfare programs and herself head of the Children's Bureau for some years, contended that the women in New Deal agencies had a difficult time. Most male administrators, according to Abbott, were prejudiced against women, and they took the advice of women associates and subordinates lightly. Moreover, when a woman proved inadequate to her job, male administrators characteristically drew conclusions about the performance of all women.[4]

Like Eleanor Roosevelt, few of the Roosevelt appointees brought to their positions a militant feminist perspective. Frances Perkins, who as Secretary of Labor was FDR's most important female appointee, was perhaps typical. Although she had followed a career path—from settlement work through paid employment with a voluntary agency (the Consumers' League) to the government bureaucracy—that had been

97 Frances Perkins, FDR's Secretary of Labor and the first woman cabinet member.

typical of many Progressive women, she did not want to be held up as an example to women. Perkins "never recommends a public career [for women]," reported the journal of the National Federation of Business and Professional Women's Clubs, because she believed "that the happiest place for most women is in the home."[5] (Yet this stance may have been the result of her own distaste for the intense publicity to which she, as the first woman cabinet member, was subjected.) She retained her maiden name throughout her career, not as a feminist gesture, but because she did not want to hinder her husband's career by having him identified with a well-known woman.

Mary Anderson, head of the Women's Bureau, charged that Perkins did everything possible to avoid aiding women. According to Anderson, Perkins was afraid of arousing the special enmity of the business community and of losing the support of organized labor, which distrusted her not only because she was a woman, but also because she had risen through social-welfare rather than labor ranks.[6] Perkins' fears were realistic. According to Eleanor Roosevelt, businessmen and politicians who did not like the pro-labor legislation of the New Deal continually accused Perkins of being a typically incapable woman, "bewildered, rattlebrained, befuddled," and "scared" of John L. Lewis, the militant labor leader. Moreover, Congress took special pains to require Perkins to testify before their committees. "Dragging Frances Perkins up to the Hill before congressional hearings, with accompanying ballyhoo in the press," according to Eleanor Roosevelt, "became a kind of a game."[7]

In her apprehension that men disliked dealing with women, Perkins was not alone among major women New Deal bureaucrats. WTUL official Rose Schneiderman, who was FDR's female appointee to the Labor Advisory Board of the National Recovery Administration, never accepted the monthly dinner invitation issued to members of the labor board by the employer's advisory board. She thought that the presence of a woman among these men would "cramp their style" and prevent them from becoming "chummy" with one another.[8]

Despite their traditionalism, Eleanor Roosevelt and other women within FDR's administration did function as advocates for women. Democratic party chairman James Farley estimated that Eleanor Roosevelt was personally responsible for the appointment of over four thousand women to post office jobs, many of which were then patronage positions. She would admit only female reporters to her press conferences, hoping thereby to generate more newspaper jobs for women. She strongly supported the efforts of Mary Dewson, a former social worker and official of the Consumers' League whom FDR had appointed head of the women's division of the Democratic party. Dewson reactivated the Democratic Women's Clubs, which had become little more than appendages of male organizations, by encouraging them to become experts on New Deal policy and publicists of it in their local communities. The plan did succeed in gaining increased prestige for women within the party, and by 1936 Dewson achieved a cherished ambition: equal representation for women on the Platform Committee at the Democratic National Convention. To what extent Dewson made a dent in the common practice of recognizing a woman in politics on the basis of "looks, money, or the late husband's service to the party"— a syndrome she herself identified—is debatable, but at least she and Eleanor Roosevelt played a major part in establishing the initial mechanisms for the equal representation of women on party committees.[9]

Eleanor Roosevelt personally served as the clearing agent for project proposals initiated by women, which came under the aegis of agencies like the Works Projects Administration. Some of these projects may have had limited social impact—like the request of the women of Kansasville, Tennessee, for aid to refurbish the public library—but in Eleanor Roosevelt's view, women's energies were being utilized. She also concerned herself with the difficult problem of the many unemployed and single women who, like men in similar positions, had taken up aimless, wandering existences—moving from one city to another, sleeping in parks and subways. Knowing that estimates of the number of transients went as high as 2 million and that of these, the number of women was as high as 200,000, Eleanor Roosevelt was instrumental in calling a White House Conference on the Emergency Needs of Women shortly after her husband became president.

To alleviate this situation of destitute women, Eleanor Roosevelt advocated numerical guidelines to assure the employment of women in New Deal programs. Working with Frances Perkins, she also acquired funds to establish a number of resident camps for unemployed young women, on the order of the Civilian Conservation Corps for young men, where job skills and basic educational subjects were taught. She was a firm supporter of the union movement and publicly advocated the unionization of domestic help.

To what extent Eleanor Roosevelt succeeded in these efforts awaits a detailed historical investigation. The evidence suggests that, as in her advocacy of the black cause, she encountered sustained resistance. For example, the young women in her retraining program received maintenance and a minimal allowance, while the young men in the comparable Civilian Conservation Corps received a regular salary, although monies were deducted for the support of parents and siblings. Moreover, when one key Washington bureaucrat was faced with the problem of how his department might employ women, he typically suggested that all clerical positions be reserved for them. Heads of federal agencies were willing to issue vague guidelines on the employment of women, but at all levels of the New Deal bureaucracy, admini-

98 Through her radio broadcasts, Eleanor Roosevelt became a familiar commentator on the American scene.

strators were responsive to the pressure and prejudices of local constituencies. In the case of blacks, a group that historians have studied in some detail, this localism often meant that they were passed over in hiring. It is probable that this was also true for women.

What cannot be disputed, considering her early life, her personal difficulties, and the obstacles she faced, is that the work of Eleanor Roosevelt on behalf of women and minorities was admirable. Granted that her suggestions were not always heeded. Granted that her role within the New Deal was most often that of ombudsman and publicist of New Deal programs rather than that of architect of change. Still in her own day Eleanor Roosevelt set a new standard of justice for politicians in the fair treatment of women and blacks. And for several decades she served as the conscience of the nation: she would not let the dispossessed be entirely forgotten.

99 Attracted by federal relief jobs, thousands of unemployed workers in New York line up at the state labor bureau building.

CHANGES FOR THE WORKING WOMAN: THE NEW DEAL, UNEMPLOYMENT, NEW UNION STRENGTH

In addition to the efforts of Eleanor Roosevelt, the social and economic reforms of the New Deal directly affected women. The Social Security Act of 1935 provided for federal funding for state programs for maternal and pediatric care as well as for state and local aid-to-dependent-children programs. Moreover, early in the New Deal, the concept of special labor laws that established maximum-hour and minimum-wage standards for workers of both sexes, rather than just women, was adopted. Under the National Recovery Act of 1933 (NRA), representatives of labor and management in each industry met with government negotiators to draft production codes that included such standards. In 1938 Congress passed the Fair Labor Standards Act, which established maximum-hour and minimum-wage standards in all industries that produced goods for interstate commerce, and state legislatures began to follow suit for intrastate commerce.

Such legislation represented a complete change in the thinking of unions and the government about the worker. For all workers, the old common law doctrine of the inviolability of contract between worker and employer was overruled. For women, the implications of the new laws were additionally significant. The massive unemployment during the depression, by threatening male as well as female labor, had given compelling support to those who argued that the government must protect all workers, not just women and children. The New Deal laws did just that, and at one blow the campaign for special legislation for women, which had divided organized women for over a decade, was brought into question. By 1933 even the Women's Trade Union League had reversed its historic stand to join other reform groups in advocating general labor legislation for minimum wages and maximum hours, although not until the 1970s would the labor movement begin to abandon its support for special health, safety, and maximum-hour laws for women in a variety of industries. The way was now open for an eventual rapprochement of numerous women's groups around the Equal Rights Amendment.

Antifeminism had not, however, been exorcised, nor had the unequal treatment of women been ended. In keeping with the discrimination against minorities in other New Deal programs, many of the codes drawn up under the NRA permitted industries to pay less to women workers than to men in similar jobs. In general, the minimum wages established by NRA codes did operate to increase women's salaries. Yet fully one-quarter of the codes contained some measure of salary discrimination, particularly those written for industries that employed large numbers of women. This had, of course, long been the unofficial practice. Moreover, the Fair Labor Standards Act of 1938 specifically exempted from its provisions many job categories, like domestic service, in which women were clustered. The argument was that such marginal work might disappear completely if wages were raised.

Behind such discriminatory legislation lay a set of venerable myths about women's work. The old argument that women worked for "pin money" and that most of them were supported by husbands and fathers again reared its head. Many employers, forced by the depression to lay

185

off workers, fired all married women employees, despite the fact that many men workers, with salaries often reduced, were not making enough to support their families. Despite the protest of women's organizations, the federal government ruled that only one member of a family could work in the federal civil service, arguing that additional jobs thereby would be made available to heads of families. The result was that thousands of women with civil service jobs, whose salaries were usually less than their husbands', were forced to resign. Bills categorically prohibiting the employment of married women were introduced in the legislatures of twenty-six states, and it took the determined resistance of women's organizations to defeat them. Louisiana actually passed such a law, but the courts declared it unconstitutional. A 1936 Gallup poll showed that nearly four out of five Americans felt that wives should not work if their husbands were employed. Among women the figure was 75 percent. The argument was not uncommon in the 1930s that women, by going to work and taking needed jobs away from men, had caused the depression. That was not all. By leaving home, so the argument went, they had weakened the moral fiber of the nation and rendered inevitable a crisis of the spirit. [10]

Despite this hostility, women remained in the work force in about the same proportions as in the 1920s, although their ratio to men in the professions fell somewhat. Indeed, although by the late 1930s more women than men were unemployed, Women's Bureau studies showed that during most of the depression there was a greater proportion of unemployed workers seeking jobs among men than among women. Partly, this situation reflected the fact that, no matter what the economic conditions, women were still cheaper employees than men. Thus many industries in financial distress would not hesitate to give them job preference. Moreover, in some industries, women's work was so identified with them that it was virtually closed to men. Nor could even unemployed men easily take on women's jobs and maintain their masculine self-esteem. One analyst of New Deal employment trends pointed to the greater "adaptability" of women workers, who could accept almost any job with little loss in prestige or self-respect. This, however, was not true of men workers. [11]

What this greater adaptability meant in some instances was that women were reduced to becoming domestic workers. Even between 1920 and 1930, a time of moderate, although not extreme, unemployment, the number of female domestic workers rose by 1 million. In 1934 Women's Bureau analysts described a pattern they thought typical: before 1930 Mary Smith made dashboard equipment in an automobile shop. After she was laid off during the early days of the depression, she spent months unsuccessfully looking for another job. Finally, she returned to her family, who lived on a farm. But the sale of crops was not bringing in enough money to support them all. In desperation, Mary Smith accepted a job as a domestic servant.[12] Assuredly, not all women followed this pattern. The number of families that could afford servants obviously decreased; labor statistics for the 1930s show no particular rise in the number of domestic workers. And although millions of women could not find jobs, 80 percent of those who wished to work managed to secure employment at one time or another, and much of this work was nondomestic. As throughout the twentieth century, the largest percentage increase of women workers in the 1930s was in the clerical field.

The 20 percent unemployed were dominated by those women who often had the least resources on which to depend—older women, single women in general, and minority women. Many companies, for example, refused to hire women over thirty-five years of age—a situation that made the campaign for social security legislation especially compelling. And although single women were often given preference over married women in employment, they were often passed over in direct relief payments in favor of families.[13] According to one observer in 1934, there were 75,000 homeless, single women in New York City alone. The pattern of their lives was similar: they spent the morning making the rounds of employment agencies; during the afternoon they rested in the train stations; at night they rode the subways. They ate in the so-called penny kitchens, cheap eateries spawned by the depression.[14] Some of them—like the poor and unemployed in general—began to organize. An Association of Unemployed Single Women was formed, which, although small in membership, put pressure on government agencies to pay attention to their needs. However, one

100   Wives of unemployed workers receive food from priests of the New Hope Mission in New York.

detailed study of the many teenage girls who had left urban homes to join the legions of tramps who roamed the nation concluded that prostitution was often their only means of livelihood. [15]

For black women the situation was especially severe. Employment on federal work-relief projects was often closed to them. Traditional discriminatory practices in employment still existed: a Women's Bureau study in 1938 found that only 10 percent of black working women were employed in manufacturing, which represented only a 7 percent gain over the figure for 1890. Clerical labor and office work were equally closed to them: social worker Ellen Terry remembered that in Harlem in 1930 all the salesclerks in the stores on 125th Street, the black shopping center, were white. [16] Black workers remained farm laborers and domestic workers, and the only remotely mitigating factor

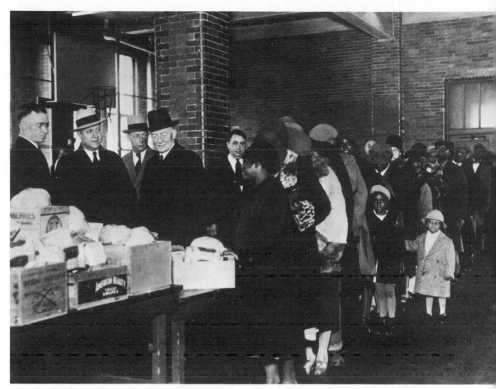

101   In Harlem, the police distribute food to the jobless.

in their situation was that they were accustomed to the economic deprivation that was a new experience for whites. Even so, whites were far better off economically: in 1939 the median yearly earnings of nonwhites were 38 percent that of whites.

In the worsening economic situation, one unexpected avenue of relief appeared. Massive unemployment plus government sympathy produced a new, more militant labor movement that was more responsive to women workers than the conservative American Federation of Labor had been. For example, the International Ladies' Garment Workers' Union, a powerful prewar AFL affiliate, which by 1930 had nearly ceased to exist, underwent a transformation within a few years. The passage of the 1933 National Industrial Recovery Act, which specifically recognized labor's right to organize, prompted the union's leadership to call a series of successful strikes. Throughout the clothing industry, hours were reduced, and wages were increased by as much as 50 percent. During 1934 union membership increased from 45,000 to over 200,000, and for the first time in many years the ILGWU treasury contained a surplus.

Most important for women workers was the formation in 1935 of the Committee for Industrial Organization. It was founded by a faction within the AFL leadership, and would emerge in 1938 as the Congress of Industrial Organizations (CIO). The CIO was not afraid to call strikes or to demand government legislation to protect unions and workers. The mass-production industries—like auto and steel, which contained small minorities of women workers, and textiles, among which 40 percent of the workers were women—were finally organized. Through effective and often bloody strikes, as well as through the

102 Over one thousand women storm an office building in St. Louis in answer to a newspaper advertisement for 150 jobs as soap demonstrators.

mediation of the National Labor Relations Board, established in 1936, employers were forced to recognize their workers' demands.

It was precisely because working women were clustered in the mass-production industries that the new labor movement became valuable to them. The CIO cannot be credited with any extensive feminist sentiment; it was simply that in order for the CIO to gain majority control in many industries, women had to be included as members. Not surprisingly, few women breached the leadership ranks of the new labor organization. Men dictated local and national policy then, as they do today. Nor was the new union organization among women workers in general ever very extensive. Even in 1973, only one-third as many women as men belonged to unions. Women clerical workers, domestic servants, and many schoolteachers have never been unionized. Nor was the new union structure any more willing to support the WTUL than the predepression AFL had been. In 1947 the WTUL was dissolved. The reason given by the leaders was that the sympathetic attitude of the unions toward women made its existence unnecessary. But WTUL official Rose Schneiderman, for one, contended that the real reason for its demise was the unwillingness of the male-dominated unions to give it any additional funding.[17] Working women profited greatly from the organization of the CIO, but its appearance did not lead to extensive feminist support among unions or within the working class.

THE SECURITIES OF MARRIAGE IN AN INSECURE AGE

Many women sought jobs during the 1930s; more remained at home, respecting society's dictate that the married woman ought not to work. But the continuation of this traditional pattern represented more than social repression or female timidity. For in this time of economic insecurity the family assumed a new importance in the social structure: the home was, after all, one place where the individual could find emotional sustenance. The number of divorces declined during the early 1930s, as did attendance at public events, travel, and membership in clubs. Partly, people were staying home and staying married because they could not afford to do otherwise. Also, the radio had become a popular form of home entertainment. In their study of Mun-

191

103   A West Virginia coal miner and his wife spend an evening listening to the radio.

cie, Indiana, for example, Helen and Robert Lynd found an increasing incidence of teenage marriage, motivated, they thought, by the search for emotional security that the depression stimulated in all Americans.[18]

Many sociologists who studied the response of families to the depression were surprised to find that economic adversity did not, as they had expected, destroy families. On the contrary, it often welded them together into more closely knit units. One city editor expressed a general sentiment when he wrote, "More families are now acquainted with their constituent members than at any time since the log-cabin days of America." And, he continued, in a characteristically antifeminist vein, "Society is not made poorer because mother is now neglecting the encyclopedia from which sprang full blown the club papers with which she formerly bored her fellow clubwomen, and is devoting more of her time to cookbooks."[19]

Severe economic adversity, however, often contributed to an undermining of traditional family roles and relationships. According to one analyst, a long-term loss of income could create an "epic demoralization" within the family.[20] Sometimes wives could find jobs when husbands could not, and this situation often increased the relative power of women in the family. One psychiatrist who observed long-unemployed miners in Pennsylvania found that the entire structure of the family there had shifted. The men hung out on the street corners and dreaded returning home. Within their culture a jobless man was considered worthless, by himself and by his family. Wives punished their unemployed husbands by withholding themselves sexually, and, according to this observer, "by belittling the men . . . [and] undermining their parental authority."[21] One thinks, however, of the Joad family in John Steinbeck's *The Grapes of Wrath,* torn apart by the process of migration from Oklahoma to California and by the terrible conditions of work for migrant families there, yet held together by the strength of the mother, who emerged in this case as a loving matriarch.

The Lynds identified a similar pattern in Muncie, Indiana. The lives of the majority of the wives were much less disrupted by the depression than were their husbands' lives. For women who remained at home,

104   A migrant family en route to California in search of work.

the household routine remained intact. Those who worked often gained increased status within the family. The men who were out of work "lost much of their sense of time and dawdled helplessly and dully about the streets." In such a situation women became the centers of stability within the family and often the arbiters of family decisions. In general, the Lynds concluded, "All sorts of temperamental variations have appeared, with women showing perspective and steadfastness under stress and men sometimes dissolving into pettiness . . . and personal rancor."[22]

Given women's increased authority within the family and in response to lowered incomes and unemployment, the birth rate dropped

105 Birth control advocates at a House Judiciary Committee hearing in 1934: (seated, left to right) Mrs. Thomas N. Hepburn, mother of the actress; Representative Walter Pierce of Oregon; and Margaret Sanger.

during the 1930s. More couples were using contraceptive measures, and by 1940 every state in the union, except Massachusetts and Connecticut, had legalized the dissemination of birth-control information. At the beginning of the decade, there were 28 family-planning clinics in the nation. By 1941 there were 746, and almost one-third received government assistance.

The increasing availability of contraceptives probably did not lead to an increase in sexual promiscuity. Among the young, the vanguard of liberated sexual attitudes in the 1920s, most studies showed that premarital intercourse was on the increase but that both men and women expected it to lead to marriage and fidelity. A 1937 questionnaire of fourteen hundred college students showed that one-half of the men and one-quarter of the women polled had had sexual intercourse by the end of their college years. But the respondents to this poll universally condemned promiscuity. Those who had had affairs explained that "true love" had motivated their deviation from standards of "purity."[23] One thinks of the "emancipated" young women in Mary McCarthy's novel *The Group*: knowledgeable about sex but shocked by the one member of their group who had lived with her lover before marriage; expectant that a sexual encounter ought to eventuate in a permanent liaison if not marriage; using condoms and douches as their only means of birth control.

The 1930s witnessed the demise of America's so-called flaming youth. Concerned about jobs and housing, people lost interest in the rebellion of youth and the new moral standards. The patterns of the 1920s were either taken for granted or forgotten. What concerned people was that a generation of young Americans were not finding jobs, that these future citizens might become despairing and embittered. Young middle-class women did not demand liberation. Caroline Bird, author of several studies of the women of the 1960s, has written regarding her college class at Vassar in the 1930s that "we did not think we had a right to a private life until we had first straightened out society."[24] A 1936 *Fortune* magazine survey of college campuses found that economics had replaced liquor, sex, and religion as the dominant issue of campus debate.[25] Reflecting the increased nationwide strength of communism, leftist movements emerged on many college campuses. Critic Pauline

Kael, a student at the University of California at Berkeley during the late 1930s, remembered that the college was then a "cauldron" of radical discontent.[26]

But the majority of their generation probably were not so oriented. While acknowledging student discontent, Kael also recalled that the conservative fraternities and sororities were immensely powerful and that they regularly acted in conjunction with the university administration in quelling radical dissent. The *Fortune* study showed that three out of five college women wanted to marry immediately after graduation. After traveling throughout the country and interviewing young men and women, sociologist Maxine Davis concluded that "in an existence that holds meager promise, they are hunting comfort and hope and stability in marriage."[27] Writer Doris Fleischman agreed. The "charming and lovable fire-eating youngsters" of the 1920s were gone, she wrote. The young women of the 1930s, Fleischman thought, were tired of the "sport of their elder sisters." But, in her view, they had not found much to take the place of the older interests. "They go to college in great numbers, but they are ashamed of being regarded as highbrows. They enter the professions and place an enormous compensation emphasis on their social activities. They seem to be stabilizing their interests into a feminine pre-occupation with the essentials of marriage and motherhood."[28]

Author Pearl Buck thought that in the face of the depression women in general—old as well as young—more than ever before were retreating into domesticity and femininity. "Women's interest in work and a profession," wrote Buck, "has not been lower in the last half century than it is now."[29] Buck's pessimism may have been exaggerated. Families may have been disoriented, and young people may have searched for stability through marriage; still the percentage of women in jobs remained constant. And, perhaps what is most significant, the percentage of married women at work once again increased during the 1930s—from 12 percent in 1930 to 15 percent in 1940. One commentator, surveying the decade, thought that there may even have been a major shift in cultural attitudes—that men, "thankful" that their wives could find a job, were no longer hostile to their working.[30] Although such a shift in values may not have been widespread, it was at the very least an important portent of change.

FASHIONS AND MOVIES: OLD AND NEW IMAGES

Among all women, working or not, a return to tradition was clearly evident in their dress. The "lady-like look" once again became the cynosure of the American woman. Women no longer wore the short skirts and flat-chested frocks of the 1920s. Although clothes remained loose and free-flowing, skirts became longer, and above all, bosoms reappeared. Indeed, to look just right, well-groomed women took again to some form of figure-molding undergarment. In the 1927 spring/summer Sears Roebuck catalogue, the source of fashion for thousands of rural women and other mail-order customers, corset advertising had been directed to the overweight woman, to the woman who wanted the "stylish 'un-corseted' effect without allowing [her] figure to spread."[31] By the fall of 1930, however, corset advertising was directed to all women. According to the Sears catalogue: "The new mode calls for a definitely higher indented waistline, long tapering hips and the molded bust. To wear the new frocks, you must wear the smart, new corsetry."[32] In the next two decades, as defined bosoms and small waistlines became increasingly fashionable, the corset would once again emerge triumphant. Its name was changed to girdle, but its function remained the same. Its apogee would be reached in that much treasured possession of the young lady of the 1950s, the "merry widow" waist-cincher.

That the new fashions with their emphasis on traditional models emerged as a specific response to the emotional insecurity of the depression is difficult to prove. Styles follow a cyclical pattern all their own, and what looked new and chic in 1920 looked old and boring by 1930. Yet for several years before the 1930s, Parisian designers had tried to lower skirt lengths and reintroduce closer fitting clothes. The new styles did not catch on until 1929. Whereas in 1920 American women thumbed their noses at a Victorian past, by 1930 they were willing to accept a new concept of elegant femininity that in some ways drew from a Victorian model. So Paris, finally, had its say.

The most influential model for the change in fashion was the movie star. Maxine Davis found that in every section of the country and within every social group the most common subject of conversation was the cinema queen.[33] Particularly in a time of social despair, people were living their lives vicariously through films. Unlike other types of entertainment, movies still attracted sizable audiences. First, Greta Garbo was the rage, then Marlene Dietrich and Bette Davis. And when Jean Harlow dyed her hair blonde, it started a fad that has lasted for decades. In the 1910s and 1920s, the vamps all had dark hair, while the virginal heroines were blonde—a literary convention that was in fact a holdover from an earlier age. But by the 1930s, this image had changed. Now the real temptresses, the true vamps, were as blonde as they could possibly be. In combining the old image of innocence with a new image of guile, the movie industry created a powerful sex symbol—a symbol that would reach its apogee in Marilyn Monroe.

In general, the films of the 1930s continued the trends started in the 1920s. There was the vamp turned temptress, such as Marlene Dietrich in *Blue Angel,* and the sweet virginal blonde, such as Janet Gaynor in a series of films beginning with her best-known *Seventh Heaven* (1927). A

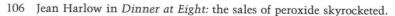

106   Jean Harlow in *Dinner at Eight:* the sales of peroxide skyrocketed.

107 Mae West, star of *Belle of the Nineties:* an exception to the rule.

new twist was the good-bad girl, who was both temptress and angel, and whose good qualities, through the help of a man, would triumph in the end. Yet in the 1930s a strict film censorship code was in force, and although violence was not prohibited, any hint that immorality was condoned could bring down the wrath of the powerful censorship board. Endings almost invariably had to be happy; adultery had to lead to marriage or be strictly punished, particularly when it was on the part of a woman.

One female film star of the 1930s, however, paid little attention to the canons about woman's proper role, and that was Mae West. Big and buxom, she mimicked all the contemporary standards of feminine beauty; she even padded her hips to make them larger. In voice and movement she exuded sexuality, and no man could resist her. No man could manipulate her either. Her attitude toward sex was masculine: sex did not imply any commitment to a man; marriage she could take or leave. A range of men from Cary Grant to W. C. Fields chased her; and to Grant's question, "Haven't you met a man who could make you happy?" her answer was classic West, "Sure, lots of times." She was strong and confident, always in command. Her sardonic dialogue was among the most clever in screen history. She wrote much of it herself, just as she took a hand in directing and editing some of her films. Her salacious dialogue was so cleverly worded that it even slipped by the strict censors of that time.

Mae West movies were, however, exceptions. The prevailing movie plots continued to deny women any real power outside of sex. In some ways, this message became even more heavily underscored than before. In the gangster film, a favorite genre of the 1930s, leading ladies were regularly mistreated by their gangster lovers. In 1931 James Cagney established the fashion by hitting Mae Clark in the eye with a grapefruit in the movie *Public Enemy*. Critic Gilbert Seldes attributed the stir created by this scene to its effect in re-enforcing the male image of masculinity, which, he contended, feminism and the depression had undermined.[34] By 1938 one analyst of movie trends thought that the mistreatment of women stars had become a stock device. "Today a star scarcely qualifies for the higher spheres," she wrote, "unless she has been slugged by her leading man, rolled on the floor, kicked down-

108 Women are kept in line in movies like *Nothing Sacred*, starring Carole Lombard and Fredric March.

stairs, cracked over the head with a frying pan, dumped into a pond, or butted by a goat."[35]

One of the most consistent movie themes of the 1930s, 1940s, and 1950s involved a hard-nosed professional woman or a wealthy woman who was taught by a strong man that sex and marriage were all that really mattered in life. The movie was made again and again. Occasionally, as in the sophisticated 1936 comedy *Wedding Present*, with Cary Grant and Joan Bennett, marriage was itself satirized and the professional woman sympathetically portrayed. More often, the opposite was the case. In *Take a Letter, Darling* (1942), Rosalind Russell gave up a lucrative and glamorous career as head of an advertising agency to travel around Mexico in a trailer with Fred McMurray. In *Lady in the Dark* (1944), magazine executive Ginger Rogers relinquished all to marry her assistant, Ray Milland, after her psychoanalyst had convinced her that only through marriage could she really find fulfillment. Spencer Tracy and Katherine Hepburn waged the war of the sexes in eight films; in most of them the battle was charmingly intense until Hepburn capitulated in the last frames. And in one of the most successful films of the 1930s, *It Happened One Night* (1934)—which catapulted Clark Gable to fame—wealthy Claudette Colbert found Gable, the virile journalist of indeterminate origins and low income, irresistible. The equation between money and power was obvious, and Gable captured both.

Although still antifeminist in their viewpoint, these films did strike a new note. The women in them were portrayed as strong-minded, quick-witted, even aggressive. Despite the fact that Bette Davis, Rosalind Russell, and Katherine Hepburn regularly gave in to men on screen, their intelligence and strength showed through. They were women of character and force, and it is impossible not to recognize this even when watching their early movies today. In fact, so much does the personality of these women dominate their films, that their ultimate surrender seems almost irrelevant to the triumph of their character. In *Middletown*, the Lynds provided an example of the effect of one of these early film stars on the first generation of young women to view her. Joan Crawford, they wrote, "has her amateur counterparts in the high-school girls who stroll with brittle confidence in and out of 'Barney's'

109　In movies like *Mildred Pierce,* Joan Crawford shows women a new kind of prototype.

soft-drink parlor, 'clicking' with the 'drugstore cowboys' at the tables; while the tongue-tied young male learns the art of the swift, confident comeback in the face of female confidence."[36]

The high-school girls at Barney's in Middletown became the WACS and the war workers of the Second World War, and then the wives and mothers of the postwar era of the 1940s. Joan Crawford and Bette Davis did not open the vision of a feminist future to them. But these actresses became part of the mythology of the culture. Their movies continued to be shown, and the emergence of the feminism of the 1960s is not unrelated to the image these women projected.

WOMEN AS PART OF THE WAR EFFORT

Both world wars created major changes in the female work force. But whereas few additional women entered the work force during the First World War, more than 6 million women went to work for the first time during the Second World War. The proportion of women in the labor force increased from 25 percent in 1940 to 36 percent in 1945. This increase was greater than that of the previous four decades combined. That the Second World War had a sizable impact on women's employment when the First did not is not surprising: the United States participated in the First World War for only nineteen months; the Second World War, and hence the shift in women's roles, lasted for four years, from 1941 to 1945.

Initially, it was not easy to persuade women that they ought to violate traditional mores and fill the jobs vacated by men. To this task the molders of public opinion in newspapers, magazines, and radio turned their considerable power. They created Rosie the Riveter, who became the lauded symbol of the woman temporarily at work. In all the media, women at work were pictured and praised, and the woman who did not at least raise a "victory garden" or work as a volunteer for the Red Cross was made to feel as guilty as the working woman had been made to feel in times past. Even the movies joined in. As part of their effort to bolster

110   Women workers bevel armor plating with acetylene torches.

national morale, moviemakers churned out a steady stream of pro-allied propaganda films. In these films the wife or sweetheart who stayed behind and went to work in a regular job or for an agency like the USO, became as familiar a figure as the valiant soldier-lover for whom she waited.

Behind the propaganda for the employment of women stood official government policy. During the war years, four times as many women as men found employment in the federal bureaucracy. The War Manpower Commission, established to utilize labor resources more effectively, sponsored local vocational-training programs in high schools, in storefronts, and on the job, and it actively encouraged women of all ages to enter these programs. State governors and legislatures suspended protective legislation for women so that they could take over the kinds of skilled labor and higher-paid jobs previously denied them. The noncombatant Women's Auxiliary Army Corps and the Navy WAVES were founded, and Americans saw women in military uniform—a traditional symbol of masculinity.

The government, too, at least paid lip service to the idea that women and men should receive equal pay and that child-care centers should be established throughout the nation. The War Manpower Commission repeatedly urged a policy of equal pay, and the National War Labor Board, established to mediate labor disputes, for a time applied this principle in discrimination cases. By 1945, 100,000 children were enrolled in federally supported child-care facilities. Moreover, within the political parties, women continued to play a larger role. With men at war, women more and more ran local and state committees, and, according to one commentator, male party leaders were finally coming to realize that women actually constituted a majority of the electorate.[37]

Although women were courted to join the work force, it was primarily to fill clerical and factory jobs, particularly in war-related industries. Some additional opportunities were available in medicine and law, but few women moved into professional careers during the war years. Women were not hired for high-level positions in business or in government; these were left for men. For example, a shortage of teachers and school administrators was caused, not so much because male instructors and supervisors went off to war, but because industry and business, desperate for administrative talent, lured men away with higher salaries. As for government directives that women's wages should be the same as men's, inexplicit wording and lack of continued strict enforcement by the National Labor Relations Board made it relatively easy for employers to disregard them. And, although FDR supported the principle of federally funded day-care centers, little money was actually allocated for them, despite the fact that Women's Bureau studies showed that a large proportion of working mothers had available to them inadequate provisions for child care while they were on the job. Federal funds supported day-care facilities for 100,000 children in 1945, but this figure represented only 10 percent of the total number of children who needed such care. Finally, women leaders charged that the government showed little interest in their recommendations. The War Manpower Commission, for example, composed entirely of men, shunted them into a Woman's Advisory Committee, which was rarely consulted.

The concern for women lacked impetus because, for the most part,

111 American Red Cross workers land in France to take up their duties behind the fighting lines.

no one really expected women to continue working after the war ended. The unstated assumption was that women, like men, were enlisting in the national service during a time of crisis, and that when the crisis ended they, like men, would take up their "normal" roles once again. Added to this was the memory of the depression, as well as the recollection that after the First World War many of the women who had gone to work returned to their homes or went back to unskilled "women's work." Typical of the national attitude, all federal funds for day-care facilities were discontinued in 1946. Few were the commentators who, like the Women's Bureau staff, suggested to the public and to the government that many women might not want to return to domesticity or to lower salaries and that arrangements ought to be made to accommodate their desires in terms of equal opportunities for advancement, equal pay for equal work, and publicly funded day-care centers. The Second World War produced women of strength, but it did not produce militant feminists.

When the war ended, many women did happily leave jobs in factories, farms, and offices to return to the homes and marriages denied them during the war years. Others were not so content to return to the home. A Women's Bureau study in 1944 showed that 80 percent of the women who had worked throughout the war wanted to continue in their jobs. After all, countless numbers of women had moved into high-paying men's work as railroad switchmen, precision toolmakers, blacksmiths, and even lumberjacks. Black women in particular had been aided by the manpower crisis: the number of black women who worked as servants fell from 72 percent to 48 percent, while the proportion in factories grew to nearly 19 percent. According to historian William Chafe, the war represented for them almost a "second emancipation."[38]

Yet cutbacks among women workers, particularly in industry, began as soon as peace was declared. This was not unexpected, since in the period of conversion from wartime to peacetime production, businesses and factories simply did not need as many workers. What was surprising was the large number of women who were laid off in comparison with men. For example, in aircraft engine plants, women had made up 39 percent of the workers, while they comprised 89 percent of those laid off; in the truck and agricultural implements industry, they had made up 13 percent of the work force, while they comprised 51 percent of those laid off. Consonant with these trends, the percentage of women in the labor force in general dropped from 36 percent in 1945 to 28 percent in 1947.

After 1947 the number of working women again began to rise. By 1951 the proportion reached 31 percent. In general, then, women either remained in the work force after the war or reentered it after a brief hiatus. Conditions in clerical work, long defined as "women's work," remained essentially stable throughout the war and the postwar years. But in manufacturing, women were often either demoted to lower-paying jobs, or they were rehired under such a classification that their seniority was denied them. Without definite equal rights legislation, there was little that they could do, since state protective laws, suspended during the war years only, could easily be interpreted as meaning that women were not capable of performing whatever labor was defined as "men's work." Or state provisions like those for special rest periods for women could be used to justify lower wages. In some instances the unions were willing to aid women members: the movement of women into war industries had caused a quadrupling of their membership in the CIO. During the war years, for example, the automotive unions had negotiated an agreement with General Motors, which the National War Labor Board had approved, that specified that there should be no difference in pay between men and women. But the male-dominated unions were only too willing, once the war had ended, to acquiesce in or even institute agreements that reserved higher-paying positions for men. General Motors, for example, reinstituted its discriminatory practices simply by changing the job classifications of "male" and "female" to "heavy" and "light." In the late 1940s, some women filed court suits demanding back pay because, according to historians Sheila Tobias and Lisa Anderson, "'certain female classifications were changed to male classifications,' so as to exclude women from keeping or returning to jobs they had held during the war."[39] Most of these suits were denied, but in 1948 thirty-one women won a retroactive wage settlement of $55,000 from the Chrysler Corporation because the company had laid them off in violation of their seniority.

Despite the discriminations imposed on women during and after the Second World War, a striking number of women remained at work. After 1953 the percentage of women in the labor force steadily continued

207

to increase: by 1973 it had reached 42 percent. The percentages of employed married women and older women continued to rise accordingly. Thus many women retained their tie to a world outside the home. The experiences of depression and war had lasting effects on the lives of women—at least on the lives of those who were now relatively permanent members of the work force.

Notes

[1] Mary Anderson, *Woman at Work: The Autobiography of Mary Anderson, as Told to Mary N. Winslow* (Minneapolis: University of Minnesota Press, 1951), pp. 210–13.

[2] Quoted in William H. Chafe, *The American Woman: Her Changing Social, Economic, and Political Roles, 1920–1970* (New York: Oxford University Press, 1972), p. 115.

[3] Eleanor Roosevelt, *It's Up to the Women* (New York: Frederick A. Stokes, 1933), pp. 202, 206.

[4] Grace Abbott, *From Relief to Social Security: The Development of the New Public Welfare Services and Their Administration* (Chicago: University of Chicago Press, 1941), pp. 361–62.

[5] *Independent Woman* (April 1933), 123.

[6] Anderson, *Woman at Work: The Autobiography of Mary Anderson, as Told to Mary N. Winslow*, p. 148.

[7] Eleanor Roosevelt and Lorena A. Hickok, *Ladies of Courage* (New York: G. P. Putnam's Sons, 1954), p. 192.

[8] Rose Schneiderman (with Lucy Goldthwaite), *All for One* (New York: Paul S. Eriksson, 1967), p. 197.

[9] Roosevelt and Hickok, *Ladies of Courage*, p. 13.

[10] Margaret Culkin Banning, "They Raise Their Hats," *Harper's*, CLXXI (August 1935), 355; Alma Lutz, "Why Discharge Women First?" *Independent Woman* (December 1931), 534.

[11] Lorine Pruette, *Women Workers Through the Depression* (New York: Macmillan, 1934), p. 35.

[12] Women's Bureau, U.S., Department of Labor, *Women at Work: A Century of Industrial Change* (Washington, D.C.: U.S. Government Printing Office, 1934), p. 48.

[13] Grace Hutchins, *Women Who Work* (New York: International, 1934), p. 183.

[14] *Ibid.*, p. 191.

[15] Thomas Minehan, *Boy and Girl Tramps of America* (New York: Farrar and Rinehart, 1934), pp. 75, 139–40.

[16] Ellen Terry, *The Third Door: The Autobiography of an American Negro Woman* (New York: David McKay, 1955), p. 88.

[17] Schneiderman, *All for One*, p. 246.

[18] Helen Merrell Lynd and Robert S. Lynd, *Middletown in Transition: A Study in Cultural Conflicts* (New York: Harcourt Brace Jovanovich, 1937), p. 152.

[19] *Ibid.*, p. 146.

[20] Paul L. Benjamin, "The Family Society and the Depression," *Annals of the American Academy of Political and Social Science*, CLX (March 1932), 142.

[21] Studs Terkel, *Hard Times: An Oral History of the Great Depression* (New York: Pantheon, 1970), pp. 196–97.

[22] Lynd and Lynd, *Middletown in Transition: A Study in Cultural Conflicts*, pp. 178–79.

[23] Dixon Wecter, *The Age of the Great Depression, 1929–1941* (New York: Macmillan, 1948), p. 197.

[24] Caroline Bird, *The Invisible Scar* (New York: David McKay, 1966), p. 139.

[25] Dorothy Dunbar Bromley and Florence Britten, *Youth and Sex: A Study of Thirteen-Hundred College Students* (New York: Harper and Brothers, 1938), p. 20.

[26] Terkel, *Hard Times: An Oral History of the Great Depression*, p. 346.

[27] Maxine Davis, *The Lost Generation: A Portrait of American Youth Today* (New York: Macmillan, 1936), p. 87.

[28] Doris E. Fleischman, "Women: Types and Movements," in Fred J. Ringel, ed., *America as Americans See It* (New York: Literary Guild, 1932), p. 117.

[29] Pearl Buck, *Of Men and Women* (New York: John Day, 1941), p. 91.

[30] Grace Adams, "American Women Are Coming Along," *Harper's*, CLXXVIII (March 1937), 372.

[31] *Sears Roebuck Catalogue*, CLIV (Spring/Summer 1927), 88.

[32] *Sears Roebuck Catalogue*, CLVII (Fall/Winter 1930), 79.

[33] Davis, *The Lost Generation: A Portrait of American Youth Today*, p. 135.

[34] Gilbert Seldes, "The Masculine Revolt," *Scribner's*, XCV (April 1934), 279–82.

[35] Margaret Thorp, *America at the Movies* (New Haven: Yale University Press, 1939), p. 76.

[36] Lynd and Lynd, *Middletown in Transition: A Study in Cultural Conflicts*, p. 262.

[37] Marguerite Fisher, "Women in the Political Parties," *Annals of the American Academy of Political and Social Science* (May 1947), 93.

[38] Chafe, *The American Woman: Her Changing Social, Economic, and Political Roles, 1920–1970*, p. 142.

[39] Sheila Tobias and Lisa Anderson, "Whatever Happened to Rosie the Riveter?" *Ms.*, I (June 1973), 94.

Bibliography

Although they do not specifically focus on the subject of women, the best general sources for the history of women in the 1930s are Dixon Wecter, *The Age of the Great Depression, 1929–1941* (New York: Macmillan, 1948); Caroline Bird, *The Invisible Scar* (New York: David McKay, 1966); Studs Terkel, *Hard Times: An Oral History of the Great Depression* (New York: Pantheon, 1970); and Helen Merrell Lynd and Robert S. Lynd, *Middletown in Transition: A Study in Cultural Conflicts* (New York: Harcourt Brace Jovanovich, 1937). One might also consult Doris E. Fleischman, "Women: Types and Movements," in Fred J. Ringel, ed., *America as Americans See It* (New York: Literary Guild, 1932), and Mary Beard, *America Through Women's Eyes* (New York: Macmillan, 1933).

Information on the League of Women Voters and women's political behavior can be found in Martin Gruberg, *Women in American Politics: An Assessment and Sourcebook* (Oshkosh, Wis.: Academia, 1968). On this subject, Eleanor Roosevelt and Lorena A. Hickok, *Ladies of Courage* (New York: G. P. Putnam's Sons, 1954) is also useful. There is no general history of women and the New Deal, and the standard works on the FDR administration, like Arthur M. Schlesinger, Jr.'s multivolume study, ignore women.

Numerous biographies of Eleanor Roosevelt are available. Among the best are Tamara Hareven, *Eleanor Roosevelt: An American Conscience* (New York: Quadrangle, 1968); James R. Kearney, *Anna Eleanor Roosevelt: The Evolution of a Reformer* (Boston: Houghton Mifflin, 1968); and Joseph Lash, *Eleanor and Franklin: The Story of Their Relationship* (New York: Norton, 1971), and *Eleanor: The Years Alone* (New York: Norton, 1972). None, however, fully analyzes Eleanor Roosevelt's relationship to women's organizations and concerns. For a representative sample of her ideas, see *It's Up to the Women* (New York: Frederick A. Stokes, 1933). There is no biography or autobiography available of Frances Perkins. Mary Anderson's autobiography, *Woman at Work: The Autobiography of Mary Anderson, as Told to Mary N. Winslow* (Minneapolis: University of Minnesota Press, 1951) sheds some light on the inner workings of women in the FDR administration. Studies of New Deal programs, including Clark A. Chambers, *Seedtime of Reform: American Social Service and Action, 1918–1933* (1963; reprint ed., Ann Arbor: University of Michigan Press, 1967); Grace Abbott, *From Relief to Social Security: The Development of the New Public Welfare Services and Their Administration* (Chicago: University of Chicago Press, 1941); and Josephine Chapin Brown, *Public Relief, 1929–1939* (New York: Henry Holt, 1940) give some information.

On the labor movement in the 1930s, see Irving Bernstein, *Turbulent Years: A History of the American Worker, 1933–1941* (Boston: Houghton Mifflin, 1970); Grace Hutchins, *Women Who Work* (New York: International, 1934); and Women's Bureau studies.

On the family and the depression, the numerous studies undertaken by sociologists at the time are particularly useful. See, for example, *Annals of the American Academy of Political and Social Science* (March 1932); Robert Cooley Angell, *The Family Encounters the Depression* (New York: Scribner's, 1936); Samuel Stouffer and Paul Lazarsfeld, *Research Memorandum on the Family in the Depression* (New York: Social Science Research Council, 1937); Winona Morgan, *The Family Meets the Depression: A Study of a Group of Highly Selected Families* (Minneapolis: University of Minnesota Press, 1939); and Mirra Komarovsky, *The Unemployed Man and His Family: The Effect of Unemployment Upon the Status of the Man in Fifty-Nine Families* (New York: Institute of Social Research, 1940). On youth during the depression, Maxine Davis, *The Lost Generation: A Portrait of American Youth Today* (New York: Macmillan, 1936); Thomas Minehan, *Boy and Girl Tramps of America* (New York: Farrar and Rinehart, 1934); and Dorothy Dunbar Bromley and Florence Britten, *Youth and Sex: A Study of Thirteen-Hundred College Students* (New York: Harper and Brothers, 1938) are interesting. Changes in fashions are difficult to pinpoint in any period, but Women's Wear Daily, *Sixty Years of Fashion, 1900–1960: The Evolution of Women's Styles in America* (New York: Fairchild Publications, 1963) is an excellent introduction to the subject. On women in films, one should consult the studies mentioned in the bibliography to Chapter 4, and Andrew Bergman, *We're in the Money: Depression America and Its Films* (New York: Harper & Row, 1971), although nothing suffices for watching the films themselves.

On women in the Second World War, there is a large literature, including studies done at the time and more recent works. One might consult with profit Katherine Glover, *Women at Work in Wartime* (New York: Public Affairs Committee, 1943); Elizabeth Hawes, *Why Women Cry; or, Wenches with Wrenches* (New York: Reynal and Hitchcock, 1943); Women's Bureau studies; J. E. Trey, "Women in the War Economy—World War II," *The Review of Radical Political Economics,* IV (July 1972), 41–57; and Sheila Tobias and Lisa Anderson, "Whatever Happened to Rosie the Riveter?" *Ms.,* I (June 1973), 94.

Feminism Comes of Age: 6
1945–1974

In the two decades following the Second World War, two central and divergent trends influenced women's lives. The first was their continued participation in the work force, which reflected changing economic, demographic, and medical factors. The second was a resurgent cultural emphasis on domesticity and femininity as woman's proper role.

A GENERAL CONSENSUS ON WOMAN'S ROLE
Women Under Attack

In contradistinction to the movement of women into the work force, and partly because of it, an emphasis on the importance of marriage and motherhood became widespread in the late 1940s and the 1950s.

112 GI's being welcomed on their return home at the end of the Second World War.

In the immediate postwar years, antifeminist rhetoric was especially virulent. During the war the nation had lauded women for their participation in the national effort, and they had emerged from the war, in the words of a contemporary, "noble, impeccable and shining."[1] But within months many opinionmakers had turned against women, criticizing them not only for having gone to work during the war, but also for having, as they saw it, destroyed the American family in the process. The attack was blatant and resembled nothing so much as the inflated antisuffrage rhetoric early in the century. The antifeminism of the 1920s and 1930s had been extensive, but subtle, and it had only rarely denied women the right to live their lives as they saw fit. But the antifeminism of the postwar 1940s held women responsible for society's ills—either because they were failures as mothers or because they had left the home for work.

As early as 1942, in his best-selling book *Generation of Vipers*, Philip Wylie accused American women of being tyrants in their homes and emasculating their husbands and sons. Taking the opposite tack in *Modern Woman: The Lost Sex* (1947), sociologist Marynia Farnham and historian Ferdinand Lundberg argued that the problems of modern society—including war and depression—could be traced to the fact that women had left the home. In their view, women had given up their essential femininity to compete in a futile battle with men, causing their children to become delinquents or neurotics, and their husbands to become alcoholics or sexually impotent. Wylie, Farnham, and Lundberg based their case, as did most antifeminists of this period, on studies that seemed to show high rates of neurosis among army draftees and career women and increasing alcoholism and impotence among American men. They concluded that the career woman was neurotic because she had rejected her natural role, while the other evils were traceable to the neurotic housewife.

Their arguments, however, grew directly out of their ideological biases. Farnham and Lundberg, for example, were Freudians. In the 1920s, Freudianism had begun to have a major influence on Americans. But the advent of behaviorism, which offered a compelling alternative, and the onset of the depression, which made it difficult for anyone to afford psychoanalysis, had considerably diluted the Freudian impact. Also, by the late 1930s psychiatrists like Karen Horney had begun to attack Freudian views about women. But among psychiatrists in the postwar years, Freudianism prevailed. The Freudians argued that women could attain emotional stability only through domesticity and motherhood. Women who worked denied their deepest needs and risked being unable to experience love or sexual satisfaction. This, in turn, threatened the family, and, according to the most apocalyptic thinkers, the whole of Western civilization. Moreover, Freudians emphasized the importance of the early years of life on total personality development. The message to mothers was clear: they ought to stay at home to oversee their children's development.

Expert Opinion: Freud and Functionalism

The bitter antifeminism of the immediate postwar years was a transitory phenomenon, but its arguments, and particularly the Freudian ideas on which it was based, echoed throughout the 1950s, forming a body of thought that few sociological writers could avoid. As late as 1956 sociologists Alva Myrdal and Viola Klein commented that conferences of school headmasters, juvenile magistrates, probation officers, and welfare workers invariably blamed mothers, and especially working mothers, for the problems of their youthful charges.[2] Child-care experts universally recommended that mothers stay at home with their preschool children and be available when their older children returned from school. Dr. Benjamin Spock, whose book *Baby and Child Care* (1946) became the standard authority on the subject, recommended that the federal government pay women to raise their children so that mothers would not leave the home.[3] College educators argued for the adoption of new curricula for women that would stress courses on marriage and the family.

Within the disciplines of sociology and anthropology, some protest against these ideas was registered. But sociologists themselves were influenced by the technique of analysis known as functionalism, itself partly an outgrowth of the conservative postwar years. Functionalism stressed the value-free analysis of existing institutions and thereby left little room for criticism of them. Not all sociologists, however, were functionalists or Freudians. In her influential book *Women in the Modern World: Their Education and Their Dilemmas* (1953), sociologist Mirra Komarovsky criticized the Freudians and the functionalists and argued that female personality traits and women's relative lack of accomplishment in comparison to men's was due to their cultural conditioning, not to their biological inferiority. She did not deny women the right to work, and she counseled that men as well as women needed training for marriage and child-bearing. Komarovsky criticized the then-current concern about the threat to men's masculinity that competition with women posed. But she clearly implied that wives, not husbands, bore the major responsibility for the home and the family. "Everything we know and believe today about the development of the child points to the importance of mother-child relations."[4] In child-rearing, the father was a secondary figure. Like Komarovsky, Viola Klein and Alva Myrdal criticized Freud, but they approved of what they judged to be the "new and exacting standards of motherhood," and they recommended that mothers stay at home with their children—at least for the child's first three years.[5] And, while cataloguing the biological evidence that women were constitutionally superior to men and counseling that the male world of work needed woman's influence, anthropologist Ashley Montagu, in his popular *The Natural Superiority of Women* (1952), wrote that a large part of women's superiority lay in their greater gentleness and humanity, while, echoing the argument of the traditionalists, he stressed the importance of "mother love" to successful human development. Even anthropologist Margaret Mead was ambivalent. In studies like *Male and Female* (1955) she criticized the rigid sex-role definitions of American culture; at the same time she glorified woman's role as mother and homemaker.

The Evidence from Popular Culture

On a more popular level, the new emphasis on domesticity was everywhere apparent. In newspapers and magazines, on radio and billboards, Rosie the Riveter was replaced by the homemaker as the national feminine model. Advertisers in particular were quick to exploit the expanded market for domestic products that the return to a peacetime economy and the appearance of a new affluence offered. It was predictable, as before, that the model woman they would project would be either a housewife eager to buy the latest home products or a seductress whose appearance suggested special pleasure from the product she displayed. In addition, according to feminist Betty Friedan in *The Feminine Mystique* (1963), Freudian attitudes infused most articles in the mass-circulation women's magazines; the vast majority of the heroines in the short stories were housewives, and nonfiction articles were devoted almost exclusively to cooking and child care.[6]

Re-enforcing society's belief that women functioned best as sweethearts, sirens, or wives, female film stars of the 1950s were either sweet, innocent, and characterless, like Debbie Reynolds and Doris Day, or, like Marilyn Monroe, projected a complex blend of innocence and aggressive sexuality. In addition, by the mid-1950s television was beginning to beam its message into countless American homes. It also portrayed the woman either as a sex object or as a contented homebody, often flighty and irresponsible. The emphasis on domesticity was

215

113, 114, and 115   Out of slacks, back into skirts: *(left)* Marilyn Monroe at the première of her film *The Seven-Year Itch*; *(right)* Christian Dior's 1947 "new look"; *(far right)* a young couple at an amusement park.

pronounced in long-running, popular shows like "I Love Lucy" and "Father Knows Best."

Women's dress styles reflected the same female images. During the war, women had worn mannish clothes: skirts were narrow; suits were popular; padded shoulders were in vogue. But in 1947 Parisian designer Christian Dior introduced the "new look," and women abandoned their masculine garb in a rush to femininity. The "new look" featured long, full skirts and emphasized a defined bosom and tiny waist, which required wearing foundation garments. By the early 1950s these fashions reached their height in the "baby doll" look. It was characterized by a cinched-in waist, a full bosom, and bouffant skirts held out by crinoline petticoats. Shoe styles emphasized ever higher heels and ever more pointed toes until, ultimately, women had difficulty walking. Not since the Victorian era had women's fashions been so confining.

The Back-to-the-Home Movement

The new arguments and styles could never have gained widespread favor had not women—and men—been willing to accept them. After

the war traditionalism was in vogue, and the patriarchal past took on a romatic hue. The deprivation of the war years made a close family life attractive; women eagerly responded to the returning soldiers' desire to re-create a secure environment in the family. Rates of marriage and of remarriage after divorce and widowhood continued to remain high. The age of first marriage rapidly dropped: in 1900 the average age of first marriage for women was 22 years, while by 1940 it had lowered to 21.5 years. The Second World War occasioned the most rapid decrease over the course of the century, and by 1962 the average age of first marriage for women was 20.3 years. The size of families, which had decreased during the depression and the war, was increasing. Families with four and five children were common: the 1940s, according to one analyst, was a period of "the most rapid family formation" in the history of the United States, and the trend continued into the 1950s.[7] In keeping with these trends was the widespread influence of two movements that exalted the joys of motherhood. One, the La Leche League, was dedicated to helping mothers nurse their infants. The other movement promoted the LaMaze method of natural childbirth,   217

116   A natural childbirth
class.

which combined a humanitarian desire to free women from the pain
of childbirth with a zealot's fervor to make it the most important
experience of their lives.

Even most college-educated women continued to see marriage as their
most important goal in life. From her vantage point at Barnard College,
Mirra Komarovsky noted that, far from taking a militant feminist
position, college women were defending marriage and motherhood with
Freudian arguments.[8] Betty Friedan estimated that by the mid-1950s,
60 percent of female undergraduates were dropping out of college to
marry.[9] One educator presciently explained this development as the
result of the overwhelming influence of movies, television, and
popular magazines, with their glorification of romantic love and
marriage. To the young, marriage seemed both a haven and an escape
from parental and social restraints.[10]

The desire to marry and to create a stable life around a romanticized version of the family (which in many ways was a middle-class luxury made possible by postwar affluence) was re-enforced by other factors. The fear that the decrease in population due to the war had weakened the nation prompted some government officials and scientists to call for a return to large families. The superficially tranquil postwar decade had its own tensions and pressures. International affairs were characterized by a series of crises and wars, including the Korean conflict, and by the perceived threat of a newly resurgent communism. Recurring cycles of inflation and depression cast an air of unease over the new affluence. As early as 1945, one analyst contended that the postwar attack against women was a classic case of scapegoating—of blaming vague fears on a definable villain.[11] Shortly thereafter, woman as virtuous wife replaced woman as villain as the central image within the cult of domesticity. But to a nation that had undergone an exhausting war and was living in a troubled peace, home as a refuge was welcome.

Also, affluent Americans increasingly clustered in suburban areas, where jobs for women were limited and domestic help was in short supply. Husbands were away from home longer because they had to commute to work, leaving wives to bear complete responsibility for the family—including the sometimes overwhelming task of transportation. With schools, stores, and the train station rarely within walking distance, the suburban housewife could spend her day behind the wheel of the station wagon, suburbia's solution to the transportation problem. The American dream of affluence in a natural, bucolic setting, away from urban squalor, often made it impossible for women to be other than housewives and mothers.

Sex and Child-Rearing The new emphasis on Freudianism also was central to the return to the home. Americans have always respected experts, particularly when "science" is their justification and when sexuality is the issue. Marriage manuals and sex handbooks have never wanted for sales in the twentieth century. After the Second World War, as after the First, Americans were once again captivated by the notion of sexual liberation, eager to learn the style and techniques

117 Suburban ritual: waiting at the station.

of physical gratification.* To this drive, Freudian theories gave the rationale: sex was an inevitable necessity of life that ruled human development. But Freudians also argued that the proper end of sexuality for women was domesticity and motherhood. Sex experts told women their mission was healthy sex; child-care experts, like Benjamin Spock, told them they must stay at home to raise their children. According to sociologist Philip Slater, this "magnification of the child-rearing role" was the most important factor in the "ultra-domestication" of the American woman in the 1950s.[12]

---

* To what extent Americans were successful in this quest in the 1950s—as in the 1920s—is debatable. One study of best-selling marriage manuals between 1951 and 1971 concluded that women had been granted the right to sexual pleasure but that men were always to play the dominant role. (Michael Gordon and Penelope J. Shankweiler, "Different Equals Less: Female Sexuality in Recent Marriage Manuals," *Journal of Marriage and the Family*, XXXIII [August 1971], 459–66, cited in Jessie Bernard, *The Future of Marriage* [New York: World, 1972], p. 47.)

Feminism in the 1950s

To the arguments of Freudians and traditionalists, the feminist rebuttal was weak. True, bold statements appeared from time to time: for example, Simone de Beauvoir's *The Second Sex* was published in the United States in 1952. More typical of the feminism of the 1950s was Mirra Komarovsky's stated purpose for writing *Women in the Modern World:* to steer a course between feminism and antifeminism.[13] In studying feminism during the 1950s, sociologists Arnold Green and Eleanor Molnick encountered few radicals. Those they did meet felt it was futile to issue manifestoes or to organize because the majority of Americans had become conservative in opinion and life style. Militant feminism in the American past had often coincided with times of general reform sentiment. But such was not the climate in the 1950s.

The old-line women's organizations continued their activities. But many had declined in strength, while disagreement over the ERA made a unified campaign difficult. The Women's Joint Congressional Committee, for example, which in the 1920s had been an important agency of social feminism, by the 1950s served as an information clearinghouse for liberal organizations. The Consumers' League was rarely heard from, while the Women's Trade Union League had disbanded in 1947. Even the Lucy Stone League, founded in 1921 to end legal restrictions against women using their maiden names after marriage and to persuade women to do so, had little impact in the 1950s. "The present young generation is not interested," wrote an early leader of the organization despairingly.[14]

With regard to the ERA, the Woman's Party, the National Federation of Business and Professional Women's Clubs, and the National Federation of Women's Clubs supported it, but the League of Women Voters, the Women's Bureau of the Department of Labor, and women in the labor movement still opposed it as being against the best interests of working women. In 1950 and again in 1953 the Senate passed the ERA. But in both years a coalition of forty-three national organizations, known as The Committee to Defeat the Unequal Rights Amendment, successfully lobbied for the attachment of riders to the bill that exempted from its provisions state protective laws for working women. Yet

221

despite their differences, the major women's organizations were instrumental in many states to the passage of equal-pay legislation. Although the Fair Labor Standards Act of 1938 had established the principle of equal pay, the government and the courts had been unwilling to apply it with any consistency. At the same time, women's organizations pressed for a broader federal law.

The Re-Emergence of Domestic Feminism

Given the climate of the 1950s, it is not surprising that the domestic feminist argument, in evidence throughout the century, found numerous adherents. Even the conservative analysts of woman's role were aware that many women were discontent at home, that they were frustrated about working at an all-demanding job for which they were paid no salary and given little recognition. But the solution of the traditionalists was not that women could rearrange their lives to accommodate their own ambitions or creative drives; rather it was that women should be educated to find more satisfaction in what was their natural role and that society should be persuaded to give recognition to the housewife. Housework must come to be recognized as a real profession was their rallying cry. "Many a girl marries unprepared either intellectually or psychologically for the lifetime job she is undertaking," wrote one supporter of professional training programs for future wives.[15] In a slight variation on the common theme, journalist Agnes Meyer revived the idea of women's superior morality and, like Eleanor Roosevelt, chided women for not organizing on their own behalf. But Meyer was not primarily interested in community concerns; she wanted women to organize behind the goal of raising the status of the housewife.[16]

There is no question that the goal of these "domestic feminists" was admirable: unquestionably homemakers—whether male or female—ought to enjoy greater recognition. But these publicists of domesticity—like those before them—had little impact on popular attitudes. They were successful in expanding training in home economics, in introducing new courses on marriage and the family in high schools and colleges, and in generating public debate on the issue. These successes, however, did not alter what feminists and antifeminists alike diagnosed as the cause of American women's discontent; they did not modify the American belief that housework is menial. Nor did they change the fact that a wife's social status is determined by her husband's occupation, not by her achievements as a homemaker.

The feminists of the 1950s did not envision a vastly altered future. They believed that women could achieve their needed equality with certain modifications in the existing social structure. Many contended that there were major biological differences between men and women, and they did not want to tamper with these arrangements. Writing in the May 1947 issue of *The Annals of the American Academy of Political and Social Science,* Margaret Bruton, a housewife and part-time historian, outlined the moderate feminist position. "Former generations," she wrote, "smothered a girl's intellectual capacities; the feminists and most of her teachers today ignore her emotional needs . . . Each woman must still learn for herself and often too late the necessity for managing somehow to find outlets for her dual needs with the limitations imposed on her by society and by her biological function."[17] It is difficult to decry the honest endeavors of the postwar feminists on behalf of women; what seems lacking were methods adequate to force the issue. By 1964 Alice Rossi, sociologist and feminist, found that the overt antifeminism of the immediate postwar years had ended, but at the same time "there was practically no feminist spark left among American women."[18] Her judgment as applied to the moderate feminists of the 1950s was harsh, but at base it was not incorrect.

EVIDENCE TO THE CONTRARY
New Economic, Demographic, and Medical Factors

At the same time that militant feminism was in decline and traditional attitudes were prevalent among Americans, more and more women were entering the work force. Throughout the twentieth century the expanding American economy had absorbed increasing numbers of women workers, primarily because of their willingness to take on low-paying, part-time work. In addition, by the 1950s changing patterns in the life of the American woman had made work outside the home increasingly possible for her. In 1900 the average woman married at twenty-two years of age and had her last child at thirty-two. With a life expectancy of fifty-one years, it was probable that child-rearing would take up most of her adult life. By 1950, however, the average woman married at twenty, bore her last child at twenty-six, and had a life expectancy of sixty-five years. Even if she remained at home until her children were grown, she still had at least twenty years of life at home without children. For many women, the reasonable alternative was to go to work. And the employment figures of married women increasingly reflected this new demographic dispensation: in 1940 the proportion of married women employed outside the home stood at 15 percent; at 30 percent in 1960; and over 50 percent in 1968.

Medical science, too, was aiding women in gaining more control over their lives. By 1960, with the marketing of oral contraceptives for women, birth-control technology made an epic advance. Women now had available a relatively inexpensive and almost foolproof method of contraception, and its popularity was attested to by the sizable number of women who began to use it. For those women who chose to use the pill, it seemed to give them their final freedom to have sexual intercourse without the fear of pregnancy, to be able to plan their children around their lives and not their lives around their children.

As early as the 1950s, it was evident that the experience of depression and war had unquestionably eroded the older notions that work for married women violated the fulfillment of their role as wives and mothers. The substantial lowering of the average age of first marriage was not only an indication of a new traditionalism but also proof that the old stigmas against working wives were ending: because the wife could work, young couples no longer felt that they had to postpone marriage. Pearl Buck, who in the 1930s had been pessimistic about women's position, now thought that husbands not only tolerated working wives, but they expected their wives to work if family finances were low.[19] Marriage rates among professional women also began to rise substantially. In 1940 26 percent of professional women were married; in 1960 (among a sampling of approximately fifty thousand) 45 percent were married.[20] Most significant was the increasing percentage of working mothers with dependent children. In the mid-1950s,

This healthy, normal baby has a handicap. She was born female.

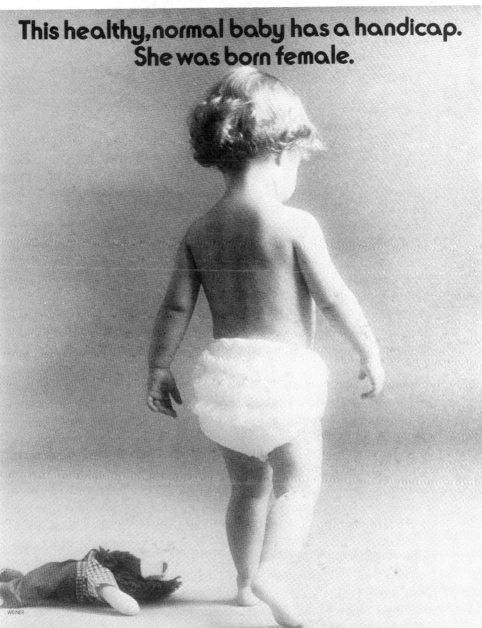

WEINER

When she grows up, her job opportunities will be limited, and her pay low. As a sales clerk, for instance, she'll earn half of what a man does. If she goes to college, she'll still earn less than many men with a 9th grade education. Maybe you don't care—but it's a fact—job discrimination based on sex is against the law. And it's a waste. Think about your own daughter—she's handicapped too.

Womanpower. It's much too good to waste.

25 percent of women with young children had jobs; by 1969 the figure had risen to 40 percent. What is more, between 1960 and 1969 the category of workers that increased most rapidly was that of mothers with preschool children. By 1969, 33 percent of these women were employed outside the home.

The New Trends: Revolutionary or Not?

To what extent this movement of women into the work force represented a revolutionary force is debatable. Historian William Chafe has argued that the increasing numbers of married women in the labor force—and particularly the participation of a significant number of women from higher-income families—is proof that a revolutionary change in outlook among women was occurring. But we need to know much more about the kinds of jobs these women were entering and their attitudes about them before we can accept his thesis.

In the first place, the old discriminations against women were everywhere in evidence. Women did not continue to move into higher-paying, skilled-labor or professional jobs after the war years. Reflecting the labor shortages during the war, the proportion of women in most professions increased somewhat between 1940 and 1950. But by and large, they did not retain these gains during the 1950s. The percentage of women doctors rose slightly between 1950 and 1960, while in law their ratio to men remained stable. The proportion of women college administrators and professors, ministers, dentists, and scientists declined.

In the second place, sociologists Ellen Keniston and Kenneth Keniston in their study of working women have argued that most women work in order to augment the family income and would gladly return to the home if given the chance.[21] Economics, not independence, is their major motivation. Indeed, the postwar years spawned a new consumerism in which all families wanted to participate, while inflationary cycles created instabilities in husbands' salaries and increased the costs of items like cars and a college education for children that had once been luxuries, but were now widely viewed as necessities. Above all, Keniston and Keniston suggest that most women are unable to regard themselves seriously as full-fledged members of the labor force.

226

They do not readily join unions; until the rise of the new feminism of the late 1960s they did not press for equal rights with men at work. They submit to enforced seasonal layoffs without complaining; they accept part-time work with a pay scale lower than that of full-time work. In 1971 only 40 percent of working women were employed in full-time, year-round jobs.

Moreover, the conventional attitudes about marriage and motherhood could be and were stretched to accommodate the new statistical reality. In many marriages, according to observers, a new relationship was beginning to emerge, based partly on women's new role as wage earner. The husband who washed the dishes and diapered the baby became a standard subject for news comment and satire. Yet more often than not, behind the new readjustment in relationship, the old mascu-

119 Sharing the housework: is it any more than "playing the part of a volunteer aide"?

line–feminine models were still dominant. Sociologist David Reisman discerned a pattern in the marriages over several generations in his own family that he judged significant of general trends. His grandmother's marriage had been patriarchal: his grandfather was the head of the household and the family's provider; his grandmother found autonomy in running the household, rearing the children, and going to concerts and plays. Within his daughter's marriage, however, childrearing, housework, and cultural pursuits were shared. Yet, he concluded, "Wives still have the main responsibility for the home, the husband playing the part of a volunteer aide, and . . . the women have made a tacit bargain with their husbands not to compete with them professionally or in career terms."[22]

The sizable movement of women into the work force in the 1940s and 1950s gives the illusion of social change, but the reality for women was not very different from what it had always been. And until the advent of the new feminists of the 1960s, there was little outspoken protest. Among educated working women cognizant of their second-class status, the new feminists would find support, but it would take the agitation of a small group of determined women to alert the nation to the unseen inequality in its midst.

THE SHIFT TO MILITANCY

In face of the virulent antifeminism of American society in the immediate postwar years and the strong appeal of domesticity in the 1950s, the rise of a militant feminism in the 1960s is surprising. Given the long-standing ambivalence of most women about feminism, why were many, at this time, willing to embrace a radical ideology?

A New Reform Climate

Most significant in the emergence of the new feminism was the appearance of a new reform mentality in the 1960s. In the late 1950s and early 1960s, studies showing the growth of crime, poverty, juvenile delinquency, and drug abuse appeared in abundance, and these problems became dominant public issues. In 1956 Rachel Carson's *Silent Spring*, a major study of environmental pollution, was published, and in 1962 the nation was shocked by Michael Harrington's *The Other*

120 Betty Friedan: her message "spread like a nuclear chain reaction."

America, an exposé of poverty. The civil rights movement burst upon America following the Montgomery, Alabama, bus boycott of 1956 (which was begun by a black woman, Rosa Parks, who refused to give up her seat when a white man demanded it), and the mid-1960s witnessed the advent of a new radicalism among the young, inspired by the civil rights protest and by increasing dissatisfaction with America's long-term involvement in the Vietnam war. Environmentalists and population experts warned that the national birth rate, which had begun to equal that of developing nations like India, would have to fall or overpopulation would destroy the nation's resources. They made a powerful case for limiting the number of children per family to one or two.

These new trends made Americans receptive to controversial exposés. Thus, when Betty Friedan's militant polemic *The Feminine Mystique* was published in 1963, it captured a mass audience. Friedan's prose was powerful, and her argument gave no quarter to the defenders of

229

women's traditional role. In Friedan's view, women were discontent, not because they were untrained to be housewives and mothers, but because homemaking was intrinsically boring. If women contributed to the ills of society it was precisely because they stayed at home, inflicting their dissatisfaction on husbands and children. Friedan saw little justification for the argument that women had a special ability to raise their own children. She refused to give any credit to the Freudians. Rather she launched the kind of bitter attack against Freud that has become standard in feminist writings ever since.

The reform mood made it difficult for readers to dismiss Friedan's book as the ravings of a selfish woman unhappy with her lot. Besides, after a decade of trying to persuade women that they ought to stay at home to raise their children, the child-care experts had not been able to prevent many of them from entering the work force. Nor had social problems been alleviated by women who heeded this advice and did stay at home. Friedan's view was fresh and different and in tenor with the times. In fact, it may have been the very emergence of a reform

121   The establishment of day-care centers has become a primary feminist goal.

mentality that impelled Friedan to write her book, for she completed it relatively late in her own life, after many years of marriage and free-lance editing and writing.

The new interest in social reform led to substantial gains for women during the administration of John F. Kennedy. Kennedy was no advocate of feminism. But he was willing to listen to the suggestion made by women both within and outside of his administration that he appoint a commission to study the position of women in the United States. The idea had its precedent in the commissions on the status of blacks, which had been a federal priority item for a decade and would continue to be so under the Kennedy administration. Furthermore, an influential 1957 report entitled *Womanpower*—which had been funded by the Ford Foundation as a result of shortages of trained personnel in professions like nursing and teaching—had urged that the government give serious attention to the needs of working women, including the possibility of federal funding for day-care centers. The time seemed right to do something for women. Between 1940 and 1960, both political parties in their election platforms had recommended passage of the Equal Rights Amendment, and neither had followed up on its campaign promise. Eleanor Roosevelt added her influence to the pressure on Kennedy. She was shocked that only 9 women were included among Kennedy's first 240 appointees to office, and she sent him a three-page list of women she judged qualified for government service. Kennedy, anxious to gain support from the Adlai Stevenson wing of the Democratic party, which Eleanor Roosevelt led, appointed her chairman of the Commission on the Status of Women, which he created in 1960.*

---

* It is useful to compare England and the United States in terms of the emergence of the new feminism. In both countries there are large numbers of educated women and working women. In both countries the same kinds of discrimination against women are in evidence. But feminism in England, in size and strength, is a full decade behind the movement in the United States. Two factors are missing in England that existed in the United States: the civil rights movement, and government studies of discrimination against women, which were largely the result of the pressure that major women's organizations put on President Kennedy, particularly through the Women's Bureau in the Department of Labor. There is no such agency in the British government.

The commission's report, issued in 1963, was not a radical document. It gave full support to the nuclear family and recommended that women should have special training for marriage and motherhood. It withheld support from the Equal Rights Amendment on the grounds that the Fifth and Fourteenth Amendments provided sufficient constitutional guarantees for women's rights. But, among other recommendations, the report called for equal job opportunities and equal pay for women, for the end to laws discriminating against women, and for the expansion of child-care facilities outside the home. Its debates and its recommendations stimulated some important action on behalf of women. In 1963 Congress passed the Equal Pay Act, a measure that had been a priority item for women's organizations for some time. After 1963 the states began to appoint similar commissions. Several presidential advisory groups composed of both private citizens and government officials also were formed. Title VII of the 1964 Civil Rights Act prohibited all discrimination on the basis of sex as well as on the basis of race. (Title VII was introduced by a Southern congressman, not out of feminist sentiment, but as a strategy to block passage of the entire bill. The plan backfired, and the amendment passed together with the bill.)

The pressure of old-line women activists was instrumental in persuading Kennedy to establish the presidential commission and the subsequent committees. The composition of the Committee on Civil and Political Rights under the 1960 commission offers a graphic example of their involvement. Members of the committee included presidents of the League of Women Voters, the General Federation of Women's Clubs, the National Federation of Business and Professional Women's Clubs, and a vice president of the International Ladies' Garment Workers' Union. Esther Peterson, who had risen through the ranks of labor to become, as head of the Women's Bureau and later Assistant Secretary of Labor, Kennedy's highest-ranking female appointee, served as vice chairman of the commission under Eleanor Roosevelt. Peterson herself had been a powerful advocate within the administration for convening such a commission. Over the years the national women's organizations represented on this commission had taken an increasingly feminist position. By 1960, for example, even the League of Women

Voters had become much more sympathetic to the Equal Rights Amendment, although they did not officially endorse it until 1972. Such action, however, did not imply any increased radicalism on the part of these groups. The League, for example, did not give up its concern for social welfare. And the National Federation of Business and Professional Women's Clubs refused to take a strong leadership role in the post-1966 women's movement because the organization did not want to be identified by the public as "feminist"—a stance that it considered too radical.[23]

New Faces and the Formation of NOW

In addition to the old-line activists, a second group of women, more militant in style and demands, emerged in the mid-1960s. Generally young, these women often turned to radical feminism because of their disillusioning experiences in the civil rights and student movements, where they found that the male leaders relegated them to housekeeping and clerical chores. Like many nineteenth-century feminists who turned from reform to feminism, they began to identify with the disadvantaged and to ask if they, too, were not objects of discrimination.

The old-style feminists worked through the existing women's organi-

122 Consciousness-raising: a feminist technique borrowed from the left.

zations and through the government commissions dealing with women. The new-style feminists moved in a different direction: they formed their own groups, often modeled after those they had recently left. Thus they opted for small, loosely structured, informal groups. They de-emphasized leadership and stressed equality. They issued manifestoes and, like the left generally, published fugitive newspapers. They conducted "consciousness-raising" meetings, where they employed the techniques of group therapy to heighten women's sensitivity to their presumed oppression.

The actions of both conservative and radical feminists came to national attention in 1966. In that year, the Third National Conference of the State Commissions on Women met in Washington, D.C. According to Aileen Hernández, a former organizer for the ILGWU who was later to serve as president of the National Organization for Women (NOW), the mood among the hundreds of delegates was bitter and angry.[24] Most felt that the government was not meeting its obligation to implement the recommendations of the various commissions on women or to enforce the laws already passed. Meanwhile women who served on federal agencies concerned with women communicated this discontent to, among others, Betty Friedan, who was present at the meeting and whose book, *The Feminine Mystique,* had gained her national prominence as a feminist spokeswoman. The consensus was that there was need for an organization to pressure the government on behalf of women in the same way that the civil rights organizations functioned for blacks. These forces came to a head in Friedan's hotel room, where plans were formulated for the National Organization for Women.

With the formation of NOW, the new feminism had its official and national birth. Other organizations soon followed. In 1968 academic and professional women formed the Women's Equity Action League (WEAL) for the purpose of ending sex discrimination in employment, education, and taxation. The Women's Political Caucus, a bipartisan group aimed at pressuring the political parties to consider women's concerns and to elect women to office, was organized in 1971. By that time job placement and counseling agencies for women, like Catalyst in New York City, had begun to appear. Courses on women's history,

234

123 Kate Millett, best-selling feminist author, one of the first of many.

psychology, and sociology were introduced in colleges throughout the nation, until in the spring of 1972 over six hundred were being offered. They soon led to women's studies programs.

Women began to express their discontent and to go into action. Feminist exposés poured from the presses. Kate Millett's *Sexual Politics* (1969) became a national best-seller. It was rapidly followed by, among others, Shulamith Firestone's *The Dialectics of Sex* (1970), Robin Morgan's *Sisterhood Is Powerful* (1970), and Germaine Greer's *The Female Eunuch* (1971). Women formed feminist theater troupes and rock groups; they made feminist movies. Throughout the nation women marched for the repeal of antiabortion legislation; they established day-care centers; and in New York and Atlantic City they picketed the *Ladies' Home Journal* offices and the Miss America pageant respectively for perpetrating myths about women. In 1972 three scholarly journals devoted to women's studies appeared. That same year marked the publication of *Ms.*, which became the first militant feminist magazine in the history of the nation to attract a sizable circulation. Events seemed to bear out Friedan's judgment that "the absolute necessity for a civil rights movement for women had reached such a point of subterranean explosive urgency by 1966, that it took only a few of us to get together to unite the spark—and it spread like a nuclear chain reaction."[25]

235

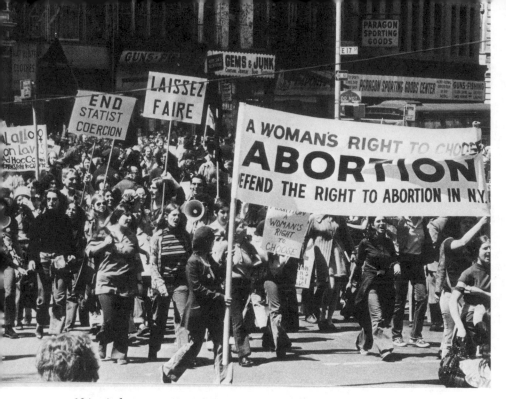

124   A demonstration at Union Square in New York.

THE CONTEMPORARY FEMINIST POSITION

The spokeswomen of the new feminism have made it their job to dis-
prove the contentions of the moderate feminists of the past: first, that
women had, indeed, made substantial progress in achieving equality
with men; and second, that women, because of their biology, had
special responsibilities to their families.

Feminist scholars and polemicists have scoured the available statistical evidence to try to demonstrate that women have made only super-
ficial gains over the past few decades. To their credit, they have found
impressive data to support their arguments. They have turned to
government reports, work force studies, and census data, and they
have made their own studies. Much of this material, particularly
statistics published by government agencies, had long been in the
public domain. In effect, the feminists have forced Americans to pay

236

attention to a deep strain of unattended discrimination against women.

Feminist analysts have drawn a dismal picture in the area of politics. Since 1920 there have been sixty-five women in the House of Representatives and ten women in the Senate—a total of 2 percent of the membership of Congress in those years. Twenty-four of the congresswomen and seven of the women senators served one term or less, and almost all of these women were themselves widows of former congressmen or senators when they ran for office. Since 1920 two women have served in the cabinet: Frances Perkins, FDR's Secretary of Labor between 1933 and 1945; and Oveta Culp Hobby, Secretary of Health, Education, and Welfare from 1953 to 1955 in the Eisenhower administration. Three women have been governors between 1920 and 1970; one woman has served as a state attorney general and three as lieutenant governors. In 1968, 3 percent of the nation's judges were women.

Predictably, where women have entered the political sphere in large numbers, they have served as library board members, as city treasurers, and as school board members. Still women hold no more than 10 percent of the school board positions in the nation. And although in the 1950s women secured equal representation with men on the governing committees of both political parties, the traditional hostilities against women are still in evidence. Shirley Chisholm, black congresswoman from New York, has stated that in her political career the greater discrimination against her has been because of her sex, not her race: "I was constantly bombarded by both men and women that I should return to teaching, a woman's vocation, and leave politics up to men."[26] The McGovern wing of the Democratic party, itself an outgrowth of the civil rights and radical movements of the 1960s, appears to have been an exception to the general rule about politics. In this organization women as leaders were highly visible.

In the area of employment, feminists have found similar evidence of inequality. In 1940 women held 45 percent of the professional positions in the nation (a figure that includes the large proportion of women professionals who are schoolteachers). In 1967 they held 37 percent. The percentage of workers in domestic service did decrease (creating a crisis for employed mothers), but it was clerical and office work into which these women moved. All indices showed that women earned less than men and that the percentage difference was sharply rising. In 1959 women's earnings were 66 percent that of men; by 1968 the figure had dropped to 58 percent. Statistics for 1970 showed that the average woman college graduate could expect a smaller annual income than the average white male who had graduated from elementary school.

As for their economic status, poverty among women was on the increase. In 1959 women constituted 26 percent of the total poor; in 1968 the figure stood at 41 percent. Black women in particular bore the brunt of poverty, but the situation was critical for white women as well. In 1965 the average income of black women was 70 percent that of white women, 50 percent that of black men, and 40 percent that of white men. In 1969 unemployment among black women seeking work stood at 6 percent. Among white women the figure was 3.4 percent; among black men, 3.7 percent; and among white men, 1.9 percent. Experts estimated that among families headed by black women, 50 percent had an income below the poverty line, compared with 25 percent of families headed by white women, less than 25 percent of families headed by black men, and about 7 percent of families headed by white men.* Finally, studies showed that most alimony payments were small and that in many cases they were not paid, that the median payment for child support was $12 per week in 1970, that most banks would not lend money to women, and that women were discriminated against in pension plans, insurance policies, and social security payments.

In education, a corresponding pattern of inequity was apparent. The proportion of women to men in college dropped from 47 percent in

---

* Changing employment patterns and the attack on discrimination in the postwar years provided some increased job mobility for black women. Nursing, saleswork, and clerical jobs—traditionally largely closed to them—became more available. Between 1950 and 1966, for example, the proportion of black women working as saleswomen and clerical workers rose from 6 percent to 13 percent. Their employment as factory workers remained fairly stable. The proportion of black women in service jobs, however, continued to remain high—approximately 58 percent. The comparable figure for women in general was 25 percent. (Women's Bureau, U.S., Department of Labor, *Negro Women in the Population and in the Labor Force* [Washington, D.C.: U.S. Government Printing Office, 1966].)

125 Something new: the storybook without sex stereotypes.

1920 to 35 percent in 1958. In 1930, two out of five B.A.'s and M.A.'s were awarded to women and one out of seven Ph.D.'s. By 1962 the figures had dropped to one in three and one in ten respectively. Textbooks in all fields customarily did not mention women, while in children's stories and readers, women were unilaterally shown in dependent roles, usually as wives or mothers. Powerful women were generally evil. In contrast, men were shown as venturesome and strong; they were the professionals, explorers, and inventors. *Sex-stereotyping* was the term feminists coined to characterize this literature, and they contended that it was a powerful force in molding adults who adhered to rigid separations in gender roles and expectations.

In law, feminists have found hundreds of state laws still on the books that variously forbade women to sit on juries, limited their right to make contracts and to hold property, and held them in minor status longer than men. Prostitution, after a half-century of often desultory action against it, was still thriving in many cities. Rape laws in many states made it nearly impossible for the rapist to be convicted.

239

In politics, employment, education, and law, feminists can make a strong case for discrimination. When it comes to questions of marriage and the family, they are on shakier ground. On this issue the moderate and radical wings of the movement divide. The radicals, like Kate Millett, argue that women can be free only when traditional patterns of marriage and family life are replaced by communal arrangements. Feminists with an inclination toward socialism insist that liberation can be won only with the fall of the capitalist economy. Some of the radicals, like Shulamith Firestone, contend that woman's function as child-bearer must be ended and the fetus brought to gestation, not in the woman's body, but in the uterus of a cow or in a laboratory setting. Others are particularly hostile to men and argue that because of their historic role as oppressors, men should be made subordinate to women. Some of these women espouse lesbianism as the most honest form of female behavior.

126   Some young women hope to find new freedom in communal life.

The more moderate members of the movement—concentrated in NOW and WEAL—share some, but not all, of these sentiments. The moderates are not especially antagonistic toward men. They are opposed neither to marriage nor to communal arrangements; they advocate individual choice in these matters. They do, however, support abortion as well as the establishment of day-care centers. A distaste for domesticity, seen as confining, pervades their rhetoric, and the professional woman is their ideal.

To uphold their view that women are not necessarily bound to homemaking and child-rearing, moderate and radical feminists point to recent scholarly studies. The consensus of the 1950s that only motherhood offered a woman real fulfillment and that the young child needed his mother at home no longer exists. Some child-rearing experts believe that in many cases either the mother-child relationship develops into a neurotic dependency, or, pressured by economic want or other personal difficulties, the mother gives her offspring insufficient attention. Citing successful examples of communal child-rearing in Israel and Russia, scholars in the fields of psychology and sociology argue that children are too valuable a national resource to be entrusted solely to parents who have little expertise in the care and education of children. On the question of domesticity, other authorities argue that this interest is learned and not innate and that working women are in fact much more content than housewives. In opposition to the postwar analysts, sociologist Jessie Bernard contends that the majority of the past and present studies of marital discontent decisively show that nonworking married women are much more prone to anxiety, depression, and mental breakdown than either married men, married working women, or single women.[27]

Although the feminist position has gained a strong foothold among experts and professionals, it has not conquered the field. Many psychiatrists and psychologists still regard the mother–child relationship during the first years of life crucial to future development. Some medical experts contend that the differing biological make-up of men and women may yet indicate a natural urge on the part of women toward domesticity and motherhood. Some recent studies, too, suggest that a pregnant woman's activities may influence the development of the fetus: we may yet see scientific proof for the Victorian notion that an expectant mother should spend her time resting and trying to think pleasant thoughts. Finally, one recent work indicates that Friedan, Bernard, and others may, in fact, be wrong about the discontent of American housewives. In her study of 571 housewifes in urban and suburban Chicago—carefully chosen to represent a variety of ages, incomes, educational backgrounds, and ethnic identifications—sociologist Helen Lopata found that the majority were not unhappy with their lot. Those for whom the role seemed restrictive were the less well-to-do, generally of working-class background and limited education. These women often were passive and found it difficult to interact with others. They resented the domineering attitudes of their husbands, while lack of obedience from their children made them feel inadequate. Middle-class Chicago housewives, however, with adequate incomes and some education, had few of these problems. Absorbed in their family and home, they nonetheless found time to do volunteer work and to make extensive friendships. They were proud of their role and felt that they functioned creatively. They were the hope of the future, Lopata implied, and not Shulamith Firestone's commune member or Betty Friedan's career woman.

Thus the debate continues. Feminists have brought to light undeniable evidence of widespread discrimination against women. Whether a root and branch restructuring of society is necessary to bring women social equality as well as personal satisfaction in their own lives, however, has yet to be resolved.

AN ASSESSMENT OF FEMINIST ACHIEVEMENTS AND POTENTIALS

Since 1966 the women's movement has achieved solid accomplishments. Equal opportunity commissions of the state and national governments have pressed sex discrimination suits filed by women: by 1971 the courts had awarded $30 million in back pay to women as a result of these suits. As early as 1970 WEAL brought class action suits against one hundred universities under an executive order requiring federal contractors to file affirmative action programs with federal investigators, committing themselves to schedules for ending sex discrimination. Faced with the cutoff of federal funds for university programs, administrators were quick to comply. The Education Act of 1972 prohibited sex discrimination in colleges and universities, while a new and expanded Equal Employment Opportunities Law was passed in the same year. Under pressure from women's organizations, many states repealed their legislation prohibiting abortion. In the spring of 1973, the Supreme Court declared abortion to be a private decision between doctor and patient, thereby substantially liberalizing its availability to women *(Doe v. Bolton; Roe v. Wade)*. Finally and most important, in the spring of 1973, fifty years after its introduction into Congress, both the Senate and the House passed the Equal Rights Amendment.

12/ The first women to graduate from a full four-year program at Yale University, June 3, 1973.

128   Some women see lesbianism as the only way to achieve liberation.

The feminist movement has aroused much attention because the media has given it extensive publicity. Particularly in the activities and rhetoric of the radical wing, newspapers, television, and magazines have found the kind of sensationalism that appeals to the public. Radicals' demands for abortion and for acceptance of lesbianism had sexually titillating overtones, and their willingness to march and to stage sit-ins had the dramatic quality that the news had lost since the demise of civil rights, student, and peace protests by 1970. The media have not generally been kind to the new feminism: in characteristically identifying all feminists as "bra-burners," they have misrepresented the movement.* But they have at least given the new feminism the kind of striking publicity it could not otherwise have achieved.

---

* The "bra-burning" charge was the figment of an overheated reporter's imagination. At the 1968 protest against the Miss America pageant, where the incident was supposed to have occurred, women did not burn their brassieres; they threw them into an ash can, thereby shedding what they considered to be a symbol of female oppression.

Still, the actual membership of feminist organizations is small. NOW had only about 30,000 members in 1973. (The membership of the League of Women Voters was about 160,000.) The Women's Political Caucus and WEAL were even smaller than NOW. Moreover, their membership has been drawn from among white, middle-class educated women of liberal persuasion. Organization is strong in cities, in the suburbs, and on college campuses. Like Betty Friedan, the older women in the movement had often devoted themselves to motherhood during the 1950s and had found that it did not satisfy them. Or they were discontent in their work and wanted to find a new image for themselves, while working for the general rights of women. The younger women, who constitute the majority of feminists, have matured during a reform-minded decade. They are often the daughters of women who worked during the Second World War and who thereafter stayed at home or who continued working in low-status, part-time positions. These young women want something different for themselves, but they often find wide discrepancies between their education, their personal aspirations, and the jobs available to them. They are prime candidates for radicalization, and books like *The Feminine Mystique* and *Sexual Politics* easily convince them that their problems are not personal but social. Instead of psychoanalysis, the standard Freudian solution for discontented middle-class women, they turn to feminist consciousness-raising.

The small number of members of NOW and the other groups is not necessarily an indication of the strength of the movement. Many women are sympathetic to certain aspects of the feminist program, while unwilling to commit themselves formally to an organization. Although they are not members of NOW or WEAL, many professional women, for example, work with feminists in identifying job and salary discrimination and in providing redress for aggrieved women. Recent studies suggest that the new feminism may in fact be having a significant impact on the American public. In 1971 and 1972 Louis Harris conducted polls on men's and women's attitudes toward a variety of issues that the women's movement had raised. His sample included a cross section of classes and groups. Although in both polls the majority of women judged homemaking to be the most important women's career, a near majority regarded the woman's movement favorably. In the first poll, 42 percent were opposed to the movement, 40 percent were in favor, and 18 percent were undecided. Only a year later, 48 percent were in favor of the movement, 36 percent were opposed, and 16 percent were undecided.[28] In statistical terms, these were sizable changes. And a January 1973 *Redbook* magazine survey of 120,000 readers (mostly middle-class) showed that 66 percent favored the movement, 45 percent credited it with having raised their consciousness, and less than 2 percent believed that women could best develop their full potential solely by being good wives and mothers.[29]

The new feminism has had considerably less influence among working-class and minority women. No organization on the order of the Women's Trade Union League has emerged to try to bridge the gap, although the limited success of the WTUL may prove that class lines are impossible to cross. Groups like the National Welfare Rights Organization, staffed primarily by women on welfare, have begun to appear, and this trend may yet prove that to achieve group solidarity, working-class and minority women can accept women of different ethnic, educational, and socioeconomic backgrounds only as allies, not as co-members of a group. NOW in particular has tried to attract other than middle-class white women as members, but it has had limited success. Most black women, for example, regard NOW as a movement of dissatisfied and selfish well-to-do women who want to find better jobs. They criticize it for taking attention away from the black movement, with which they identify. To a certain extent these black women are correct. The educated white women who run the feminist organizations, preoccupied with the working out of their own personal identities and futures, often forget the problems of other groups.

Differences in opinion between moderates and radicals have caused some tension in the movement. In the spring of 1973, personal and ideological disputes arose among major feminists in New York City, where many of the ideologists of the movement live. Betty Friedan, herself an acerbic personality, was at the center of the controversy. The radicals resented her attacks against the supposed influence of lesbians in the movement, while they argued that she had failed to

129 Jeanette Washington of the National Welfare Rights Organization: can black women and white women work together?

see that a complete restructuring of social institutions, including the family, must take place before liberation could be achieved. Such open disagreement, however, has been rare. In their organizations, feminists have been able to maintain a broad coalition of groups from left to right, even including the League of Women Voters and the National Federation of Business and Professional Women's Clubs, on issues like abortion and the ERA.

One of the major reasons for this success at coalition has been that, unlike the feminists early in this century, the radical wing of the movement has exerted leverage over the center to maintain a strict feminist position. The radicals initially launched the attacks of the mid-1960s against the male power structure; they coined the term *sexism*, modeled after the word *racism* (which itself was a product of the black movement of the 1950s and 1960s); they went to the heart of women's oppression. The radical feminists have not avoided the full implications of their search for equality. By insisting in one way or another that the structure of society and its institutions must be fundamentally

247

changed, they have continually forced moderate feminists to question their own values and their own compromises with the established order.

The new feminism may be one of the few liberal movements in modern American history that has been so completely permeated by the tactics and the ideology of the left. The course followed by NOW is an example. NOW has dedicated itself to the complete eradication of all sex-role subordination of women, whether in textbooks or in the media, in business or in politics. The platform of its national convention in February 1973, not only endorsed the struggles of lesbians to achieve liberation, but, recognizing that sexist and racist attitudes toward minority women constitute a double burden of discrimination, it also made the eradication of poverty a priority issue. NOW was a major lobbyist in the spring of that year behind the ultimately unsuccessful attempt to raise the minimum wage and to extend it to domestic workers. The emphasis of NOW on consciousness-raising is also borrowed directly from the left.

These, then, have been the strengths of the new feminism: it has remained unified on major issues; it has kept to feminist goals; it has avoided the error of the suffragists by not placing all emphasis on one goal, such as the ERA; it has made a sizable impact on middle-class women and some impact on working-class women. However, the feminist movement has suffered setbacks. In the spring of 1973 President Nixon vetoed the family assistance bill, which would have provided federal funds for day-care centers, despite the statistics that show that over one-third of mothers with children under six years of age are at work. His arguments were based on a tired but venerable theme: encouraging women to work outside the home would undermine the family and thereby the moral fiber of the nation. And after passage in the legislatures of thirty states, the Equal Rights Amendment began to meet severe reversals, inspired in large part by the same fear. Conservative Phyllis Schlafly, who in the winter of 1972 formed the National Committee of Endorsers Against ERA, gained widespread attention with her success in establishing local state groups as well. Her views, like Nixon's, echoed those of the Victorians: women are happiest at home; they need protection at work; chivalry promotes the position of women;

and the true American way is one in which "a man's first significant purchase is a diamond for his bride, and the largest financial investment of his life is a home for her to live in."[30]

By the summer of 1973 there was growing sentiment throughout the nation, spurred on by the Catholic Church and conservatives in general, for an amendment to the Constitution that would make abortion illegal once again and thereby nullify the Supreme Court ruling. Furthermore, the federal government, besieged by suits filed by white males who charged that they had been discriminated against in employment in favor of women, seemed to drag its feet in prosecuting sex discrimination suits filed by women with the Equal Employment Opportunities Commission, established under the 1964 Civil Rights Act.

130 Like any movement that disturbs the status quo, feminism has its share of detractors.

Given women's position in the early 1970s in the United States, what will the future of feminism be? Will it have a substantial impact on American life, or, like its predecessor of the early twentieth century, will it disappear in a decade or two, the victim of internal divisions and of the antifeminism of American culture? Any such prediction is difficult to make, for it must be remembered that the feminism of the early twentieth century fell prey to events unleashed by the First World War, while the depression and the Second World War further weakened its potential. In assessing the strengths and weaknesses of the feminist movement of the 1960s and 1970s, one cannot foresee the possible variable of a national calamity that could quickly change the thinking of the country.

It can be said that the feminist movement has resulted in action and legislation; that in consciousness-raising it has found a new technique of self-realization; that at its very best it has counseled that men as well as women should be able to do and to be whatever they wish—and that if this involves men staying at home while women work, so be it. To what extent traditional social structures can tolerate such change remains to be seen. How will professions like law and college teaching, for example, in which women have never constituted more than 7 percent of the membership and which today have a surplus of trained personnel, handle the demands of women for parity in hiring and promotion? How will the economy in general, which has been built on the exploitation of marginal workers—women and blacks—cope with the demands of these groups for better pay and better jobs? Can the nuclear family survive a situation in which both parents work or in which the father stays home while the mother works? Or will society ultimately have to turn to communal arrangements or take up Charlotte Perkins Gilman's idea of large apartment complexes in which all home services are provided by professionals?

Such solutions, all of which fly in the face of tradition, seem far in the future. In the meantime, the feminist movement could dissipate. It is difficult to believe that the current generation of feminists will tire of feminism, that they will retreat to other reform pursuits or to the home. Yet it must be remembered that much of the strength of the feminist movement in the 1960s and 1970s lay in its appeal to those young women who, born in the 1940s and 1950s, were raised by mothers who accepted the conventions of those years. To a certain degree each generation rebels against the practices and values of the previous generation: to the young women of the 1920s, the feminist concerns of the prewar generation had seemed out of date; that the new feminism emerged in the 1960s had much to do with this fact of generational conflict. When Kate Millett wrote *Sexual Politics*, for example, she was criticizing, not only the values of her society, but also those of her middle-class parents. Even if the feminists do retain their feminist values, will their own children rebel against them?

These are questions that one can pose but not answer. That the feminist movement has achieved widespread strength in government, in education, and in politics and has not spent its efforts in one single crusade, as did the suffragists and feminists early in the century, is encouraging for the future. What direction it will take remains to be seen.

Notes

1 Harrison Smith, "Must Women Work?" *Independent Woman* (December 1947), 34.

2 Alva Myrdal and Viola Klein, *Women's Two Roles: Home and Work* (London: Routledge and Pauls, 1956), p. 134.

3 Benjamin Spock, *Baby and Child Care* (1946; reprint ed., New York: Dell, 1957), p. 570.

4 Mirra Komarovsky, *Women in the Modern World: Their Education and Their Dilemmas* (Boston: Little, Brown, 1953), pp. 297–98.

5 Myrdal and Klein, *Women's Two Roles: Home and Work*, pp. 125–30.

6 Betty Friedan, *The Feminine Mystique* (1963; reprint ed., New York: Dell, 1970), pp. 29–63.

7 John Sirjimaki, *The American Family in the Twentieth Century* (Cambridge, Mass.: Harvard University Press, 1953), p. 55.

8 Komarovsky, *Women in the Modern World: Their Education and Their Dilemmas*, p. 94.

9 Friedan, *The Feminine Mystique*, p. 115.

10 Kate Hevner Mueller, "The Cultural Pressures on Women," in Opal P. David, ed., *The Education of Women: Signs for the Future* (Washington, D.C.: American Council on Education, 1957), pp. 50–51.

11 Abraham Myerson, "Woman, the Authorities' Scapegoat," in Elizabeth Bragdon, ed., *Women Today: Their Conflicts, Their Frustrations, and Their Fulfillments* (New York: Bobbs-Merrill, 1953), p. 305.

[12] Philip Slater, *The Pursuit of Loneliness: American Culture at the Breaking Point* (1970; reprint ed., Boston: Beacon, 1971), p. 66.

[13] Komarovsky, *Women in the Modern World: Their Education and Their Dilemmas,* p. viii.

[14] Doris E. Fleischman, "Notes of a Retiring Feminist," *American Mercury,* LXVIII (February 1949), 161–68.

[15] Helen Sherman and Marjorie Coe, *The Challenge of Being a Woman: Understanding Ourselves and Our Children* (New York: Harper and Brothers, 1955), p. 17.

[16] Agnes Meyer, "Women Aren't Men," *Atlantic,* CLXXXVI (August 1950), 33.

[17] Margaret Bruton, "Present-Day Thinking on the Woman Question," *Annals of the American Academy of Political and Social Science,* CCLI (May 1947), 14.

[18] Alice Rossi, "Equality Between the Sexes," in Robert Jay Lifton, ed., *The Woman in America* (Boston: Houghton Mifflin, 1965), p. 99.

[19] Pearl Buck, "Changing Relationships Between Men and Women," in Beverly Cassara, ed., *American Women: The Changing Image* (Boston: Beacon, 1962), pp. 5–6.

[20] Cynthia Fuchs Epstein, *Woman's Place: Options and Limits in Professional Careers* (1970; reprint ed., Berkeley, Calif.: University of California Press, 1971), p. 97.

[21] Ellen Keniston and Kenneth Keniston, "An American Anachronism: The Image of Women and Work," *American Scholar,* XXXIII (1964), 355–75.

[22] David Reisman, "Two Generations," in Lifton, ed., *The Woman in America,* pp. 72–97.

[23] Judith Hole and Ellen Levine, *Rebirth of Feminism* (New York: Quadrangle, 1971), p. 81.

[24] Kate Stimpson, ed., *Women and the "Equal Rights" Amendment: Senate Subcommittee Hearings on the Constitutional Amendment, 91st Congress* (New York: Bowker, 1972), pp. 38–39.

[25] Hole and Levine, *Rebirth of Feminism,* p. 81.

[26] Kirsten Amundsen, *The Silenced Majority: Women and American Democracy* (Englewood Cliffs, N.J.: Prentice-Hall, 1971), p. 86.

[27] Jessie Bernard, *The Future of Marriage* (New York: World, 1972), pp. 26–27.

[28] Louis Harris and Associates, Inc., *The 1972 Virginia Slims American Women's Opinion Poll.*

[29] *Spokeswomen,* III (February 15, 1973), 10.

[30] Nick Thimmesch, "The Sexual Equality Amendment: Will Nine More States Approve? *The New York Times Magazine* (June 24, 1973), 56.

Bibliography

The best source for the history of women in the 1950s is Betty Friedan, *The Feminine Mystique* (1963; reprint ed., New York: Dell, 1970). Although Friedan's feminist analysis may seem outdated, her historical sense is still excellent. An insightful assessment of the feminism of the period is Arnold W. Green and Eleanor Melnick, "What Has Happened to the Feminist Movement," in Alvin W. Gouldner, ed., *Studies in Leadership: Leadership and Democratic Action* (New York: Russell &

Russell, 1950), pp. 277–302. Eric Goldman, *The Crucial Decade—And After: America, 1945–1960* (New York: Knopf, 1960) provides a good sense of the troubled nature of the decade.

The major statement of the Freudian position is Helene Deutsch, *The Psychology of Women: A Psychoanalytic Interpretation* (New York: Grune and Stratton, 1944–45). Some popular statements of the various feminist positions can be found in Viola Klein, *The Feminine Character: History of an Ideology* (Urbana, Ill.: University of Illinois Press, 1946); the May 1947 issue of *Annals of the American Academy of Political and Social Science;* Helen Sherman and Marjorie Coe, *The Challenge of Being a Woman: Understanding Ourselves and Our Children* (New York: Harper and Brothers, 1955); Elizabeth Bragdon, ed., *Women Today: Their Conflicts, Their Frustrations, and Their Fulfillments* (New York: Bobbs-Merrill, 1953); and Beverly Cassara, ed., *American Women: The Changing Image* (Boston: Beacon, 1962).

On the emergence of the new feminism of the 1960s, Judith Hole and Ellen Levine, *Rebirth of Feminism* (New York: Quadrangle, 1971) is indispensable, although it is weak on the role of the various national and state women's commissions and on the relationship of the emergence of the new feminism to more general social events of the decade. On this topic, one might also consult Marlene Dixon, "Why Women's Liberation," *Ramparts,* VIII (December 1969), 58–63. For a general understanding of the position of women in the 1960s, government studies provide an excellent starting point. The 1963 report of the President's Commission on the Status of Women was published as Margaret Mead and Frances Bagley Kaplan, eds., *American Women: Report of the President's Commission on the Status of Women and Other Publications of the Commission* (New York: Scribner's, 1965). Another useful compilation is Kate Stimpson, ed., *Women and the "Equal Rights" Amendment: Senate Subcommittee Hearings of the Constitutional Amendment, 91st Congress* (New York: Bowker, 1972). Equally illuminating are Kirsten Amundsen, *The Silenced Majority: Women and American Democracy* (Englewood Cliffs, N.J.: Prentice-Hall, 1971); Cynthia Fuchs Epstein, *Woman's Place: Options and Limits in Professional Careers* (1970; reprint ed., Berkeley, Calif.: University of California Press, 1971); and Caroline Bird, *Born Female: The High Cost of Keeping Women Down* (New York: David McKay, 1968).

On the new feminism, the outpouring of literature from the movement speaks for itself. In addition to Kate Millett, Shulamith Firestone, and Germaine Greer, one might also consult with profit Robert Jay Lifton, ed., *The Woman in America* (Boston: Houghton Mifflin, 1965); Robin Morgan, *Sisterhood Is Powerful: An Anthology of Writings from the Women's Liberation Movement* (New York: Random House, 1970); Vivian Gornick and Barbara K. Moran, eds., *Women in Sexist Society: Studies in Power and Powerlessness* (New York: Basic Books, 1971); and Jessie Bernard, *Women and the Public Interest: An Essay on Policy and Protest* (Chicago: Aldine, Atherton, 1971). On the attitudes of black women, particularly black militants, see Toni Cade, *The Black Woman: An Anthology* (New York: New American Library, 1970). Among the scholarly journals of note are *Feminist Studies,* 417 Riverside Drive, New York, New York 10025, and *Women's Studies,* Department of English, Queens College, Flushing, New York 11367. A number of weekly feminist newsletters have also appeared. The *Spokeswomen,* 5464 South Shore Drive, Chicago, Illinois 60615, is representative. An impressive amount of material on the contemporary movement, including newsletters, pamphlets, and records of local feminist groups, has been collected at the Women's History Research Center Library, 2325 Oak Street, Berkeley, California 94708. A representative sampling of the collection, entitled *Herstory,* is available on microfilm, published by Bell and Howell.

On subjects like women and the family, sexual attitudes, women in education and law, a large body of literature exists written by scholars and popularizers that will soon pass into the historical record. Among the more insightful are William J. Goode, *After Divorce* (New York: Free Press, 1956), *World Revolution and Family Patterns* (New York: Free Press, 1963), and *The Family* (Englewood Cliffs, N.J.: Prentice-Hall, 1964); Mirra Komarovsky, *Blue-Collar Marriage* (New York: Random House, 1964); Jessie Bernard, *Academic Women* (University Park, Pa.: Pennsylvania State University Press, 1964); Leo Kanowitz, *Women and the Law: The Unfinished Revolution* (Albuquerque, N.M.: University of New Mexico Press, 1969); Vance Packard, *The Sexual Wilderness: The Contemporary Upheaval in Male–Female Relationships* (New York: David McKay, 1968); and Helen Znaniecki Lopata, *Occupation Housewife* (New York: Oxford University Press, 1971).

General Bibliography

Among the few general works that were published prior to the recent resurgence of interest in the history of women are Robert Riegel, *American Feminists* (Lawrence, Kans.: University of Kansas Press, 1963); Andrew Sinclair, *The Better Half: The Emancipation of the American Woman* (New York: Harper & Row, 1965); and Eleanor Flexner, *Century of Struggle* (Cambridge, Mass.: Harvard University Press, 1959), although her excellent work focuses mainly on the suffrage movement.

Some of the more important general works published since that time include Carl N. Degler, "Revolution Without Ideology: The Changing Place of Women in America," in Robert Jay Lifton, ed., *The Woman in America* (Boston: Houghton Mifflin, 1965). In his essay, Degler presents the debatable argument (which is standard in studies of modernization and economic growth) that women's changing position in America has been primarily due, not to individual initiative, but to the process of industrialization. He further argues that the woman's movement had been devoid of any real ideology—a point that William O'Neill, *Everyone Was Brave: The Rise and Fall of Feminism in America* (New York: Quadrangle, 1969) challenges. My own thinking about feminism has been greatly influenced by O'Neill's argument. In addition to Degler and O'Neill, one might also consult with profit Gerda Lerner, "New Approaches to the Study of Women in American History," *Journal of Social History*, III (1970), 53–62, and Page Smith, *Daughters of the Promised Land: Women in American History* (Boston: Little, Brown, 1970), although the book is antifeminist in interpretation. For any study of women, Janet Wilson James and Edward T. James, *Notable American Women, 1607–1950*, 3 vols. (Cambridge, Mass.: Harvard University Press, 1970), which is a collection of brief and perceptive biographies, is essential. Finally, for women in the twentieth century, William Chafe, *The American Woman: Her Changing Social, Economic, and Political Roles, 1920–1970* (New York: Oxford University Press, 1972) is indispensable. I have relied on Chafe's work throughout my study, particularly on his data regarding women in the war effort and in the labor force.

254

THE
POWER OF A
WOMAN

Appendix
Women in the Labor Force

Women in the Labor Force

	Percentage of all workers	Percentage of all women
1890	17	18
1900	18	20
1920	20	23
1930	22	24
1940	25	28
1945	36	37
1950	29	32
1955	31	34
1960	33	36
1970	40	44

SOURCE   Esther Peterson, "Working Women," in Robert Jay Lifton, ed., *The Woman in America* (Boston: Houghton Mifflin, 1965), p. 145.

Women in Selected Professional Occupations

Percentage of all workers

Occupation	1900	1910	1920	1930	1940	1950	1960
Lawyers		1.0	1.4	2.1	2.4	3.5	3.5
College presidents, professors		19.0	30.0	32.0	27.0	23.0	19.0
Clergy	4.4	1.0	2.6	4.3	2.2	8.5	5.8
Doctors		6.0	5.0	4.0	4.6	6.1	6.8
Engineers					0.3	1.2	0.8
Dentists		3.1	3.2	1.8	1.5	2.7	2.1
Biologists						27.0	28.0
Mathematicians						38.0	26.4
Physicists						6.5	4.2
Librarians		79.0	88.0	91.0	89.0	89.0	85.0
Nurses	94.0	93.0	96.0	98.0	98.0	98.0	97.0
Social workers		52.0	62.0	68.0	67.0	66.0	57.0

SOURCE Cynthia Fuchs Epstein, *Woman's Place: Options and Limits in Professional Careers* (1970; reprint ed., Berkeley, Calif.: University of California Press, 1971), p. 7.

Percentages of Women Employed in Professions and Occupations, 1910–1930

Percentage of employed women

	1910	1920	1930
Professional	9.1	11.9	14.2
Clerical	7.3	16.6	18.5
Manufacturing	22.6	22.6	17.5
Trade (including saleswomen)	5.9	7.9	9.0
Transportation and Communication	1.3	2.6	2.6
Domestic (including waitresses and beauticians)	31.3	25.6	29.6
Agriculture	22.4	12.7	8.5

SOURCE   Grace Hutchins, *Women Who Work* (New York: International, 1934), p. 24.

Percentages of Women Employed in Professions and Occupations, 1940–1962

	1940	1950	1962
Professionals	13	11	13
Managers, officials	5	5	5
Clerical	21	26	31
Manufacturing	18	19	15
(craftsmen, foremen)	1	1	1
Sales	7	9	7
Service workers (including waitresses)	11	13	15
Private household	18	10	10
Agriculture	6	5	3

SOURCE Esther Peterson, "Working Women," in Robert Jay Lifton, ed., *The Woman in America* (Boston: Houghton Mifflin, 1965), p. 155.

Occupational Groups of Employed Men and Women, 1962

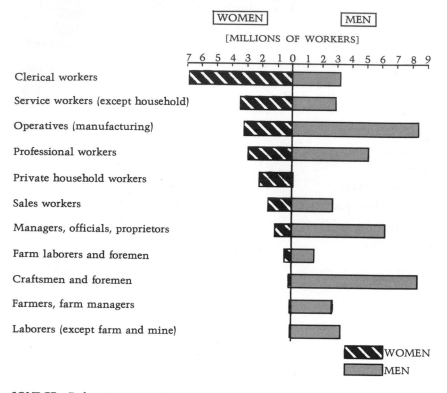

SOURCE Esther Peterson, "Working Women," in Robert Jay Lifton, ed., *The Woman in America* (Boston: Houghton Mifflin, 1965), p. 154.

PHOTO CREDITS

261

262

Index

263

271

272

275

A 4
B 5
C 6
D 7
E 8
F 9
G 0
H 1
I 2
J 3